MY KARST AND MY CITY
AND OTHER ESSAYS

THE LORENZO DA PONTE ITALIAN LIBRARY

MY KARST AND MY CITY

AND OTHER ESSAYS

SCIPIO SLATAPER

Edited, with an Introduction and Notes, by Elena Coda

TRANSLATED BY NICHOLAS BENSON AND ELENA CODA

UNIVERSITY OF TORONTO PRESS
Toronto Buffalo London

Toronto Buffalo London
utorontopress.com
Printed in Canada

ISBN 978-1-4875-0822-7 (cloth) ISBN 978-1-4875-3779-1 (EPUB)
ISBN 978-1-4875-3778-4 (PDF)

The Lorenzo Da Ponte Italian Library

Library and Archives Canada Cataloguing in Publication

Title: My Karst and My City and other essays / Scipio Slataper; edited, with an introduction and notes, by Elena Coda; translated by Nicholas Benson and Elena Coda.
Other titles: Essays. Selections. English.
Names: Slataper, Scipio, 1888–1915, author. | Coda, Elena, editor, translator. | Benson, Nicholas, 1966–, translator.
Series: Lorenzo Da Ponte Italian library.
Description: Series statement: The Lorenzo Da Ponte Italian library | Includes index.
Identifiers: Canadiana (print) 20200280716 | Canadiana (ebook) 20200280775 | ISBN 9781487508227 (cloth) | ISBN 9781487537791 (EPUB) | ISBN 9781487537784 (PDF)
Classification: LCC PQ4841.L4 A2 2020 | DDC 858/.91209 – dc23

This volume is published under the aegis of Agincourt Press Ltd. and with the financial assistance of Dr. Berardo Paradiso and Casa Italiana Zerilli – Marimó of New York University.

Agincourt Press

CI ZM
Casa Italiana Zerilli - Marimò
New York University

University of Toronto Press acknowledges the financial assistance to its publishing program of the Canada Council for the Arts and the Ontario Arts Council, an agency of the Government of Ontario.

Canada Council for the Arts
Conseil des Arts du Canada

ONTARIO ARTS COUNCIL
CONSEIL DES ARTS DE L'ONTARIO
an Ontario government agency
un organisme du gouvernement de l'Ontario

Funded by the Government of Canada
Financé par le gouvernement du Canada
Canada

FSC
www.fsc.org
MIX
Paper from responsible sources
FSC® C016245

Contents

Acknowledgments

This translation would have not been possible without the collaboration of Nicholas Benson, my co-translator. His commitment to this project and his skills as a translator have been essential to seeing this project come to fruition. Throughout this long process he has been an enthusiastic, patient, and insightful collaborator. An earlier version of the first segment of *Il mio Carso*, translated by Nicholas Benson, appeared in the *New England Review*, volume 32, no. 3 (2011). Nicholas Benson would like to thank Stephen Donadio, Rick Jackson, Tzvi Rivlin, and Domenic Stansberry for their support and advice at that early stage of the translation.

Un grazie di cuore to Luigi Ballerini, general editor of the Lorenzo Da Ponte Italian Library, for having believed in this project and for his encouragement and friendship throughout the years.

I am very grateful to the College of Liberal Arts at Purdue University for the research and travel grants made available to me to spend time in the libraries and archives in Trieste.

Many friends and colleagues on both sides of the ocean have helped me throughout this process. A special thank you goes to Jennifer William, currently head of the School of Languages and Cultures, for her constant support, friendship, and sense of humour. Maren Linett was very generous with her time, and I appreciated her comments on a first draft of my introduction. Rebekah Klein-Pejšová gave me useful insights on the section of the introduction that deals with Slataper's political writings. In Trieste, I am particularly grateful to Riccardo Cepach, director of the Museo Sveviano, for always making me feel welcome in his city and to Fulvio Senardi for inviting me to participate in a symposium on Slataper, and for keeping me up to date with the latest research on Slataper and turn-of-the-century Trieste. I would also like to thank the staff of the Biblioteca Civica Attilio Ortis for their kindness and helpfulness and Dr. Claudia Colecchia at the Fototeca e Biblioteca dei Civici Musei di Storia ed Arte for providing the photo for the cover of this volume.

I am indebted to the anonymous readers for their careful comments and feedback and to Mark Thompson at University of Toronto Press and Terry Teskey, copyeditor, for their advice and assistance throughout the publication process. A special thanks also to Susan Clawson for her help with the final proofreading and indexing.

Finally, I would like to thank my family in Italy and in Austria for their love and support. I wish to dedicate this book to my husband Ben Lawton, my best friend and companion in many adventures still to come. Without him none of this would have been possible.

Introduction
"This Little Corner of Europe": Slataper's Reflections on and around Trieste's Cultural and National Identity

ELENA CODA

When in 1909 Scipio Slataper, a young university student, published in the Florentine journal *La Voce* his *Lettere triestine* (*Letters on Trieste,* in this volume), in which he analysed and criticized the cultural and political situation of his native city, he was still completely unknown both in Trieste and in Italy. Who was this young man questioning the traditional Italian perception of Trieste as a wealthy Italian *città irredenta,* literally, an "unredeemed city" that longed to be reunited with its motherland but was still under the yoke of Austrian domination? How could he accuse the Triestines of lacking any cultural tradition, and of being so obsessed with their Italian identity that they ignored the Croatian and Slovenian population in their midst? And how dared he criticize the bourgeois, business-oriented mentality of the city, when it was that very mentality that allowed the city to grow and prosper, and to become one of the wealthiest cities in *fin de siècle* Europe?

And yet, the twenty-year-old Slataper who dared to reflect publicly on his city in the pages of *La Voce* was the product of the complex and conflictual essence of Austrian Trieste, and his letters offer a window into the irresolvable political, cultural, and social tensions present in this border city at the beginning of the twentieth century.

***Fin de siècle* Trieste**

In order to understand the importance of Slataper's *Letters* and the mixed reactions that they received, we must first understand the complex and often contradictory features of the city at that time. In 1909 when Slataper started his collaboration with the Florentine journal, Trieste was still part of the Austro-Hungarian Empire, having submitted to the Habsburgs in 1382 for fear of being seized by the expanding Republic of Venice. Situated on the north-eastern Adriatic coast, on the western edge of the Austrian Empire, Trieste remained for centuries an insignificant fishing town.[1] Its destiny changed drastically when Emperor Charles VI saw the hidden commercial and financial potential of this coastal town and granted it the status of free port in 1719.[2] This significant fiscal privilege was followed in subsequent years by remarkable investments in Trieste's infrastructure, which permitted the construction of a bigger harbour, new roads, and railroad lines that connected the city to its Austrian hinterland. Moreover, in order to attract investors, experienced merchants, and labourers to the city, Charles VI issued a series of patents that permitted individuals from "any nation, social standing or religion" to settle in the city of Trieste to do business without any restrictions (Mainati 142).[3]

Furthermore, the government was willing to forgive debts that the relocated merchants had incurred in other countries and give them a clean slate from which to start their business (Mainati 163). Additional edicts specifically aimed at encouraging wealthy Austrian Jews to relocate to Trieste and to invest their capital there soon followed. The Theresian Diplomas of 1771 ensured the exceptional status of Triestine Jewry when compared to other Jewish communities within the Dual Monarchy. In Trieste, Jews did not have to wear any distinguishing sign, they could own real estate outside the ghetto, and they were allowed to worship in public and to engage in any kind of work or business. Moreover, they did not have to pay extra taxes for toleration or for travelling to other cities.[4] In sum, they could participate *tout court* in the financial and cultural growth of the city. Of pivotal importance for the development of a multi-religious and multi-ethnic Trieste was the Edict of Tolerance of 1781, which allowed the settlement of Protestants and Eastern Orthodox Christians in the city. As a direct result of these policies and financial investments, the city grew into a powerful commercial and financial

1 Luzzatto Fegiz noted that "at the beginning of the eighteenth-century Trieste counted about 600 houses and a population of 5700 unities" (15), all living inside the walls of the medieval town. All translations from Italian are mine unless otherwise noted.

2 Joseph Cary defines a free port as "a port free of the usual protectionist devices (dock restrictions and custom duties; wharfage, portage, and storage charges) by means of which a modern port normally assures itself of order, upkeep and profit. The aim of a free port policy is, through the offer of optimal trade conditions, to attract an unusually large volume of business, which will outweigh the loss of conventional revenues" (96).

3 The text of the original patents is reprinted in Mainati's *Croniche*, a valuable early-nineteenth-century volume on Trieste's early history.

4 On the impact of the patents and the development of the Jewish community in Trieste see Dubin 40–62.

centre that attracted people from all over Europe: the city's population grew from 5,000 inhabitants in the early 1700s to 176,000 in 1890 and reached 250,000 people in 1914. By the middle of the nineteenth century its population comprised not only Italians but also Slavs, Germans, Austrians, eastern European Jews, Greeks, and Turks, giving it that multiethnic and multicultural quality that by the end of the century would become one of its most distinct characteristics.[5]

In the years following the declaration of the free port, the physical physiognomy of the city also changed drastically. The Maria Theresa and the Joseph quarters, erected outside the walls of the old medieval city and named after the two emperors who supported their development and construction, exemplified with their perpendicular grid of wide avenues flanked by neoclassical buildings the commercial ethos and wealth of the new city.[6] By the mid-nineteenth century the city was an established site of major financial and insurance companies, such as the Assicurazioni Generali, the Union Bank, and La Riunione Adriatica di Sicurtà, which attracted large investments from all over Europe.[7] It also housed a thriving exchange market, hosted since 1844 in the grandiose palace of the Tergesteo, whose glass arcades also housed the "Merchant Society," making it the epicentre of the financial life of the city.[8] Here the groups of marble statues adorning the top of both facades of the building featured Mercury and Neptune, the gods of commerce and sea, reminding the businesspeople and merchants who came to buy stocks,

5 The poet Umberto Saba (1883–1957) captured the cosmopolitan essence of turn-of-the-century Trieste: "Its greatest charm lay in its variety. Turning a corner of the road meant changing continent. There was Italy and the desire of Italy, there was Austria (not nearly as bad as one thought), there was the East, there was the Levant with its merchants in red fez, and still many other things" (1089). On the city's economic development see Apih, *Trieste* 7–21; Ara and Magris 18–42.

6 The Borgo Teresiano, situated outside of the walls of the old medieval town, was built between 1754 and 1788, while the Borgo Giuseppino was erected along the coast between 1788 and 1825.

7 See Hametz 48.

8 The importance of the Tergesteo in the life of the city is testified to by its predominant role in Italo Svevo's masterpiece *Zeno's Conscience.* Zeno Cosini, the protagonist of the novel, frequents the offices of the bourse in the hope of gaining access to and understanding the intricate world of business that rules the city, and thus becomes a respectful member of Triestine society: "I had come to the Tergesteo building on the advice of Olivi, who told me that I would get my commercial activity off to a good start by spending some time at the Bourse, and that I might also garner there some useful information for him. I sat down at that table [...] and I never left it afterwards, since it seemed to me, I had really come upon a classroom of commerce, such as I had long been seeking" (62).

make deals, socialize, and hear the latest financial news and gossip who were the true patrons of the wealthy and cosmopolitan city.

Yet this city, which was at the turn of the twentieth century "one of the richest cities of this wealthy empire" (Bazlen 243) because of a strong and solid bourgeoisie, was also a city of poor immigrants: "the harbor where castaways find shelter and the promise of a new life [...] consolatrix afflictorum et refugium peccatorum: this is Trieste for its immigrants" (Pittoni 26). Slataper saw this refuge differently, describing it bitterly in one of his articles as a "true asylum for crooks" ("Trieste Has No Cultural Traditions," in this volume, 81). The city's financial and industrial development led also to a dramatic increase of its proletarian and sub-proletarian class, composed of both Slovenes who abandoned the nearby countryside to try to improve their economic conditions and, in a later wave, Italians from the Friuli region: between 1864 and 1909 the city population doubled, from 112,000 to 224,000 inhabitants.[9] This ever-increasing number of unskilled immigrants who moved to Trieste as cheap labour found refuge in "*città vecchia*," the old medieval town, a maze of small and dark alleys flanked by old, crumbling houses unfit for habitation, and in the adjacent district of San Giacomo, also overpopulated and lacking necessary infrastructure. Though the two poor quarters were geographically situated next to the new, thriving cosmopolitan city, which housed wealthy entrepreneurs and clever businesspeople in large and elegant palaces, their social and economic fabric made them a world apart. These were the poorest and sickest sections of the city, where the child mortality rate was one of the highest in all Europe and where tuberculosis, syphilis, and alcoholism abounded.[10] Even the police avoided their dark, narrow alleys, allowing both petty and more serious criminals to act and move freely (Cattaruzza, *Proletariato urbano* 160). Although the bourgeoisie maintained their distance from these dangerous districts, with the exception of nightly anonymous rendezvous in the

9 Immigration from Carniola, the western region of Slovenia, was prominent until 1890 and was made up predominantly of peasants and day workers. After that date, with the extension of the port and aggressive industrial development, the city attracted factory workers, coming also from Italy. See Cattaruzza, *Trieste nell'ottocento* 125–7.

10 Compared to the rest of Europe, Trieste continued to witness "an abundance of infectious diseases" (Scartabellati 136) such as tuberculosis, diphtheria, and venereal diseases, which claimed the lives of a high percentage of the general population and an even larger percentage of young children. As Scartabellati noted, the major cause of infant and early childhood mortality was what the doctors defined as "congenital weakness," a euphemism that referred to the conditions of extreme indigence and horrific malnutrition in which the poor of *città vecchia* lived (135–7). See also Cattaruzza, *Proletariato urbano* 63–4.

many brothels that thrived in the area, the wealthy city could not ignore the existence of the poor. The unemployed, the vagrants, the petty thieves, and the drunkards moved freely within the affluent districts, their presence calling into question the seeming coherence and strength of Trieste's bourgeois ethos (Cattaruzza, *Proletariato urbano* 163).

Throughout the nineteenth century, doctors, hygienists, public officials, and various governmental and philanthropic associations tried but mostly failed to improve the conditions of the proletarian and sub-proletarian class. For instance, a housing institute created to alleviate the housing problem of the poorest part of the population, although commendable in its efforts, was unable to offer an effective solution to the increasing number of poor residents. In 1902 doctor Achille Costantini wrote a disparaging report to the housing committee, noting that the density of the population per dwelling continued to be much higher in Trieste than in many other great cities, while most residences in San Giacomo and *città vecchia* continued to lack running water. Constantini concluded his report by remarking that the "unhealthiness of the dwellings for the lower classes exacerbates the overall mortality and the mortality due to transmissible diseases."[11] In spite of the increasing wealth of the city as a whole, the persisting lack of decent housing coupled with a poor diet and constant job insecurity led one of the authors of a 1908 report on the city's indigent population to note that the circumstances of the poor in Trieste not only had not improved from the previous century, but were actually getting worse every year (Scartabellati 132).

In 1910 Silvio Benco, one of the most outspoken and prolific Triestine intellectuals of the time, having described the modern city with pride and satisfaction as a site full of activity where "the restlessness of its working class people is spreading in all its districts" (52), condemned the old, morally decrepit section of Trieste. Here he witnessed

11 Achille Costantini, *Relazione e parere del Protofisico civico dottor Costantini* 1, cited in Scartabellati 124. See also the article "Il veicolo del colera" (The vehicle for transmission of cholera), *L'Indipendente*, 19 February 1893). Here the journalist exhorted the city's health officials to attend the next international health convention and use this venue to address the vulnerability of the city and the need for an organized worldwide system of quarantine that could identify and isolate infected individuals. The situation did not improve in the next decade, and in 1910 the newspaper *Il Lavoràtore* published an article entitled "Le disastrose condizioni sanitarie di Trieste" (The disastrous health conditions of Trieste) in which the journalist wrote that deaths from cholera and tuberculosis in the old part of the city were still higher than in other Austrian cities (27 August 1910).

> [a] mixture of misery and dirt in which human life festers [...]. The odor of deteriorating old masonry, the stench of viscous infiltrations, the miasma of the rotten air coming from dark doorways, they all blend together in a thick atmosphere [...] where the smell of cobwebs and rats, unkempt beds, grease, junk shops, alcoholism and prostitution lingers. (49)

Even the brightness of sunrays is tarnished in this environment, while the "sickly, contaminated air" impregnates everyone and everything (50–1). The moral debasement of the district is mostly visible at night, when "throngs of seamen" seek in its many brothels and lurid taverns the pleasures of the "obscene goddess" (51). Benco ends the description of the neighbourhood by demanding its *sventramento*, literally its disembowelment, the urban practice started by Haussmann in Paris, and embraced by nineteenth-century hygienists and urbanists who saw the demolition of a whole city quarter as a drastic but necessary surgical procedure needed "to save a badly infected urban organism" (Çelik et al. 10). The infection that Benco and others saw propagating from *città vecchia* and that had to be stopped was not just physical, but also moral. The many prostitutes and brothels that plagued the old quarter were a constant reminder that moral and physical degradation were intrinsically connected and just a few steps away from the beautiful cafes frequented by the proper wives and daughters of the wealthy bourgeoisie.[12]

Moreover, the proletarian and sub-proletarian uprisings and demonstrations that broke out time and time again in the city reminded the ruling class that the urban masses were very difficult to control, and that they could easily threaten the bourgeois order and productivity of the city. The strikes and popular uprisings of 1902 and 1907 are a case in point: they revealed the sense of anger and frustration that incited the poorest part of the population, and the fragile relationship that the city of wealth and commerce had with its indigent inhabitants.

In 1902 the Austrian Lloyd stockers' union strike turned quickly into a mass uprising that the socialist party, which had organized the strike, was unable to contain. Within twenty-four hours, the lumpenproletariat, including women and children, were in the streets rioting and protesting. In the words of an anonymous journalist:

12 Many philanthropic associations tried, without success, to limit the practice of prostitution and reduce the number of people affected by venereal diseases. In his study of prostitution in Trieste, Schneider noted that prostitutes were the "embodiment of human and social error, failure and intractability" (152).

> These were not Friday's strikers. It was a crowd made up of disparate elements who appeared, as if by magic, from the poorest slums, the stigmata of poverty on their forehead. A crowd that seemed summoned by the desire to avenge itself, [...] to vent their hate without really knowing against whom or why. [...] That crowd represented the rage of the abject against all of society; it was the lowest social class advancing on the tragic scene shouting, "I am here before the firing squad, ready to be executed, because I have nothing to lose." (Domokos 121–2)[13]

The journalist concluded his article by drawing a clear distinction between the socialist demonstrators, who had a class consciousness and protested for better working conditions and social reforms, and the unpredictable mob that lacked class identity and was indifferent to the socialist cause and ideals. Although the journalist recognized that the latter were the forgotten victims of capitalism, he was also quick to disown them as thugs, as "barbarians," living outside the parameters of civil society, beyond any possibility of rehabilitation or redemption (123). Only five years later, on 13 September 1907, another major uprising undermined the tranquility of the city, and this time it did not need the pretext of a strike. Incensed by the rising prices of bread and other basic goods, a mob of poor and disenfranchised men, women, and children vandalized public buildings, looted stores, attacked carriages, and destroyed many of the cafes situated in the centre of the city and frequented by the bourgeoisie.

Il Lavoratore, the organ of the Lega Socialdemocratica, as the Triestine socialist party was called, constantly denounced the tragic conditions in which the poor lived.[14] The socialists wished to strengthen a supranational party that, leaving aside the various national identities of its members, could tackle and resolve the serious social problems that afflicted the proletarian population. The desire to construct a proletarian identity that transcended national Italian and Slovenian loyalties inspired activists and intellectuals such as Giuseppina Martinuzzi and Angelo Vivante, who in their works not only fought against the bourgeois financial elite,

---

13 This is a quote from an article that appeared in the socialist newspaper from Trento, *Il Popolo*, and that the journalist Lajos Domokos (1877–1903), who was at that time editor-in-chief of *Il Lavoratore*, reprinted in his detailed account of these events in his book *Trieste: I fatti di febbraio* (Triest: The events of February).

14 For an analysis of both strikes, see Cattaruzza, *Proletariato urbano* 137–47. While *Il Lavoratore* insisted on separating the riots from any socialist doing, the irredentist-nationalist *L'Indipendente* maintained that the socialists were directly responsible for the riots. See *L'indipendente*, 14 September 1907, 2.

but also emphasized the economic and social potential inherent in the multi-ethnic identity of Trieste. In her articles and public lectures, Martinuzzi (1844–1925), a writer and a journalist who taught elementary school in *città vecchia*, advocated for the education of the underclass. She underscored the futility of nationalistic identities and denounced the exploitation of the capitalist class that oppressed Italians and Slovenians alike. For her, "there are no distinctions between the two nationalities"; both proletarian groups should become conscious of their class struggle and come together to undermine the "capitalistic arrogance" of the ruling bourgeoisie (Martinuzzi 222). Starting from similar premises, Vivante (1869–1915) in his volume *Irredentismo adriatico* (Adriatic irredentism), published in the same year as Slataper's *Il mio Carso (My Karst and My City*, in this volume) and favourably reviewed by Slataper in the pages of *La Voce*, noted that Italians and Slovenians should realize their best interests were served by a supranational state where both groups could live and thrive peacefully while maintaining their specific cultural identities. For Vivante, the multi-ethnic Habsburg Empire would not only guarantee the continuous financial and commercial well-being of the city but could also become the foundation for a new socialist confederation of diverse ethnic and national groups.

Martinuzzi's and Vivante's work brought to the fore the nationalistic tensions that existed in the cosmopolitan city. Trieste's rapid population growth not only caused dramatic socio-economic clashes and urbanistic concerns within the city; it also fomented nationalist and ethnic conflicts. By 1900, almost half of the city's population had been born elsewhere.[15] The two largest groups living in the city at this time were Italian immigrants from the Friuli and Veneto regions and Slovenians from the surrounding countryside. Although in different numbers and percentages, both groups participated actively in the commercial and financial growth of the city.[16] Like all the other ethnic and national groups living in Trieste, they were well aware that the economic success of their businesses and enterprises was linked to the Habsburg's patronage of the city; however, starting in the second half of the nineteenth century, nationalist ideologies superseded the cosmopolitan identity of the city

15 The population of the city in 1900 was 178,599. Of these only 59 per cent were born there, while 30 per cent came from the surrounding Austrian territories, with a large Slovenian and Croatian population (such as Istria, Dalmazia, Carniola, and the area of Gorizia); the remaining percentage came from Italy and other states (Luzzatto Fegiz 22).

16 For a detailed analysis of the development of a Slovenian bourgeoisie in Trieste, see Cattaruzza, *Trieste nell'ottocento*, 136–7.

(Minca 164; Hametz 26–7). The nationalist sentiments that shaped the identity of Trieste's citizens were based on their sense of cultural, emotional and political identification with the nation state that embodied their ethnic group. Thus the Triestines who felt psychological ties to Italy because of their shared language, culture, and kinship, identified themselves as Italians, even if their own perception of Italy was more imagined than based on actual knowledge of that country. The same can be said of all the other ethnic groups present in the city. However, because the Italians represented the largest ethnic group living in Trieste and controlled the local government, the city's overall Italian identity remained unchallenged until the turn of the twentieth century.[17] Furthermore, the overwhelming majority of Italian Triestines, in spite of their strong national identity, did not embrace the irredentist cause (the political movement to incorporate the city of Trieste into the Italian nation state) until the early twentieth century because they enjoyed the autonomous administrative status of the city,[18] they appreciated the financial opportunities that Austrian Trieste offered them, and they recognized that it was unrealistic to think that Italy (still a young country, and an ally of Austria-Hungary)[19] would fight for the political annexation of the city.[20]

Nationalist ideologies became more radicalized in Trieste from the 1890s, when Slovenians refused Italian assimilation and the idea of a Slavic national identity started to take hold within a wider percentage of the population. Moreover, the Slovenians' allegiance to Austria-Hungary rendered the Italian nationalists suspicious of their fellow citizens.[21] The

17 On the cultural and emotional development of irredentism in Trieste, see Todero 59–84.

18 Trieste was since 1850 a "*reichsunmittelbare Stadt*," a city that answered directly to the Austrian monarchy but could control its local government. "The Adriatic city possessed the right to raise taxes and had administrative responsibility for military conscription, the local police, urban planning and infrastructure, health, welfare, schools, and scientific institutions" (Cole 220).

19 The Triple Alliance was forged secretly between Italy, Germany, and the Austro-Hungarian Empire in 1882. It stated that each member would grant its support in case of military attack by another power. The Alliance was renewed until the beginning of World War I.

20 See also Della Venezia Sala 84–6. Alberti in his 1936 study on irredentism noted that only 2 per cent of the population identified itself as irredentist: "circa five thousand people over 250,000 inhabitants. Ten percent of this irredentist elite, that is, about five hundred people, was actively pursuing an irredentist agenda"; cited in Todero 59.

21 For a more detailed critical analysis of the political and nationalist tensions between Italian and Slovenian Triestines, see the section of this introduction where I discuss Slataper's political writings.

Austrian government, in order to undermine the Italian identity of the city and further assure the loyalty of the Slovenians in Trieste, favoured the hiring of Slovenians in the financial and political administration of the city. This dramatic increase of Slovenians holding important positions in the local government raised suspicion among the Italian community that they were the de facto controlling hand of the Austrian government (Gayda 83). In addition, the fact that most priests and bishops officiating in Trieste were Slovenians who supported the Austro-Hungarian Empire and thus could influence the Catholic masses was seen as another threat to the Italian identity of the city.[22]

The increasing number of Slovenian cultural associations, private schools, and powerful financial institutions reminded the Italian leadership of the city of the potential uncertainty of their political prominence. The most powerful symbol of Slovenian ethnic and cultural identity in the city was the Narodni Dom, the Slovenian Cultural Centre, built in 1904 in the centre of the city in Piazza della Caserma, next to the terminal of the tramway line that led to the predominantly Slovenian village of Opicina, located just a few miles above Trieste, in the Karst plateau. The large, elegant Art Nouveau building held a theatre, a hotel, two restaurants, a cafe, a reading room, the offices of the Slovenian newspaper *Edinost*, and a bank. Its presence reminded Italians of the success of the Slovenian Triestines, who could not be easily forgotten or dismissed as "a people without a history," as the Italians tended to do.[23] By 1910, more than 30 per cent of the Triestine population was Slovenian, and they saw

22 From 1831 until 1919, all bishops (except one) officiating in Trieste were Slovenian (Apih, *Trieste* 26).

23 Friedrich Engels used the term "nations without history" to identify the Slavic national groups that were part of the Austro-Hungarian Empire. Engels perceived Austrian Slavs as barbarians who were incapable of establishing independent nation states because they were inherently politically and culturally inferior: "We repeat: apart from the Poles, the Russians, and at most the Turkish Slavs, no Slav people has a future, for the simple reason that all the other Slavs lack the primary historical, geographical, political and industrial conditions for independence and viability. People which have never had a history of their own, which from time to time when they achieved the first, most elementary stage of civilization already came under foreign sway, or which were forced to attain the first stage of civilization only by means of a foreign yoke, are not viable and will never be able to achieve any kind of independence" (367). Engels here adopted Hegel's concept of "non-historic people." According to Hegel, only a people who had the necessary cultural and spiritual strength to establish itself as an independent state could play an active role in historical progress. For a critique of Engels's ideas see Rozdolski.

the city, which had a larger Slovenian population than Ljubljana, as their moral and material capital.[24]

In order to undermine the increased social and financial status of the Slovenian minority, the Italian liberal-national party constantly refused to recognize the national rights of the Slovenian population or the use of Slovenian as an official language in public offices; they also obstructed the construction of Slovenian schools. The Italian nationalists, ignoring or disregarding the distinct Slavic national identities, referred to the Slovenian Triestines with the demeaning epithet "Slavs," which denoted a menacing ethnic group whose national identity and political claims had to be repressed to preserve the Italian identity of the city, and the potential political unification of the city with Italy (Chmiel 108).[25] While the Italian nationalists felt threatened by the Slovenian inhabitants, the Slovenians felt besieged by the Italian population and increasingly frustrated by their lack of political control within the city government. The large number of Italian and Slovenian cultural, political, and social associations that emerged in Trieste during these years testifies to both groups' intellectual and cultural yearning to express and identify their national character. For its part, the Austrian government, although it gave the city ample local independence, did not want to nurture the nationalist longings and ideals of its subjects. As a consequence, it never allowed the founding of an Italian university in Trieste, perceiving such an institution as a nationalist threat to the empire, and instead carefully played Italian and Slovenian identities against each other.[26]

While ethnic and national tensions informed Triestine politics, its culture was deeply influenced by its border status. Successful Triestines were bilingual or trilingual: while Slovenian was spoken in the countryside

24 In 1910 there were more than 56,000 Slovenians in Trieste, as opposed to the 35,000 in Ljubljana (Valdevit 7). See also Cattaruzza, "Slovenes and Italians in Trieste."

25 For an example of anti-Slavic rhetoric see Frà Giordano's article "L'università italiana in Austria" (The Italian university in Austria). The author here noted how the Slavs, "an inadequate people, without history or hope," incited by the Austrian government, "descended on the city like marauders, driven by a savage instinct of destruction" (1218).

26 The city council petitioned the Austrian government to establish an Italian university in Trieste as early as 1866, and in 1899 it created a special fund for the erection and maintenance of the university. Other neighbouring Austrian provinces with a sizable Italian population (Istria, Gorizia, Trento) joined the project wholeheartedly, and by 1902 the foundation included a capital of 50,000 krone. In spite of the financial efforts and political pressure by the Italian representatives in the parliament in Vienna, the government never approved the construction of an Italian university in Austria. See Presidenza municipale di Trieste 102–3, and Hortis; see also Sondel-Cedarmas.

surrounding the city, the Triestine dialect was the lingua franca for any business transactions. Moreover, knowing German was an important asset, and in spite of the fact that prestigious primary and secondary Italian schools were available, many members of the bourgeoisie preferred to send their children to the German gymnasium because it opened up possible careers in other parts of the empire, careers closed to anyone not proficient in the language. In his lyrical autobiography *My Karst and My City*, Slataper recounted his frustration at having been overlooked for a position at Union Bank because he attended the Italian high school instead of the Commercial Academy and his German was not fluent enough. Nevertheless, German and Austrian culture were easily accessible to Triestine intellectuals, who could read German texts in the original. The philosophical works of Schopenhauer and Nietzsche, the psychoanalytical theories of Freud, the cultural analyses of Nordau, Simmel, and Weininger, together with canonical and contemporary German-speaking writers from Goethe to Kafka, found in Trieste an attentive audience and greatly influenced Triestine intellectuals, affording them an unfiltered access to Mitteleuropean culture that would have been impossible in Italy.[27] They also had access to excellent German translations of Scandinavian works before they were available in Italian. Slataper's critical monograph on Ibsen, his essays and translations of Hebbel, his interest in Weininger, his awareness of contemporary German literary and cultural debates could only have developed in Austro-Hungarian Trieste.

Although Triestine intellectuals benefited from the multicultural fabric of this border city, they perceived the lack of a coherent, homogenous cultural and national identity as a disadvantage that they had to overcome. The poet Umberto Saba lamented the cultural backwardness of Trieste vis-à-vis Italy, stating that being born in Trieste in 1883 was like having been born in Italy in 1850 (115). While Italy at the turn of the century was experiencing a literary and cultural renewal, the Italian culture available in Trieste, complained Saba, was still imbued with the

---

27 As Elizabeth Schächter noted, "Trieste's cultural elite at the turn of the century […] had access, through their multi-linguistic patrimony, to a far richer cultural diet than their counterparts in Italy" (12). Although the impact of Freud's theories is essential to understand authors like Svevo, Saba, and Voghera (to mention only the most important ones), there is no evidence that Slataper knew Freud or engaged with his theories in his work. Slataper died in 1915, while Freud's influence in Trieste started after the end of World War I. Edoardo Weiss, who introduced Freud's theories in Trieste, did not receive his medical degree until 1914. By then Slataper's interests had shifted to political issues.

antiquated romantic rhetoric of the Risorgimento.[28] Giani Stuparich, a close friend of Slataper and the author of the first monograph dedicated to Slataper's work, clearly stated the sense of uncertainty and disorientation that characterized his generation: "Being born in these areas meant being born with an unsteady legacy, which needed to be propped up constantly. Walking meant clashing. There was no place, not a single one, where one could rest in contemplation" (19). In this complex border city, it was no longer possible to advance steadily towards a prescribed objective: walking meant constantly crashing into obstacles that frustrated and diverted the very possibility of a teleological aim. In Trieste uncertainty and doubts replaced dogmatic truths.[29] Years later, after the end of World War II when Trieste was facing geopolitical uncertainties once again, Bobi Bazlen, reflecting on the cultural milieu of Austro-Hungarian Trieste, noted with irony the unsolvable contradictions of his city. The image of the "melting pot" in which all differences are absorbed into a homogenous, organic society couldn't be applied to the reality of Trieste. As Bazlen pointed out, Trieste should be understood instead as a "sounding board" in which tensions coexisted and played against each other, producing

> [a]ttempts, approximations, haphazard figures, God's unfinished experiments. People with different premises, who must try to reconcile the irreconcilable, which of course they were unable to do, and thus created strange characters,

---

28 The Triestine critic and intellectual Bobi Bazlen described with irreverence and irony the absurd and exaggerated veneration that the Triestines displayed for anything connected to Italy: "The situation was quite delicate: a city that speaks a Venetian dialect, surrounded by a countryside where people speak only Slovenian. The most intellectual part of the bourgeoisie, which feels isolated from the country it believes it should belong to in terms of language and culture [...] is compelled, in the twentieth century, to resort to a nineteenth-century rhetoric from the Risorgimento, which still believes that Italian is the 'sweet sounding and pure idiom' of yore, and Florence the city of flowers." He continued describing how, when the Teatro Comunale staged Verdi's *Nabucco* (whose famous chorus "Va Pensiero" became during the Risorgimento a popular anthem for the Italian people, expressing their longing for political freedom from Austria), "the thoughts of all businessmen, bank managers, insurance company directors, doctors, lawyers, importers and exporters sitting in the stalls, as well as those of middle school teachers in the gallery, of students and seamstresses [...] in the top gallery, all flew on golden wings [towards their distant homeland], and their enthusiasm was such that it brought down the theater" (247–8).

29 It is telling that Zeno Cosini, the great anti-hero of Svevo's *Zeno's Conscience*, is constantly limping, getting lost, or bumping into obstacles that distract him from his well-intentioned aspirations.

adventurers of culture and life, with all the oddest and most tormented failures that derive from such a background. (251)

Trieste's fragmented and contradictory national identity and its decentered position vis-à-vis a coherent, totalizing political and cultural centre rendered it a unique modern metropolis that stimulated and inspired its writers to reflect on and express the crisis of modern individuals who could no longer filter their particular reality through preestablished values and truths. The works of writers such as Slataper, Stuparich, Svevo, and Saba who were active in Austro-Hungarian Trieste at the beginning of the twentieth century cannot be divorced from the modern urban environment that inspired them. All these authors shared a vision similar to the one elaborated by another Austrian subject, the novelist Hugo von Hofmannsthal, who in an essay published in 1906 reflected on the existential crisis of his time: "the essence of our epoch is ambiguity and uncertainty. It can rest only on what is unstable, and it knows that it is unstable, whereas other generations have believed in things that were firm" (37). This unstable and shifting cultural and social environment undermined individuals' ability to believe in traditional values, such as the importance of religion or the respect for long-established authority, that once sustained and guided society. Giuseppe Prezzolini captured this generational crisis when he wrote that

> modern man lives without the faith of the past and without any faith in the present and often without any faith in the possibility of a future faith. [...] He recognizes his tragedy [...] but he cannot overcome his own complexities. Hence the dismay, the darkness, the nihilism of so many souls. The church has fallen apart and on its immense ruin we are building haphazardly. The individual is no longer supported by social constructs [...] and every day he finds himself facing the possible alternative of becoming either the master of the world or the last rag that a blind force has seized to sweep the streets. [...] From this modern desperation, uncertainty and anguish we must create the heroism of modern man. ("Parole di un uomo moderno" 349–50)

Slataper's texts included in this volume – from his irreverent criticism of the Triestine cultural status quo in his early *Letters on Trieste*, to the lyrical prose of *My Karst and My City*, to his later essays on World War I – bring to light the ambiguity and uncertainty that informed the cultural and political milieu in which he lived, and gave voice to the existential crisis that plagues the modern individual.

Letters on Trieste and *La Voce*

A few months before the publication of the *Letters*, in the fall of 1908, Slataper, a fresh graduate of the Italian Classical Gymnasium in Trieste, had moved to Florence and enrolled at the prestigious Istituto di Studi Superiori, where he intended to pursue a degree in literature. Faced with the choice of pursuing a university degree in Austria or in Italy, many Italian Triestines chose Florence because the Italian city epitomized Italian cultural and national identity. Florence was the cradle of the Italian language, and many Triestines wanted to spend time in the city of Dante and Boccaccio to improve their linguistic abilities and absorb what the city had to offer.[30] The choice of Florence, although not original, is nonetheless quite indicative of Slataper's intentions. In Florence, Slataper sought not only to pursue a university degree, but also to find a national cultural milieu in which he could develop intellectually and spiritually. For the "peripheral" Slataper, Florence represented a modern literary and cultural capital where he could find artistic inspiration and quench his intellectual thirst.

It was a fortunate coincidence that his arrival in Florence corresponded with the beginning of a new journalistic and cultural enterprise. In 1908 a group of Florentine intellectuals, led by Giuseppe Prezzolini, launched the journal *La Voce*, whose goal was, as Prezzolini pointed out in his editorial of 27 December, "to be honest and sincere":

> We feel strongly about the ethical foundations of intellectual life, and we are disgusted to see the misery, the narrow mindedness and the revolting trade that has become of all spiritual matters. [...] We want to work. We will follow certain social movements, which are influenced by different ideologies, such as modernism and syndicalism; we will inform you [...] of the best achievements abroad; we will propose reforms and improvements for public libraries. We will devote ourselves to the moral crisis of Italian universities; we will identify the literary works that are worth reading and we will comment on the degradation of contemporary life. [...] However, we need the public to respond. We want to stay in touch with the public, especially with the public in the provinces, in the small towns in the

30 The presence in Florence of the Triestine scholar Solomone Morpurgo, who was at that time the director of the Central Library of Florence, facilitated the growth of a small community of Triestine students in the Italian city: among them were Guido Devescovi, Augusto Hermet, Enrico Elia, Giani and Carlo Stuparich, Biagio Marin, Carlo Michelstaedter, and Giorgio Fano. On the relationship between Florence and Trieste, see Pertici.

> countryside where the air is less skeptical than in the Italian big cities. ("La nostra promessa" 5)

The article emphasized the need for an in-depth analysis of contemporary life and its cultural institutions while welcoming the concerns and perspectives coming from peripheral areas, regions that were not, at least according to Prezzolini, as predisposed to the sensual aestheticism of D'Annunzio or to the emphatic poetic style of Carducci, the two most influential writers in Italy at that time. The main goal of the journal was to renew the cultural and sociopolitical fabric of contemporary Italy by establishing a new intellectual class attuned to the political and cultural changes occurring outside of the peninsula.[31] *La Voce*'s young collaborators were weary of Giolitti's government and its inability to solve Italy's most pressing social problems, while at the same time feeling frustrated by the provincialism of the dominant intellectual class.[32] They felt that the Italian intelligentsia remained fossilized in Italy's century-long tradition and were ignorant or suspicious of contemporary literary and cultural developments happening abroad. On the contrary, the *Vociani* were eager to read and publish modern foreign writers and debate the most important events occurring in the rest of Europe.[33]

It was *La Voce's* openness to other literary experiences coupled with Prezzolini's call for a more authentic and honest discussion of contemporary issues that moved the young Slataper to contact him. With youthful enthusiasm, he wrote to the editor introducing himself:

> I am from Trieste. Which bookstore sells your journal? Maybe you would be interested in some advertisement in Trieste? I would be happy if my city, which is cut off from Italy's intellectual life, became familiar with *La Voce*. And maybe you would be pleased by an exposé on our unique conditions both in art and science. (*Epistolario* 18)

---

31 As Francesca Billiani noted, *La Voce*, like other journals published in Florence at that time, aspired "to cross the boundaries between ethics, aesthetics, and politics, and create a modern, inter-discursive, and interdisciplinary intellectual space of debate" that "challenged the traditional divide between cultural and political engagement." These journals became "a meeting point for both the political and intellectual elites, the bourgeoisie, and the growing general public of the new Italy" (445–6).

32 As Gentile explained, although the period of Giolitti's government – which lasted from 1903 to 1914 – was a time of "economic progress, civil modernization, cultural renewal and democratic reforms," the new generation saw it as a "reflection of political corruption, a crisis of the state, a weakening of the nation and serious moral decay of individual and collective conscience" (11).

33 See also Billiani 463–8.

Slataper was not just interested in making the journal available to Triestine readers. He was also eager to be recognized as an engaged intellectual who could help shape the discourse on Triestine's national and cultural identity on both sides of the border. In a letter written to his friend Marcello Loewy only a few months before leaving Trieste for Florence, he already envisioned his intellectual mandate: "I was born to give shape to clay. My thumb is steady: one stroke never erases the previous one. All of you who know me [...] will carry my imprint" (*Epistolario* 104). For Slataper, *La Voce* became the ideal platform from which he could offer to both the Triestine and Italian public a fresh and dispassionate analysis of his distant city, whose intricate cultural, social, and political physiognomy was overlooked by the Triestine intelligentsia and misunderstood by the majority of Italians. While the traditional Italian nationalist discourse revolving around Trieste emphasized a hegemonic and synthetic image of an irredentist city longing to be absorbed within Italy's borders, Slataper questioned such normative assumptions and strove instead to escape established interpretations of Trieste in favour of more unconventional and problematic visions of his city. At the same time, he was well aware that this would not be an easy task, as he confessed to Loewy:

> In Florence Prezzolini and Papini – two feisty characters that I love – are publishing *La Voce* [...]. I am thinking of writing about Trieste, about our situation. But I choose to be stoned. I am tired of half-truths: I want to expand them. I want to be surrounded by so many conflicts that if I overcome them it will mean that I am worth something. (*Epistolario* 47)[34]

"Trieste Has No Cultural Traditions," the first article of the series *Letters on Trieste*, was published in the winter of 1909, and gave Slataper the opportunity to dwell upon the cultural fabric of his city without the platitudes and clichés that typically informed such discourses, and without any qualms about offending some of his fellow citizens. Moreover, this first article already showed an intellectual trait that Slataper continued to pursue throughout his career. He was not interested in developing an organic and totalizing analysis of Trieste and its many challenges, but in offering multifaceted, often contradictory readings of his city that could stimulate critical debates and dialogues (Patruno 124). His *Letters* did not attempt to offer a synthetic solution to the "Triestine problem." Instead, they became a useful intellectual platform to engage in the contemporary

34 Giovanni Papini (1881–1956) was an Italian journalist and intellectual. He was one of the founders of the journals *Leonardo* and *Lacerba*. In 1912 he became the director of *La Voce*.

debate about the changing role of culture in a modern urban society. In the same years in which Slataper was writing his *Letters on Trieste*, German sociologists and architects were reflecting on the sociocultural impact that modern city life had on the individual and on how the new metropolitan experience drastically altered the production of culture. Ferdinand Tönnies, in his pivotal work *Community and Civil Society* [*Gemeinschaft und Gesellschaft*, 1887], recorded the dissolution of the harmonic, organic existence that informed the life of the *Gemeinschaft*, the term he used to identify the traditional communities in which people lived and worked together joined by bonds based on family, shared traditions, and culture. In this traditional community, all individuals were part of an organic whole in which they could identify themselves.[35] However, the world of *Gemeinschaft* had been replaced by a modern urban society (*Gesellschaft*), "a purely mechanical construction" (17) where relationships were characterized by their individual nature and dictated only by selfish needs and rational calculations. Whereas in the small village knowledge and culture were transmitted to the next generation through example and experience, and their intrinsic value resided in their traditional capital, in modern societies everything was transformed into a commodity whose value depends only on its marketability.[36] Georg Simmel expanded on Tönnies's ideas, noting that in the modern metropolis every human relation was reduced to its exchange value (Simmel, "Metropolis" 71) while, at the same time, the new urban experience fostered a blasé attitude that protected city dwellers from the overwhelming bombardment of violent stimuli that would otherwise swallow them up into the metropolis's "socio-technological mechanism" (70). Ruled by an impersonal money economy, life in the metropolis has become "an arithmetical problem" where all "qualitative values" that once informed and anchored the life of the small town are now reduced to mere "quantitative terms" (72). For Simmel this also had a devastating effect on the cultural production of the metropolis, which privileged specialization, fragmentation, technological advances, and rational thinking at the expense of a traditional worldview that favoured instead intuition, wholeness, and classical ideals.

35 "Wherever human beings are bound together in an organic fashion by their inclination and common consent, Community of one kind or another exists" (Tönnies 28). For a detailed analysis of the discourses on the metropolis at the turn of the twentieth century, see Dal Co. For an analysis of Slataper's appropriation of the metropolitan discourse, see also Coda, "Representation of the Metropolis."

36 "In the big city, in the capital, and especially in the metropolis, family life is in decline. [...] The mechanism of money [...] seems to overcome all resistance, to accomplish all desires, to eliminate all dangers and to heal all ills" (Tönnies 255).

The tension between the alienated life of the metropolis and the organic world of the village is also reflected in the dichotomy between *Kultur* and *Zivilisation*, which occupies much of the discourse on the metropolitan experience at the beginning of the twentieth century. While *Kultur* represented everything that was authentic and organic and originated from the rooted world of small communities, *Zivilisation* was instead the product of the modern metropolis, defined by alienation, inauthenticity, and mechanization.[37] The conflict between *Kultur and Zivilisation* found a fertile ground in a city like Trieste which, as we have seen, did not undergo an organic urban evolution throughout the centuries, but instead came into being "artificially" in the eighteenth century out of the financial, strategic, and economic interests of the Habsburg monarchy (Apih, *Trieste* 21; Cova 9).

Slataper in his letters brought to the fore the tension between *Kultur* and *Zivilisation* that plagued his city. Against the status quo that saw Trieste as unquestionably Italian, he recognized the impossibility of creating a traditional, homogenous Italian culture in a city that, in his own words, "cannot contain all its contradictions within a single frame of thought" ("The Life of the Spirit," in this volume, 87). While Slataper's recognition of Trieste's complexity led him to try to formulate a new cultural identity for his city, he continued at the same time to waver between *Kultur* and *Zivilisation*, between tradition and modernity. It is precisely in his attempts to come to terms with Trieste as a modern metropolis that Slataper reveals a modern sensibility and emerges as a unique modernist intellectual.

The provocative implication embedded in the title of his first *Letter on Trieste*, "Trieste Has No Cultural Traditions" (in this volume), indicated

37 *Kultur* and *Zivilisation* are the traditional terms used by German urbanists and philosophers at the beginning of the twentieth century to describe the tension between the traditional, organic culture of the past and the disjoining, alienating forces of modernity. As Dal Co noted, for many early-twentieth-century intellectuals the modern metropolis "represents a mortal challenge to culture" (55). In his 1911 essay "On the Concept and Tragedy of Culture," Simmel described how modern technological processes, together with the current drive towards "extreme and total specialization," have rendered the possibility of a unifying meaningful culture obsolete (43). For modern man everything has become interchangeable, nothing holds an absolute value: "Thus, the typically problematic situation of modern man comes into being: his sense of being surrounded by an innumerable number of cultural elements which are neither meaningless to him nor, in the final analysis, meaningful. In their entirety they depress him, since he is not capable of assimilating them all, nor can he simply reject them, since after all, they do belong *potentially* within the sphere of his cultural development. [...] [M]an has become richer and more overloaded: *Cultures omnia habentes, nihil possidentes* (cultures that have everything own nothing)" (44).

Slataper's position in the debate on the cultural fabric of his city: Trieste suffered an intrinsic dissonance between its quick economic and urban growth and its antiquated cultural expressions. Moreover, the bourgeois, financial ethos of the city had always taken precedence over anything else, de facto undermining the possibility of any imaginative endeavour: "Slave to her compulsive thirst for profit, [Trieste] could never look ahead boldly and imaginatively, not even to open new routes for her commerce; she never had even a minor version of Christopher Columbus or Marco Polo" (84).

At the same time, the cosmopolitan, multinational character of the city further hindered any homogenous artistic or intellectual growth: "But how can we think about the development of the city's [Italian] culture when a great number of families are neither Triestine nor Italian? And our surnames (like mine! pure Slavic) are evidence of this fact" (83). For Slataper, the lack of a homogenous national identity undermined the possibility of a totalizing, hegemonic culture in which all Triestines could easily recognize themselves. The linguistic fragmentation of the city and the predominance of the Slavic element, which weakened the Italian character of Trieste, were obstacles that should have propelled the city to define and imagine its own unique cultural character outside of any predetermined national identity. But the Triestines, Slataper pointed out with bitter irony, comparing them to a sheltered and inexperienced Parsifal, were unable to "accord [their] life to another rhythm, beyond the blows of a steam engine, and delight [themselves] with something more than the melody of silver coins jangling inside the pockets of [their] bulging vest[s]" (81). Like the character in Wagner's opera, the Triestines remained ignorant of the complexities of the world they inhabited and were incapable of critical thinking; and like Parsifal, they were too disoriented and lost to envision a distinctive Triestine identity that could help them fulfil their cultural potential.

After defining in the first article the crux of the Triestine cultural situation, Slataper proceeded in the following two articles – entitled "Cultural Means" and "More Cultural Institutions" – to describe in detail the city's cultural institutions. Fully aware of the stir that his essays would cause among his fellow citizens, before tackling the task at hand he pre-emptively presented himself as a resolute individual who could single-handedly build the foundations upon which to establish a new Triestine culture. Drawing a comparison between the recent collapse of Trieste's newest and largest pier, whose foundations were not solid or deep enough to sustain its weight, and the cultural background of his city, Slataper noted that he had the strength and the will to provide the much-needed footing upon which to build a new, innovative Triestine culture. His weak and inept fellow citizens should not bother him with their empty criticisms. Instead, they should move aside and let him do his job.[38] Slataper's belief in his artistic and ethical mandate to rejuvenate the cultural stagnation of his city followed closely the cultural mission of *La Voce*, whose aim was to explore the many political, social, and cultural issues that concerned contemporary Italy from different, often contradictory perspectives.[39]

For Slataper, culture in Trieste was a superficial capitalist enterprise that did not expand with the multicultural development of the city to enhance the intellectual and spiritual growth of its inhabitants. The various cultural associations, theatres, and artistic initiatives present in the city catered only to the shallowest and most fashionable desires of its population. Culture in Trieste was defined by money alone and, "just like in America, it too often mistook face paint for a life-giving tonic" (*Lettere triestine* 24).[40] Moreover, culture was reduced to the by-product of the Italian dominant business class, which was only interested in endorsing its own nationalist values. The only noteworthy exception to this sad state of affairs was the socialist Circolo di studi sociali (circle of social studies), which housed a good library and hosted interesting conferences

38 As Angelo Ara and Claudio Magris have noted in their seminal work on Trieste, "the historical significance of Slataper's denunciation consists in its unilateralism, which is typical of any individual or group that wants to found a new culture, and must therefore reject […] the previous one" (9).

39 Reflecting on the experience of *La Voce*, Prezzolini described the group of the *Vociani* and their journalistic endeavour: "*La Voce* in its first year brought together very different people: by origin, by age, by purpose, by culture. The rapports [were] often violent, the statements contradictory. Their attitudes clashing among themselves. […] Yet why did the public feel a family air, a sense of unity, something that bound everyone to the same task? We do not know how it happened, but it happened. Or better, we do know how it happened: this unity, this family really existed, in contrast with the disorganization of [our] schools, parties, religions, everything. The previous generation was an unbelieving, sceptical generation. Now these collaborators of *La Voce* were different: one way or another, they believed, arbitrarily or rationally, striving towards the universal or shrinking within themselves, with or without prejudices, with a dogmatic or philosophical approach, but they believed. One felt that life was in and of itself serious, and they took it seriously" (*Italia 1912* 83–4).

40 It is interesting to note that here as in many other articles, Slataper embraced a common European criticism against American society as being defined by unrestrained consumerism and industrialization. The lack of homogenous historical roots together with "the predominance of a commercial mind-set, the enthusiasm for business and moneymaking, and the subordination of all moral, spiritual and aesthetic values to the dollar […] constitute a favorite Romantic objection to the United States" (Gulddal 26). This negative romantic perception of America continued to flourish in Europe in the early twentieth century.

on timely socio-political and economic issues that addressed both Italian and European concerns.[41] It is thanks to this institution that the Triestine public was introduced to the ideas of some of the most interesting intellectuals active in Italy at that time, but the Triestine intelligentsia and conservative political class, threatened by the circle's socialist ideology, boycotted it and favoured instead the more stodgy and conservative Minerva Society, which favoured the Italian nationalist agenda and maintained its elitist standing by allowing only members to participate in its series of lectures and other programs (*Lettere triestine* 28).[42]

After having summarized in detail the shortcomings of the various cultural institutions present in the city, in "The Life of the Spirit" (the fourth article in the series, in this volume) Slataper insisted on the need for a more objective and comprehensive investigation of the complex cultural and political problems that burdened his city. Slataper recognized that the multi-ethnic growth of Trieste led to a profound crisis of its collective Italian cultural identity. He asserted that his detractors should look at this reality and confront openly the intellectual stagnation of Trieste instead of hiding behind their irredentist and nationalist rhetoric for fear of being judged negatively by their Italian brothers and sisters. Slataper made clear that the multi-ethnic and commercial identity of the city should not be perceived as an obstacle to the city's cultural development. On the contrary, Trieste's cosmopolitanism and economic ethos were unique assets upon which the city could build its own original traditions, which should be influenced by its role as a dominant financial and commercial hub of the Austrian Empire. Instead of passively absorbing its culture from Italy, Trieste should try to forge its own distinctive voice. However, Slataper asserted, the Triestines were lazy and cowardly; they would rather yield to the Italian canon than interrogate and explore their own contradictory nature: "we are afraid of what surrounds us: if our spirit were to dwell on it, it would be shattered. There is a terrible anxiety in our affairs, but we keep it hidden, we do not probe it with any analysis" (in this volume, 92). For Slataper the Triestines were afraid to face their own diversity, because by doing so they would

41 "We must be grateful to the Socialists if we became acquainted with Lombroso, Ferrero, Salvemini, Labriola, Zerboglio, Sergi, Battelli [...]; if we heard, for the first time Salvemini and Ferri speak about Mazzini and Garibaldi" (*Lettere triestine* 27–8). The events and conferences organized by the circle were very successful in Trieste, "often attracting more than 1,000, sometimes more than 2,000 people – and not only workers – in the name of internationalism" (Rutar 97).

42 For an analysis of the irredentist associations present in the city, see Rutar, and Millo, *L'elite del potere* 133–41.

destroy the precarious sense of cultural and national wholeness that they had forged for themselves. Against the superficial irredentist ideology embraced by Trieste's bourgeoisie, Slataper contrasted a more complex and tormented image of his city, which must continually seek out the causes of its own restlessness. Trieste should not deny its cultural connection with Italy, but it should do so without disregarding its own unique peripheral perspective: "we must [...] accept that Trieste is Italian in a different way from other Italian cities. [...] Then we need to express this difference" (92).[43]

Trieste could thrive culturally and artistically only if it embraced what its diverse ethnic groups could offer and if it recognized the pivotal role that its financial institutions and the Austrian Empire played in its economic survival. Truth be told, noted Slataper, it would be a financial disaster for Trieste if it became Italian. Thus, Trieste should accept its double Italian and Austrian souls (93) and learn how to negotiate them. Here lay the tragic modernity of Trieste, a multi-ethnic and multicultural capitalist city that could no longer aspire to a coherent and totalizing identity: "This is Trieste. Composed of tragedy. In sacrificing the possibility of a straightforward existence, Trieste gains her own anxious originality. We must sacrifice our peace in order to give it expression. But express it we must" (94). The tragic modernity of Trieste was also what rendered it a potential laboratory for a modern cultural enterprise, one that combined both literary and artistic endeavours with the many commercial and entrepreneurial activities of the city. Instead of looking with nostalgia towards an organic wholesome cultural identity, Slataper recognized the alternative and innovative cultural potential of his city. In other words, he realized that it could become the site where *Kultur* and *Zivilisation* could find their own unique mode of expression. From this perspective, if we follow Deleuze and Guattari's insights on "minor literature," Trieste could also be understood as the place where a new, minor literature could take place, a literature "that is radically heterogeneous" with respect to a national canon (Deleuze and Guattari xv). Similarly, Slataper concluded that Trieste should "strive for a Triestine art capable of reproducing, through joyful clear expression, our fragmented and difficult existence" (in this volume, 94). This could be accomplished only by bringing together in a confident and uncompromising manner Trieste's Italian, German, and Slovenian voices and perspectives: its workers, powerful businesspersons, and financiers; the bourgeoisie living and working in the modern quarters of the city; the poor of *città vecchia*; and

43 On Slataper's cosmopolitan outlook, see Pizzi 45–57.

the Slovenian population living and thriving in the city (168–9). Furthermore, Slataper's particular stylistic choice of emphatic short phrases coupled with syntactical inconsistencies and unexpected shifts of register highlighted his preoccupation with creating a personal style that countered the prevailing decadent movement of the turn of the century, epitomized by D'Annunzio's aestheticized prose. Slataper's work poses a particular challenge to the reader (and to his translators) because, like Kafka's oeuvre, his "expression ... break[s] forms, encourage[s] ruptures and new sprouting. When a form is broken, one must reconstruct the content that will necessarily be part of a rupture in the order of things" (Deleuze and Guattari 28).[44] Thus, through his innovative use of language Slataper was able to question the cultural and political fabric of his city and redefine the role of the intellectual, while maintaining his own sense of otherness vis-à-vis traditional Italian literature.

Slataper's articles on Trieste spurred quite a controversy both in his native city and in Italy. *La Voce* received angry letters that ignored Slataper's attempt to understand Trieste as a modern metropolis that needed to foster its multifaceted cultural identity and focused instead on his political views and his lack of support for the irredentist cause. Mostly, these articles brought forth the anti-Slavic sentiments that fomented discord in local politics. *Il Piccolo*, the most widely read local newspaper, criticized by Slataper for presenting an outdated view of the national issue in Trieste (*Lettere triestine* 43–7), publicly attacked Slataper's views and *La Voce*. Prezzolini himself intervened in defence of his young collaborator, while Slataper, in an unpublished article entitled "Letters on Trieste: Why Do I Write Them?" noted that the foremost reason for writing about his city was to debunk the irredentist myth that Trieste had constructed and exported to Italy, a myth that undermined the multicultural potential of his city and hindered the possibility of truly understanding its identity and unique potential. The irredentist narrative that shaped the local perception of the city was not based on an objective understanding of Trieste's history and present situation, but was instead the product of a bourgeois mentality that was moved by fear: fear of the new socialist forces that were gaining popularity in Trieste at that time, and fear of the Slovenian minority living in their midst.[45]

---

44 As Giuliana Minghelli also noted "The 'arte impura' [impure art] of Svevo, Saba and Slataper contains all the disruptive and innovative force of what Deleuze and Guattari theorized as 'minor literature,' a force that opens Italian Literature to modernist experimentation and contamination, making of it *something other*" (13).

45 "I am convinced," wrote Slataper, "that Trieste is not irredentist, and that irredentism can no longer be awakened in any way" (*Lettere triestine* 60). See also Coda, *Slataper* 21.

After the controversy created by the *Letters*, Slataper continued to write for the Florentine journal, establishing strong intellectual relationships with some of its most important collaborators, whose artistic and philosophical work influenced his development as a writer and a critic. Slataper's friendship and close collaboration with the philosopher Giovanni Amendola and Prezzolini were pivotal in helping him further develop the ideal of an intellectual ethically and culturally engaged with current social and political issues. In his writings Amendola emphasized the philosophical importance of the ethical will. He stated that the ethical value of one's existence depended on one's will, understood as a moral act able to bring unity and coherence to one's personal, empirical life, which Amendola perceived as a mass of unruly and impulsive tendencies that if left unchecked would lead to existential chaos.[46] What attracted Slataper to Amendola's theories was above all the philosopher's emphasis on the "terrible seriousness of every individual act" (Amendola, "Il convegno nazionalista" 686), which should become the foundation for the regeneration of the whole society. Against the "inertia, the scarce sense of responsibility, the lack of active and constructive energy" (686) that characterized Italy's political leadership at the time, he stressed the necessity for every individual to strive towards the "highest ethical value," which would allow Italian citizens to renew and reinvigorate their newly unified country and fulfil the Risorgimento's ideals. On the other hand, Amendola recognized that if such ethical drive "did not arise and flourish in individuals, they would remain isolated and divided, since they would not have within themselves the ability to overcome the boundaries of a single individuality and bring them together." The result would be an alienated "collection of individualities," not a functioning and organic society (687). Meanwhile, Prezzolini continued to articulate in his articles and editorials his suspicion towards "any piece of writing that is purely artistic" ("Relazione del primo anno" 134). In a long editorial piece published at the end of the first year of the journal's publication, Prezzolini noted how *La Voce* did not want to give too much space to mere literary concerns or to fashionable contemporary artistic expressions. Instead, he invited aspiring young artists to concentrate on critical thinking, on the study of history, and on the investigation of contemporary issues (134–5).

The article "To Young Italian Intellectuals" (in this volume, 97), published by Slataper shortly after his *Letters*, reflected Slataper's own ethical and

---

46 The tension between empirical life and ethical will is a common concern for many early-twentieth-century writers. For a superb analysis of this existential issue and its aesthetic ramifications, see Harrison. See also Amendola, *La volontà è il bene.*

aesthetic concerns and showed his intellectual debt to Amendola and Prezzolini's ideas. Here the author exhorted young intellectuals to desist from publishing their early works. They should instead use their writing skills first and foremost to question themselves and resolve their own inner dilemmas. Only then should they worry about publishing: "We write: but to clarify for ourselves who we are" (98), noted Slataper, underscoring the existential anxiety that afflicted this new generation of intellectuals who could no longer solve their ontological quests with simple, coherent answers. Slataper's statement indicated the ethical importance that he assigned to introspective journal writing, a practice that he maintained throughout most of his life.[47] This practice became a valuable tool to question himself and his beliefs and offered him the opportunity to give voice to his fears and doubts. At the same time, the diary never became for him a form of solipsism or escapism. In more than one instance, the author confessed his yearning to participate in life and play an active role in current events: "acting among people, that's my diary!" (*Appunti e note* 133). Similar concerns informed his address to the new generation of intellectuals. To gain a sense of who they are, young writers should articulate their thoughts, explore their ideas, and question themselves and others within the privacy of their journal, while at the same time they should not shy away from participating in all different aspects of practical endeavours and should not be afraid of confronting the cacophony of contemporary life with all its contradictions, noises, and crises. In this way, writing could become a useful tool not only to interrogate oneself and mature intellectually, but also to examine the cultural stagnation that afflicted contemporary life. Like Amendola and Prezzolini, Slataper also believed that superficiality and conventionalism dominated present-day culture. As a consequence, young authors would never be able to question and undermine the bourgeois cultural status quo unless they first fostered their inner strength and learned how to critique the world that surrounded them. "To continually push forward and clarify this reality," concluded Slataper, was the responsibility and the challenge that every intellectual should embrace ("To Young Italian Intellectuals," 100).

Slataper's frustration with the dominant intellectual class became the underlying theme of many of the articles he wrote for *La Voce*. In general, he attacked the intellectuals' careerist obsession and mocked their

47 Giani Stuparich, who edited and published Slataper's diaries and notes, observed that the author was not interested in creating a sentimental or aesthetic diary; instead he strove to produce a "moral diary" where he could address and express freely his ethical and political concerns (Slataper, *Appunti e note* 10).

desire of becoming full-fledged members of a cultural elite that was as snobbish as it was vacuous.[48] He favoured instead the work of Hebbel, whose play *Judith* and a selection of his *Tagebücher* (Diaries) he translated together with Marcello Loewy, making them available to an Italian audience for the first time.[49] For Slataper, Hebbel was still relevant to contemporary readers because he was able to give voice to the existential anxiety that plagued contemporary society. In his introduction to the play, he emphasized how Judith and Holofernes, the two main characters, were driven by doubts and existential uncertainties: Judith knew that she must kill Holofernes despite his being the only man whom she might be able to love, while Holofernes no longer believed in the traditional values that still informed his actions. Hebbel's *Judith* expressed the crisis of pre-established values and became for Slataper a predecessor of Nietzsche's *Übermensch.* Hebbel was, like Nietzsche, critical towards tradition, Christianity, and authority, and recognized the fragility of a world that had lost its foundations. However, following Amendola's philosophical ideals, Slataper believed that to provide a fulfilling aesthetic expression the play should also aspire to overcome the moment of crisis and transform it into "a new law" (*Scritti letterari* 145) that could guide the individual towards an ethical vision of life. While Slataper felt a strong affinity towards the heroes torn by doubts that inhabited Hebbel's tragedies, he also believed that the aim of the artist was to go beyond the simple representation of the existential anguish of the single individual. The artist should instead be willing to envision "a whole metaphysical system" (*Epistolario* 268) where ethics and aesthetics came together. As he wrote in his review of Claudel's *Partage de midi,* "art is the triumph of cosmos over chaos" (*Scritti letterari* 266). Ultimately, he argued, artists like Claudel and Hebbel failed because they offered us only the struggle, the degradation of the individual who lost his bearing in the chaos of a fragmented existence, and not his redemption (266–7).

Yet Slataper was very aware, as he had already made clear in his articles on Trieste, that the complexities of modern existence could not be easily absorbed into a totalizing organic whole that eliminated all discrepancies

48 See Slataper's articles "Il solidificatore del vuoto" (The solidifier of emptiness; *La Voce 1908–1913,* 425–6) and "La claque letteraria" (The literary claque; *Scritti letterari* 11), where he railed against intellectual poseurs who had nothing culturally or socially innovative to offer to society.

49 Hebbel's diaries, translated by Slataper and Loewy, were published in 1912 for the Carabba editions (Lanciano). Hebbel's *Judith,* translated and edited by Loewy and Slataper, came out in 1910 in the Quaderni della Voce, the publishing house affiliated with *La Voce.*

and contradictions. This is why he looked for inspiration in the works of Goethe, Dante, and Shakespeare, authors who, he felt, were able to integrate the alienated experience of the single individual within a wider ethical perspective and bring to life a polyphony of individual voices while maintaining an overarching unity true to the artists' own beliefs. It was especially Goethe's ability to represent a world that comprised both complexity and unity that influenced Slataper's artistic vision. In 1911 Slataper published a review of Goethe's *Wilhelm Meisters Theatralische Sendung* (Wilhelm Meister's theatrical mission), the original version of the first six books of his famous Bildungsroman *Wilhelm Meisters Lehrjahre* (Wilhelm Meister's apprenticeship), which had been lost and was rediscovered in 1910. These first books, written between 1777 and 1785, which Goethe later rejected, recounted the adventures and passions of the young Wilhelm, who wanted to dedicate his life to the creation of a national theatre. For Slataper, the significance of this manuscript surpassed his purely literary or philological interest: it demonstrated Goethe's intellectual and ethical growth and his willingness to dismiss a text that no longer satisfied the intellectual and emotional maturity of its author. When Goethe revisited the novel nine years later, after his Italian journey, he changed it completely. In the finalized *Lehrjahre*, Goethe transformed Wilhelm Meister from a single-sided character solely driven by passions to a full-fledged human being, well integrated within society. In the final version of the novel, the protagonist renounces theatre and chooses instead to become a surgeon, a profession that was gaining more respect at that time.[50] However – and here, according to Slataper, resided Goethe's brilliance – although the mature Goethe recognized the limits of the young passionate Wilhelm, and of his world populated by "overgrown puppets full of nerves, ignorance and phoniness," he was still able to appreciate and forgive "these people he knows are false. [...] Goethe's serious mind now condemns unrestrained passion, – but those feelings and passions are still his. It's foolish – but it's wonderful to live in this way" (*Scritti letterari* 257–8). Slataper's admiration for Goethe derived from the poet's ability to transform the contradictions, tensions, and passions that inform human existence into a coherent work of art while still embracing the complexity and multiplicity of the world. Goethe became for the critic a symbol of modernity and a meaningful model to emulate because he was able to "solve from its roots the anxiety of his century" (278) by integrating all aspects of life with his artistic endeavours: Goethe

50 On the debate about the medical profession during Goethe's time and the author's fascination with medicine, see Tobin.

did not chose to be secluded from the world he inhabited, but instead remained interested in the world of sciences, was socially engaged, and participated actively in the political life of Weimar, taking on various political and civic duties. Goethe's ability to overcome the dichotomy between life and art was the lesson that Slataper aspired to apply to his own existence. As he wrote in a letter to Gigetta:

> [T]o live, organically, all the complexity of human life (through its history and its people, through friends and through adversaries), such that I'll be able to express myself, and to work for all. *To be a man.* Whatever else life gives me, I would not be completely content when my time comes, I would not have arrived, I would be lacking. Art would not be enough for me. Action would not be enough. Nor would knowledge. And not a formal plan; but the blood of the earth, harmonized in my veins. So that it would make no difference if I were writing, speaking, acting, thinking, wanting, desiring. [...] Also, if I am not able to encompass all the complexity of human life, witnessing and participating in all its apparently contradictory forms, commerce and literature, salon and tenement, Karst and pavement, Slovene and Italian, I am not a *poet.* (in this volume, 168–9)

Slataper's *Lebensphilosophie* clearly conveyed the cultural climate of his times and echoed the cultural discourse on Goethe and geniality that was being articulated in different ways at that time within the group of *Vociani* working with him in Florence and by German and Austrian sociologists and philosophers such as Otto Weininger and Georg Simmel. On both sides of the Alps Goethe's ability to "encompass all the complexity of human life" – to use Slataper's words – was viewed as both an artistic and an ethical model whose example could be followed to confront the mechanization and fragmentation of modern life. In Florence, Prezzolini and Spaini appreciated the inventiveness of Goethe's *Lehrsjahre* and admired its social and ethical lesson. The novel emphasized the spiritual development of Wilhelm Meister, who abandoned a life only concerned with pure aesthetics, as represented by his commitment to the theatre, in order to pursue an ethical existence dedicated to action among other human beings.[51] Otto Weininger's reading of Goethe was filtered instead by his misogynistic and anti-Semitic views. In his text *Sex and Character*

51 Alberto Spaini and Rosina Pisaneschi translated Goethe's *Lehrjahre* into Italian and published it in two volumes (1913 and 1915) for the publishing house Laterza. The translation included an introduction in which Spaini expressed the ethical importance of Goethe's novel. For a detailed analysis of the importance of Goethe for the *Vociani*, see Biagi 143–53.

(1903) Weininger blamed "Jew" and "Woman" for the crisis of traditional values that he was witnessing in *fin de siècle* Vienna and called for a new era in which Aryan, masculine, and Christian principles could heal "the spiritual emptiness of Viennese life" (Sengoopta 459). He upheld Goethe as the perfect example of a genius able to experience "a conscious connection with the whole universe" (149)[52] and put an end to the alienating and disintegrating forces at play in contemporary society. In Berlin, Georg Simmel offered instead a subtler interpretation of geniality, closer to Slataper's own reading of Goethe. For Simmel, Goethe's geniality did not derive from condemning the sense of ambiguity and uncertainty of his time, or by embracing anti-Semitic views, as Weininger postulated, but instead from embracing "difference and the whole" as "two twin primal motors of Life in its constant journey of discovery and turmoil" (Harrington 185). Simmel saw in Goethe's life and work the poet's ability to overcome the mechanistic duality of subject-object, and embrace instead "Life" as the principle that encapsulates all the forces and potentialities of a lived experience. As Simmel explained in an article published in Berlin in 1914:

> The marvel of Goethe's existence is that subjective life naturally flows into objectively valuable productivity in art, knowledge and practical conduct. The fundamental tone [*Grundnot*] of his life rings out in the wonderful harmony of personal existence and self-development with the objective image and the ethical structuring of things. ("Goethe and Youth" 88, revised)

What made Goethe remarkable for Simmel was the fact that he maintained a living relationship (*Lebensverhältnis*) with the world in its multifaceted, everchanging expressions, and thus questioned the viability of a synthetic system of thought that, "following its own absolute logic, would erase all differences and expressions of multiplicity to give way to a rigid and sterile unity in which all thought ceases to exist" (Simmel, *Goethe* 94). Goethe understood the consequences of this synthetic view, and he did everything to avoid it because "nothing could come from this rigid and lifeless unity" (94). Thus, even "all the great maxims or formal ideas" are useful only as "means to represent the unity of the world as a living entity" (94).

52 Weininger's work was first reviewed in Trieste's newspaper *Indipendente* in 1905. In 1910 it was reviewed by *La Voce*, and his theory of geniality as presented in *Sex and Character* appealed to the *Vociani*, who found in his writing a "satisfactory answer to their quest for a unified ethical personality" (Cavaglion 35).

In the letter to Gigetta quoted above, Slataper expressed a similar aspiration. Yet while Goethe was blessed with a "tremendous instinctual certainty, [... a] confidence in the simple, autonomous process of his life" (Simmel, "Goethe and Youth" 89), for the young Slataper the certainty and confidence that informed Goethe's work and worldview remained a constant struggle that not only influenced him as a critic and as a poet but also defined his political choices.

His yearning to find an artistic form that would capture the complexity of modern life while at the same time preserving an overarching ethical vision informed the many articles he wrote for *La Voce.* It was, however, a desire that at times hampered his critical judgment. Thus, he remained quite critical towards the new poetic trends that were developing in Italy at that time, especially those that criticized Dannunzian aestheticism. He did not understand the new poetics of the crepuscular poets and remained suspicious of Marinetti's futurist movement. His position was not unique; it followed the path traced by Prezzolini and *La Voce.* Although Slataper and *La Voce* were against the cultural and aesthetic status quo of Italy's highly conservative and elitist academic tradition, they questioned the innovative literary elements expressed by the crepuscular poets who at the beginning of the twentieth century were proposing a new, anti-Dannunzian aesthetic and a more intimate and ironic worldview. As Slataper noted in his article on crepuscular poetry, their lack of engagement with the world at large and their indifference towards the regeneration of society rendered them ineffective, their existential plight futile and meaningless ("Crepuscular Confusion," in this volume, 106). Similarly, he was frustrated by the futurists' bombastic rhetoric and their obnoxious self-promotion, which, according to him, hid their lack of an authentic vision and of "true spiritual content" ("Futurism," in this volume, 102).

The futurist movement, which began on 20 February 1909 with Marinetti's publication of "The Founding and Manifesto of Futurism" on the front page of the French newspaper *Le Figaro,* rejected traditional artistic expressions and celebrated instead a new aesthetic based on technological progress, the power of speed, movement, and violence. The futurists called for a rejuvenation of Italy by repudiating the bourgeois values of their society and Italy's overwhelming veneration of its classical past. Italy's "passatist" attitude not only stifled the imagination of the new generation of Italian artists, but also hindered the progress of Italy as a modern nation. Thus, they asked for the destruction of cultural institutions such as academies, museums, and libraries, which they saw as mausoleums celebrating a derelict past that had nothing more to offer to a modern society.[53] Although the *Vociani* and the futurists shared the same frustration towards the bourgeois conservative society of early-twentieth-century Italy and agreed that Italy's strong classical tradition stifled progress and innovations in the arts and in society, Slataper and the *Vociani* did not believe that the futurists' bombastic and violent approach could offer a serious alternative to Italy's social and cultural stagnation. As Emilio Gentile explains, while "the futurist threw himself into an assault on the world armed with a destructive will, a savage aggressiveness and [...] an idolatrous faith in modernity" (35), the *Vociani* challenged the shortcomings of their society through "serious and severe" work. The *Vociani* "did not exalt physical force, [they] did not develop a cult for sports, [they] did not glorify militarism and imperialism, [they] did not become apologist[s] for violence" (35). Moreover, the *Vociani* accused the futurists of insincerity and charlatanism. In April 1909, only a few months after the publication of Marinetti's futurist manifesto, Ardengo Soffici made fun of it in a satirical piece entitled "La ricetta di Ribi buffone" (The recipe of Ribi the buffoon) where he criticized the artificiality of the movement and its lack of originality. According to Soffici, futurism was nothing more than a badly mixed concoction of French influences combined with modern technologies and spun into a vacuous fabrication ready to be consumed by the Italian public.[54]

Slataper's critique of futurism followed a similar path, further emphasizing the insincerity of the movement whose success was defined only by outrageous statements, publicity stunts, and the financial support of Marinetti. Futurists lacked the "interior drama" necessary to express the complexity of the cultural and historical epoch in which they lived. Their vision of modernity remained superficial and focused only on reality's "exterior appearance: the haste, the quick consumption of energy,

53 On museums Marinetti wrote: "Museums: cemeteries! Identical, really, in the horrible promiscuity of so many bodies scarcely known to one another. Museums: public dormitories in which someone is put to sleep forever alongside others he hated or didn't know! [...] To admire an old painting is the same as pouring our sensibility into a funerary urn, instead of casting it forward into the distance in violent spurts of creation and action" (Rainey et al. 52).

54 "Here we go: Grab a kilo of Verhaeren, two-hundred grams of Alfred Jarry, one-hundred of Laforgue, thirty of Laurent Tailhade, five of Viélé-Griffin, a handful of Morasso – yes, even some Morasso – a pinch of Pascoli, a little phial of Nunzian water. Grab again: fifteen cars, seven planes, four trains, two steamships and two bicycles, various electrical generators, a few red-bot boiler engines: add your best flower of impotence and pomposity; blend it all into a lake of grey matter and aphrodisiac dribble, bring the mixture to a boil in the emptiness of your soul, over the fire of American charlatanism and then offer it over as drink for the Italian public" (Soffici, cited in Gentile 30).

Americanism, etc." (in this volume, 104). Slataper ended his article by dismissing their cultural and historical significance. He believed that their movement would pass without leaving any meaningful trace: "Because of this thoughtlessness, their books are read without any liberating joy. I do not believe at all that Marinetti's movement has any purpose, not even a historical one" (105).

Slataper's faith in the regenerative power of artistic endeavour and his suspicion of any aesthetic expression that did not take into account "the concreteness of life" (Gentile 34) explains also his indifference towards literary works that were being published in Trieste at that time. Not only was he unaware of Italo Svevo, who by 1909 had already published (albeit without any success) his novels *A Life* (1892) and *Emilio's Carnival* (1898), but he was also unable to recognize the literary novelty of Umberto Saba's poetry, although the two writers shared similar modernist concerns and were critical of the normative poetics of their time. Although in his *Letters on Trieste* Slataper showed critical acumen towards the cultural ambience of Trieste and was able to address the sociopolitical and cultural complexity of his native city, he offered quite a narrow and ungenerous reading of Saba's poetry. In 1911 Saba published his first book of poetry and Slataper reviewed it negatively for *La Voce*, denouncing the poet's lack of regenerative vitality. Slataper dismissed Saba as a member of the crepuscular movement and compared the poet to a weak and disoriented insect that can be either destroyed or pitied:

> I paused, feeling at first a bit of the indulgent pride and complacency that every large animal feels when it stops in order not to squash the tiny insect that gropes confused in the blinding whiteness of the street pounded by the constant racket; then, feeling a sympathetic sadness, a desire to offer a helping hand to hold his tired head. (*Scritti letterari* 212)

Saba in his poetry used the city of Trieste as a modern poetic site in which to confront his own fears and doubts. Slataper misunderstood Saba's poems as a gratuitous display of meekness and anxiety. While Saba's "meek, pale, and a bit anxious poetry" (213) could inspire in the reader some sympathy, that did not make it morally acceptable: his weariness remained for Slataper ethically repugnant, while his inspiration was too derivative, too much influenced by Pascoli's intimate subjectivity and too close to the aesthetic vision of the crepuscular poets. Slataper's inability to understand Saba's poetry was confirmed by his refusal to publish Saba's article "Quello che resta da fare ai poeti" (What remains for poets to do) in which the poet explained his poetic and existential vision, which underscored the necessity for poets to free themselves from the burden of literariness in order to find an "honest" expression that could help reveal one's true self. Like Slataper's own interpretation of poetic language as a way to gain self-examination, Saba's poetics of sincerity, honesty, and originality led to "a daily scrutiny of conscience" that ultimately produced a better understanding and a more "honest" representation of reality (Saba 676–7). We do not know why Slataper refused to publish an essay that was so much in line with his own aesthetic concerns, but his refusal, as Saba himself noted in his *Storia e cronistoria del Canzoniere* (in *Tutte le prose*), hindered the critical reception of Saba's poetry (146). His essay remained unpublished until after his death, in 1959.

Ibsen

Slataper's monograph on Ibsen can also be filtered through his perception of geniality as embodied by artists like Goethe, and it reflects Slataper's own aesthetic, intellectual, and ethical concerns. The volume developed from his university thesis and was later revised and expanded during his stay in Hamburg, where he had moved in 1913 as an Italian lecturer at the university. He finalized the manuscript in 1914 and made the last corrections on the proofs during World War I, while fighting on the Italian front. The revised manuscript was published posthumously two years later. Slataper's fascination with Ibsen was part of the wide appeal that the Norwegian playwright exercised on modernist intellectuals, who recognized in his plays the attempt to resolve the tension between "society and the individual, state and church, reason and faith, old and new, flesh and spirit" (Walker 152). Slataper was not the first Triestine writer to publish a study on Ibsen. In 1893 Alberto Boccardi had published *La donna nell'opera di Ibsen* (The representation of women in Ibsen's work) based on a conference that he held at the Minerva Society in Trieste. The book focused on Ibsen's reception in Italy and noted the Italian audience's difficulty in accepting Ibsen's complex female characters. Slataper was unaware of Boccardi's work and had no knowledge of the sporadic work by Carlo Michelstaedter on the Norwegian playwright. In fact, although Michelstaedter was from nearby Gorizia, and overlapped with Slataper at the Istituto di Studi Superiori, the two young men never met.[55] In an article on Tolstoy published in 1908, Michelstaedter had already noted the pivotal role that the individual will played

55 Carlo Michelstaedter (1887–1910) was born in Gorizia, a small town not far from Trieste that also belonged to the Austro-Hungarian Empire. Slataper became aware of Michelstaedter's work only after the latter's death. He published a short review on Michelstaedter's poetry and *Dialogo della salute* in 1912 in *La Voce*.

in Ibsen's work: Ibsen "wants man to break free from the circle of lies that chokes him. He wants man to know how to own his truth and make it triumph; he must fight the lies that are in him and must educate his will to the struggle" (*Opere* 653). What attracted Michelstaedter to Ibsen's characters was their drive towards what he called "persuasion," the determination to strive for an uncompromising authentic self as the only possible alternative to what he perceived as the world of "rhetoric," where individuals are lost in the deceiving and distracting multiplicity of everyday life, and one's meaning and value are imposed from without (Campailla 57).[56] For Michelstaedter, an individual can find redemption only within him or herself, never in another person.

The work of the Norwegian dramatist became for Slataper, as for Michelstaedter, a means to explore the unresolvable dichotomy between life and art, and the tension between the belief in an authentic, ethical self and the multifarious inauthentic world that surrounds us. However, while Michelstaedter refused to compromise his quest for authenticity and strove to turn empirical life "into a coherent totality that is governed by the ethical will" (Harrison 182), Slataper maintained a much more complex and nuanced approach towards contemporary reality, its fragmentation, and its loss of absolute values. It is telling that even Weininger, whose work Slataper admired and read with attention, did not convince *tout court* the Triestine critic. As Slataper noted in his analysis of Ibsen's *Peer Gynt*, Weininger's schematic oppositional worldview that claimed that morality, wholeness, coherence, and totality belonged to a superior masculine principle, whereas women were defined by amorality, incoherence, distraction, and fragmentation and were therefore intellectually and morally inferior, led Weininger to a misreading of Ibsen's drama.[57]

Slataper's interest in history and philosophy led him to filter his analysis of Ibsen through the lenses of the literary critic Francesco De Sanctis and the philosopher Giovanni Amendola, whose works satisfied him better than Weininger's philosophy. While Amendola's ethical perspective

56 See also Michelstaedter, *Persuasion & Rhetoric*. On Michelstaedter's work in English see Bini; Harrison; and, more recently, Angelucci. For a comparison between Michelstaedter and Slataper, see Camerino.

57 Weininger dedicated a whole chapter of his book *Über Die Letzen Dinge* (On last things; 1904) to Ibsen's *Peer Gynt*, a play that he had seen performed during his stay in Christania in August 1902. His reading of the play was informed mainly by Kant's moral interpretation of the individual will and Weininger's own misogyny. Slataper noted: "Because of his schematic dualism [Weininger] did not understand the meaning of Solveig in *Peer Gynt*, as he did not understand all the women characters in Ibsen, just like he did not understand women in general. [...] Therefore, I lean on him, but on my own legs" (*Ibsen* 113).

informed his overall judgment of Ibsen's plays, from De Sanctis Slataper learned the necessity of situating every work of art within the specific historical moment that produced it, and the inseparable correlation that existed in a work of art between ethics and aesthetics.[58] In this light, Slataper considered Ibsen's plays effective only if they expressed a historical truth and brought to the fore the importance of actively engaging with the multiplicity of experiences that life could offer.[59]

Thus, the critic privileged works like *A Doll's House* or *The Wild Duck*, where the artist was able to express a coherent, self-contained world, albeit one ruled by social and psychological deceptions. The controversial play *A Doll's House*, one of Ibsen's most acclaimed works, was for Slataper also one of his most accomplished dramas because the artist was able to give a vivid historical representation of the theoretical core of the woman question as it unfolded at the turn of the twentieth century.[60] Comparing Ibsen to the genius of Dante, Slataper emphasized the artist's ability to create a work of art that was convincing, true to itself, and ethically charged, and that as such transcended time and place. Nora, the heroine of the play, who abandons her husband and children because she does not want to continue to live a lie, exposes the crisis of every human being who strives to find a sense of authenticity in a bourgeois world built on lies and conventions. A similar critical stance can be found in *The Wild Duck* and *Rosmersholm.* Ibsen's creative imagination turned the wild duck with its broken wings into a powerful symbol of the predicament of all the characters and their claustrophobic

58 In a note from 1911 Slataper wrote: "I never write an article on aesthetics, but I always pay attention to man and history. I cannot conceive of anything that is not complete" (*Appunti e note* 141).

59 For De Sanctis the modern individual must recognize the limits of contemplation and the necessity to participate actively in the unfolding of existence: "The starting point is no longer – as was the case at the time of Dante – ignorance, the dark forest, but [...] the inadequacy of contemplation, the need for an active life. The wise Beatrice is transformed into the ignorant and naive Margherita; and Faust does not contemplate but works; in fact, his sin was precisely contemplation, the study of science, and the remedy he seeks is to be born again in the fresh waves of life" (153).

60 The Triestine bourgeoisie enjoyed attending theatrical performances, as the many theatres present in the city attest. It is therefore not a surprise that Ibsen's dramas found a very receptive audience in Trieste, where many of his plays were performed. *A Doll's House* was staged for the first time in 1892, with Eleonora Duse in the main role. A year earlier the famous actress had appeared in *The Wild Duck* at the Teatro Comunale, and the company Vitaliani Salsilli decided to open its Italian tour of *Hedda Gabler* in Trieste (Coceani and Pagnini 151).

environment.[61] Furthermore, the symbol illuminates the whole play and gives it unity and coherence. Rosmer and Rebecca, the doomed protagonists of *Rosmersholm,* in the moment when they open themselves to one another, express the intrinsic value of every human being who longs for meaningful connections. In their doomed relationship, all these characters foreground an ethical project: "the good truth that can educate humankind" (271). Slataper saw in the representation of this desperate communion of human beings the same greatness that informed the work of Leopardi. Both Leopardi and Ibsen were able to give voice to the fragile, flawed existence of a humanity condemned to live in a world that no longer offers any metaphysical certainty.

These favourable reviews were, however, exceptions in Slataper's analysis of Ibsen's work. The critic's aesthetic and ethical vision could not but be at odds with many of the characters and situations portrayed in Ibsen's dramas. Although Slataper recognized that Ibsen was the artist who best represented the fractures brought forth by modernity, with its dissolution of traditional beliefs, the playwright's inability to overcome the sense of unredeemable alienation that permeated many of his characters and plays frustrated the critic. His reading of the epic play *Brand* is a clear example of his struggle to come to terms with the Norwegian playwright.[62] On the one hand Slataper understood Brand's aspiration to a world of authenticity freed from the standards of bourgeois society where "everything is a compromise" (67), but he was also suspicious of Brand's moral fanaticism, which negated any possibility of redemption. The volitional act that pushed Brand in all his choices, his categorical "all or nothing," never led him to an ethical act that could expand into the lives of other individuals; a moral life that takes into account only oneself is not truly moral – it reduces everything to a desert (96). In his solipsism Brand was unable to reconcile his ethical quest with the modern bourgeois world that he inhabited. He refused the inauthentic world that surrounded him without understanding that it was only through the love of his fellow human beings that he could have assumed the prophetical role he aspired to. Slataper condemned Ibsen's moral rigidity and

61 "The Ekdals and the rest of the characters are like the wild duck, which is completely domesticated, but still needs to imagine itself wild" (Slataper, *Ibsen* 248).

62 The play tells the story of Brand, a clergyman who sacrifices every human connection and defies the local religious authority for his obsessive love of God. His rigid, unforgiving attitude leads to the death of his family. Unmoved, he exhorts his flock to follow him to the mountains where he wants to build an "ice church" that will bring him closer to God. After he is abandoned by his people, who stopped believing in him, he dies in an avalanche. Before dying he hears a voice "crying through the thunder-roar" "God is Love" (Ibsen, *Brand* 223).

noted how Brand “tries to be the new Christ who dictates a pure moral law. He offers only suffering” (99–101).

However, even *Peer Gynt*, whose freshness and playfulness captivated the critic, was considered a failure because the playwright did not offer a satisfying, comprehensive solution between the two existential possibilities that inform the play: the moral imperative to be true to oneself against the motto of the trolls that try to lure the protagonist into their world of pleasure and deceit where “it is enough to be as you are” (114).[63] Gynt’s final realization of his worthlessness and his encounter with Solveig, the woman who has loved him and waited patiently for him all her life, do not bring to the play the kind of spiritual uplifting that Beatrice could inspire in Dante. Even in a play as fantastic and as carefree as *Peer Gynt*, Ibsen cannot resist judging and condemning his character according to his rigid worldview. As a result, the play as a whole remains “disharmonious” and “unconvincing,” its ethical tensions unresolved (121).

His final judgment on the Norwegian writer that, with few exceptions, informed all of Slataper’s critiques of Ibsen’s theatrical production, was already present in his reading of *Peer Gynt*. At the end of his analysis he compared Ibsen to Goethe and Dante: “Ibsen is not a poet of Goethe-like epics. […] He is profound, morally profound, he knows the essential truth: but his intellect does not grasp this truth in its multidimensional forms. He is an insightful personality, not a genius.” On the contrary, works like *The Divine Comedy*, or *Faust*, which gravitate around an ethical centre that informs their values and worldview, can grasp and illuminate every aspect of life (120).

This criticism is later reiterated in the pages dedicated to the play *Ghosts*, where Slataper contrasted the claustrophobic, anguished world inhabited by Ibsen’s characters to the open, multidimensional world full of life and possibilities that defined Shakespeare’s plays. Like the works of Dante and Goethe, Shakespeare’s dramas and comedies become the perfect example of a work of art in which the characters can fully express themselves without the author constantly wanting to curb them because of an ethical will imposed from the outside. To the unforgiving Ibsenian world conditioned by “Lutheran aridity,” where the characters are always torn between unresolvable tensions (authentic and inauthentic life in *Brand*; mendacity and truth in *Doll’s House*; courage and cowardice in

63 In the play, the troll king that Peer encounters explains to him the difference between trolls and men, a difference that Peer in unable to see: “Just as morning’s different from evening, / So there’s a real difference between us, / And I will tell you what it is. Out yonder / Under the skies men have a common saying: ‘Man, to thyself be true!’ / But here, ’mongst Trolls, ‘Troll, to thyself be – enough!’ it runs” (Ibsen, *Peer Gynt* 62).

Ghosts; joy and duty in *Peer Gynt*), Slataper juxtaposed the serene genius of the English playwright who allowed his characters to express all their complex humanity:[64]

> Reading, rereading Ibsen over and over again, you are suddenly seized by an indescribable restlessness: give me some air! some blood! Go back to Shakespeare. Look at this joyful poet, who lets all his characters roam around the world, without a worry, without fear of losing control! The good shepherd does not keep his sheep locked next to the arid rock where he is sitting, but lets them graze free on the mountains, each searching out the grass it likes best. Live as masters of your own lives, my brothers! Attend to your business, your loves and your sorrows – cocky and strong, beaten and hesitant, ridiculous, bestial, or delicate – but always filled with your rich and full potential. Get lost, as you please, in the world. The poet loves you just as you are. He has only love for you. He gives himself wholly to you. We cannot find Shakespeare, the poet, in you, because he disappeared in you, and has identified himself with our life. He had so much faith in himself that his genius, with his cheerful voice, could instantly summon all his creatures back to him. (in this volume, 117–18)

Although Slataper analysed Ibsen's work through De Sanctis's literary historiography and contextualized his plays historically and culturally, emphasizing the stifling milieu in which Ibsen lived and against which he rebelled, he did not use the same critical approach with Shakespeare. Instead, Slataper filtered Shakespeare's work through his own modernist lenses in order to find in his plays a key to solve the rigid dichotomy of Ibsen's worldview: "His kingdom is wide, and every vice and virtue has free access there, because vice and virtue are connected within this certain, internal, essential faith. Life, all of it, is truly holy. Ibsen aspires to this holy life, but he is unable to enjoy it: he needs to judge it" (in this volume, 118). The great lesson that Slataper learned from Shakespeare, Dante, and Goethe was that our participation in the world that unfolds around us must be filtered through love, a generous, non-judgmental love for our fellow human beings in their daily toils, struggles, and limitations. Thus, he concluded, "It is not society that ruins us, but serving it falsely, with an impure heart" (*Ibsen* 171). The crisis of modernity and the centrifugal forces that it unleashed can be overcome only if we are willing to turn our eyes away from the uncontaminated heights of the mountaintops where Brand hoped to find his authentic, uncompromising self,

64 See also Coda, *Slataper* 89.

and to embrace instead the multifaceted, kaleidoscopic experience of everyday existence. It is only here, in the rootlessness of the modern condition, in the daily toil and in the love for fellow human beings, that the artist can capture a deeper meaning of life and then transform it into a work of art.

In December 1912, just a couple of weeks after he concluded his dissertation, and the same year of the publication of his *My Karst and My City*, Slataper wrote to Elody Oblath – the friend who had engaged Slataper in an intense intellectual dialogue throughout his critical and literary endeavours – and reflected on the underlying perspective that had informed both *Ibsen* and *My Karst and My City*. From the top of the barren Mount Morello, the highest mountain near Florence, Slataper took in "the view of the golden Tuscan plains below" and wondered why they produced such a sense of peace and happiness in his tumultuous soul. The answer was that the ploughed fields below expressed "solution, fertility, [and] wealth" (*Alle tre amiche* 265). They represented humankind's accomplishments, its need for constructive work and a sense of purpose that could alleviate its existential sorrow. "I defend bread and work," he continued, and noted that meaningful work could be accomplished only in a well-functioning society that must defend itself from its disintegrating elements. He asserted the importance of becoming an active member of society and of taking responsibility for its well-being: "the funny thing is that everyone benefits from society, but only few are willing to take on the burden" (266). However, being the "armed champion" of engaged work is not enough. Love, as he already noted in his *Ibsen*, must enter the equation as well: "a love that extends to every moment and every creature" (264).

My Karst and My City

"We yearn to love and to work" are the concluding words of *My Karst*, the "lyrical autobiography" that explored his own existential crisis and his relationship with the modern urban environment of Trieste.[65] However, as the author noted on more than one occasion, the text defied any facile classification, and it should not be read as a simple autobiography; this was a mistake that the influential critic Emilio Cecchi made in his review of the

65 In a letter to Marcello Loewy, Slataper defined the various parts of his new work: "Now I am working at *My Karst.* Subtitle: Lyrical Autobiography. Three parts: Child, Adolescent, Young Man. Two intermezzi: *The Descent, The Ascent*, and an end: *Among Men*; more or less" (*Epistolario* 91). However, Slataper eliminated all the titles for the publication.

work. Cecchi's unforgivable error, noted Slataper in a letter he drafted but never sent to the critic, was to identify the author with the protagonist, and he thus failed to understand that the story presented in *My Karst* departed from personal experiences to artistically express a more universal truth.[66] However, this universal truth could not be expressed any longer in a traditional linear style. For Slataper, a modern, "lyrical" autobiography did not aim at capturing the totality of a particular individual, but only certain angles and facets filtered through the eyes of the author.[67] Slataper closely followed the aesthetic tendencies of many collaborators of *La Voce*. As Prezzolini observed, positivism, naturalism, and aestheticism had nothing more to offer to the generation born around 1880: Carducci, D'Annunzio, and Sighele, with their aloof and arrogant intellectualism, did nothing but restrict the creativity and originality of the new generation that had to find its own voice and mode of expression (*Italia 1912* 58–9). The autobiography and the fragment became for the *Vociani* the genre and the style that could best render their modern sensibility: "where could they find a more authentic truth than in one's intimate heart and for a brief moment?" asked Prezzolini (*La Voce 1908–1913* 107).

The prose fragments produced around 1910 by *Vociani* such as Jahier, Rebora, and Papini testify to their need to break free both ideologically and stylistically from a tradition that they found stifling, while allowing them to explore new ways to give voice to their own intimate and subjective experiences and bring forth a renewal of culture and society. The same can be said for Slataper's *My Karst and My City*. As a fragmented lyric autobiography it erased chronological continuity to give way to the instant as an incisive moment, essential to express a new vision of existence filled with conflicting moments (the contrast between present and past, the self and the world, the countryside and the city, the desire to sublimate reality and the attempt to express the unsolvable multiplicity of human becoming) that refused to be absorbed into a coherent whole.[68] At the same time, Slataper composed the text according to a precise ethical and social trajectory already outlined in a letter to Marcello Loewy: from a carefree childhood in contact with nature, to the relationship with the mountain as a site of ethical inspiration, to the acceptance of the city as the only place where he could live a meaningful life among other human beings.

---

66 See Martignoni.

67 In a letter to a friend he noted: "[This] book is not at all my autobiography, but the life of anyone (even mine) seen from particular visual angles, [...] which exaggerates some characteristics and forgets many others; so that it is more myth than history" (*Epistolario* 323).

68 See also Milanini.

However, while the novel's overarching trajectory might appear to borrow the traditional telos of the nineteenth-century *Bildungsroman*,[69] in which we witness the urbanization of the protagonist who "becomes enlightened by experience and successfully and unequivocally integrated into society" (Summerfield and Downward 108), here Slataper offered a more modern rendering of *Bildung*, as defined by Claudio Magris in his collection of essays *Journeying* (*L'Infinito viaggiare*). In the introduction to his book Magris notes that while the protagonist of the traditional *Bildungsroman* embarks on his journey in order to "discover his own truth" and "find himself through the journey" (7) in a trajectory that inevitably leads back to a sense of home and authenticity, the modernist *Bildungsroman* did not allow its protagonists such a fulfilling destiny. This modern version of the novel unveils the impossibility of its protagonist's gaining a sense of univocal identity "within the increasingly complex [...] workings of society" (7):

> Soon enough something in the relationship between the individual and the totality that surrounds him cracks; [...] the journey uncovers the precarious nature not only of the world, but also of the traveler, the lability of the individual "I" whose identity and unity begin to break up. (7)

Similarly, the protagonist's temporal and geographical journey does not end with a return to a reassuring sense of coherence and totality, but instead propelled him into losing his fixed, singular identity and embracing instead the multiplicity of Trieste and its many voices, linguistically emphasized by the change of the narrating subject: from the first person singular at the beginning of the story ("I would like to tell you"; *My Karst*, in this volume, 5) to the first person plural with which it ends ("We yearn to love and work"; 78).

The powerful incipit "I would like to tell you ...," repeated three times as a seductive refrain, not only functions as an effective rhetorical strategy to capture the reader's attention, but also problematizes, right from the beginning, the possibility of embracing a coherent identity that could still be conveyed through a highly evocative prose:

> I would like to tell you that I was born in the Karst, in a hut with a thatched roof blackened by rain and smoke. [...]

69 Lukács identifies the *Bildungsroman* as a narrative that describes how the individual growth of the protagonist is achieved only through his active engagement within society, noting that "the development of qualities in men [...] would never blossom without the active intervention of other men and circumstances" (134).

> I'd like to tell you that I was born in Croatia, in a great oak forest. In winter everything was white with snow, the door would open only a crack, and at night I heard wolves howl. [...]
>
> I'd like to tell you that I was born on the Moravian plain and would run like a hare through the furrows, startling chattering crows into the air above. (5)

The narrator *would* like to assume one of these identities and narrate his story from one of these exotic perspectives, but this would be nothing more than a lie. The timeless impression evoked in the first three paragraphs, emphasized by the use of the imperfect tense that dominates the narrative structure, is abruptly countered by the return to the simple past that, with its strong temporal connotation, highlights the gap between the imaginative beginnings and the actual reality: "Then I came here, tried to tame myself, learned Italian, made friends with the most sophisticated young people; but I'll have to return home soon because I'm miserable here" (5). The narrator, in Florence, surrounded by the sophisticated young *Vociani*, must recognize his own alterity and his frustrated attempt to assimilate into the new social setting by appearing more exotic than he really is (5–6). And yet, despite admitting the futility of his deception, in the first part of his narrative he adopts a sensual, aestheticized style, similar to the one used in the incipit, to recount the story of his childhood. Tired of listening to the clever discourses of his Florentine friends, the protagonist lets his mind wander back to his childhood, spent in contact with a reassuring and benign natural setting centred on the country house where his grandmother still lived.

The reverie of his childhood dwelling is strongly linked with an idealized vision of the feminized natural world where the young Slataper experienced a sense of wholeness and belonging that his current life in Florence has rendered impossible. The old patriarchal house and its natural surroundings are described as a space of bucolic serenity with a fairytale flavour, "a felicitous space" to use Bachelard's famous phrase (xxxv), "a maternal paradise" (6) "that gives mankind proofs of illusions of stability" (17). Stylistically, this is achieved both by the soothing repetition of the phrase "there was" used to enumerate the many different trees and flowers growing on the estate, and by the exotic names associated with them. Nature is not only a specific setting that the young child can explore in his games and adventures, but is also represented as a benign mother, ready to nourish the hungry child. The repetition of the verb *ciucciare* (to suckle), with its strong onomatopoeic connotation, further emphasizes the maternal relationship that exists between the child and the natural world that surrounds him, a relationship that also embraces the many female figures who love and protect him. Slataper here clearly embraces the common early-twentieth-century gendered construction of space that sees femininity as existing within an organic, natural community that functions outside the realm of modernity.[70] Within this feminine space everything is order and clarity, including his faith in God and in an idealized, distant Italy: "At that time I believed in God, and [...] I prayed for my beautiful Italy, [...] over there, across the sea" (8).

The fairy tale atmosphere of this first part of the narrative is also captured by the never-ending story that the narrator tells the other children in the hot summer afternoons.[71] The hero of the story, identifiable with the protagonist, has all the attributes traditionally bestowed on such heroes: health, strength, and beauty. He is the beloved leader of his companions, ready to lead them in many adventures. The fragment that follows describes one of these playful adventures: the children rush to the sea and attack a group of German tourists who, unaware of the children, are enjoying swimming off the coast. This episode departs stylistically from the evocative description of the bucolic setting in order to capture in a style and language that closely recalls futurist narratives the liveliness and strength that define the young protagonist as he leads

70 Georg Simmel in his essays "The Relative and the Absolute in the Problem of the Sexes" (1911) and "Female Culture" (1911) described the close link between masculinity and modernity. For Simmel, woman, because of her undifferentiated essence, was excluded from the objective social and cultural forms of modernity: "our objective culture is thoroughly male. It is men who have created art and industry, science and commerce, the state and religion" ("Female Culture" 67). The neurologist and cultural critic Paolo Mantegazza (1831–1910) in his book *Il secolo nevrosico* (The neurosic century) maintained a similar position, underlining the restorative role of women in modern society, precisely because they can bring back a sense of order and serenity to the life of man, subjected to the disruptive stimuli of society. In his essay "The Uncanny," published in 1919, Freud noted the restoring power of the female body as "the entrance to the former Heim [home] of all human beings, to the place where each one of us lived once upon a time and in the beginning. There is a joking saying that 'Love is home-sickness'; and whenever a man dreams of a place or a country and says to himself, while he is still dreaming: 'this place is familiar to me, I've been here before,' we may interpret the place as being his mother's genitals or her body" (245). For a recent analysis of femininity and modernity, see Lichtblau; Felski; and Witz.

71 Slataper proved his hand at writing fairy tales, such as "The Rose Petal," published in 1909 in the *Giornalino della Domenica*, a popular children's periodical, and "Professor Ausserleben and His Soul," published in *Riviera Ligure* in 1911. Highly influenced by German romanticism, especially by the works of Kleist, Tieck, and Novalis, Slataper saw the fairy tale as a way to express the totality of the world where peace and harmony were still accessible to the uncorrupted imagination of children.

his friends into battle.[72] However, the description of the battle and the children's victory against the bathers is unexpectedly juxtaposed with a sudden return to a much more sombre present. Years later, Steno, their leader, who became a professor, suffers from a nervous breakdown and kills himself. The interpolation of the present within the playful and carefree description of the children pestering the vacationers shows the impossibility of remaining absorbed in the idyllic world of an idealized past. The present, kept at bay by the narrator's recollections, resurfaces, exposing the fragile essence of the human condition.

Similarly, the sensual episode of the grape harvest, which focuses on the protagonist's infatuation with Vila, the young niece of the farmer who lives on his family estate, is suddenly interrupted by the narrator's realization that there is something disturbing and violent that surrounds her family. Unlike the protagonist's harmonious household, centred on his loving mother and other female relatives, the world inhabited by Vila is characterized by physical and moral decrepitude. Instead of the airy rooms full of light of the narrator's home, Vila's house is characterized by a disorder "reeking [...] of rags, bottles, and boxes, with plaster walls peeling from the damp" (15). The behaviour of Vila's grandmother and uncle mirrors the decrepitude of their physical surroundings: the grandmother is described as a hateful decaying animal with "the eyes of a barn owl [...] steady and full of cunning," while the uncle, when drunk, cursed and "spat in his mother's face" (15). Vila's world of moral decay is also morally infectious: not only does the protagonist start acting as a thief as soon as he enters Vila's house, but he also shows absolute indifference when he finds out about the uncle's brutal behaviour towards his mother.

The narrator's attempt to stop these disturbing recollections ("But I don't want to talk about those people!" [15]) reveals how difficult it is to retain a bucolic image of his childhood. The sudden return to the present tense introduced by the adversative clause and his attempt to deflect his memories towards a more pleasant past by focusing on his infatuation for Vila do not allow him to regain the sense of Pan-like immersion with nature that he previously experienced. The "[p]recious days [...] full of love and glory" (16) that marked his relationship with the young woman within a benign natural setting unexpectedly come to an end as Nature unveils its own mystery and vulnerability: "Because the

72 In a letter to Marcello Loewy, Slataper recognized that, in spite of his dislike for the futurist movement, he felt close to their aesthetics of violence: "You know what a violent man I am. [...] I am in a futurist mood. The only difference is that I am intelligent while the futurists are not" (*Epistolario* 76).

earth is full of suffering. [...] All trunks bear a scar or wound" (21). The narrator must finally accept that his attempt to reconstruct a fictional rendering of his childhood only further emphasized his present sense of displacement: "Where am I going? My country is far away, the nest is shattered" (22).

The irrevocable loss of his childhood, and the sense of irremediable homelessness that pervades him, marks the turning point of *My Karst and My City*. From now on the text underscores the crisis of the modern individual who must live in the alienating, fragmented world of modernity. Trieste, the multi-ethnic, cosmopolitan metropolis with all its contradictions and complexities, replaces the organic sites of his idyllic childhood. However, before being able to confront the chaos of the modern city, the protagonist needs the reinvigorating force of Mount Kâl, the mighty peak rising on the barren Karstic plateau that surrounds the city. It is worth noting that the symbolic transition from childhood to youth is marked by nature's switch of gender: from the organic feminine principle that defined his childhood to a powerful masculine principle that will enable him to gain the power and strength necessary to withstand the disaggregating forces of the city and to bring new life to the weakened and decadent urban society. Following closely the traditional image of the mountain as a site of moral and physical rejuvenation, the author presents the protagonist's ascent as an initiation rite that transforms him into Alboino, the king of the Lombards, who led his tribe from the eastern plains into Italy. In his description of the mountain as a site of ethical and moral inspiration, Slataper clearly had in mind both Ibsen's poem "On the Heights" and Nietzsche's *Thus Spoke Zarathustra.*

The protagonist of Ibsen's epic poem, which Slataper analysed in detail in his monograph dedicated to the Norwegian playwright, abandons his old mother and fiancée in the valley below and finds refuge on the mountaintop where he decides to live and pursue his aesthetic ideals, forever breaking off the emotional ties that bound him to the life of his native village. From up above he witnesses the death of his mother and the wedding of his former fiancée, but nothing makes him abandon the heights of the mountain: "I am clad now in steel, I follow the commandment/ that bids me to wander in high-country! / I have lived out my lowland life / Up here on the heights there is freedom and God / down there the others are groping."[73] Slataper, however, as we have already seen in his analysis of Ibsen, did not perceive the rarefied world of the mountain as his ultimate goal. Like Zarathustra, he saw the solitude of the mountain

73 Ibsen, "On the Heights," cited in Moi 174.

as a necessary stage to gain the ethical strength needed to descend into the valley and bring his teaching to the people living down below. However, as with Zarathustra, his attempt to redeem mankind soon revealed its inefficacy: the narrator's efforts to incite the Slovenian peasants who live in the Karst to descend with him into Trieste fail miserably, and he must realize that he needs to be more than Alboino, the strong warrior and leader. He must become *Pennadoro* ("golden pen," the literal translation of the word "Slataper"), the poet who can combine the might of the mountain and the courage and strength of Alboino with the narrator's creative and philosophical aspirations. Yet the protagonist becomes quickly aware that even as *Pennadoro* he cannot fully negotiate the urban chaos that surrounds him. The first encounter with the urban environment quickly overwhelms him: the crowds, the red lights, and the architectural structures close in on him, producing a sense of threat and claustrophobia: "you're not really free to walk in the city. In the city, your every step is observed by spies who pretend they're not watching. [...] And though I'm well covered by my cloak, these eyes, this covert surveillance oppresses me. The street lamps light up with a blinding red glow; the big rectangular houses press in. Why not just stretch out here, on the cobblestones? I'm exhausted. I turn around abruptly. Up there is Mount Kâl. Why did I ever come down?" (30). The view of the mountain allows him to recover his strength, at least momentarily, and to confront the most threatening part of the city, the infamous *città vecchia,* to prove to himself that he can indeed redeem, through his poetic language, the lost humanity that lives there. The episode that follows, which takes place in the old quarter of town, and the protagonist's attempt to interact with the drunks in the old tavern only further demonstrate the inherent contradiction between his lofty ideals and the squalid reality that surrounds him. His claim at the end of part I, "I'm among thieves and murderers; but if I leap onto a table and Christ inspires my words, I can destroy and remake the world with them" (31), remains unanswered, followed only by the empty page that marks the end of the narrative's first section.[74]

In an attempt to distance himself from the decrepitude of the Old Town, the narrator shifts his attention to Trieste as a site of excitement, wealth, and opportunities, the place where "the future of the world is being decided" (32). However, the image of Trieste as a modern metropolis made wealthy by its ports and its international trade, bustling with possibilities, noises, and colours, is countered by more subdued images

---

74 On the episode in the tavern in *città vecchia,* see also Coda, "Representation of the Metropolis"; and Bond.

of the city as a site of political frustrations and economic uncertainties. The protagonist's eagerness to participate in the political life of Trieste is quickly deflated once he realizes that the diverse groups that make up the political structure of the city, with their disorganized meetings and ineffective protests, lack a clear political vision. The city also unveils the tragic outcomes of a world that is ruled by financial institutions and an unstable money economy. He describes the financial distress incurred by his family, the humiliation of having to move to a small apartment, the worsening of his mother's illness, and his frustrated attempt to find a job at the "Credit," the Triestine branch of the prestigious Austrian Bank. In a desperate effort to escape his predicament, the narrator introduces a fragment in which he returns to the Old Town looking for a prostitute, "hoping to find some dirty fun" and distraction (42).

Here the protagonist seems to embrace the "blasé attitude" described by Georg Simmel in his essay "The Metropolis and Mental Life." Slataper asserts that he understands the money economy that rules modern cities and sees prostitution as simple commerce, void of any moral judgment; he also seems to accept the monetary exchange that his interaction with the prostitutes implies (43). However, this attitude comes to a quick end the moment he comes face to face with these women. Their sickly appearance, emphasized by the heavy make-up, greasy hair, and strong perfume, makes him retreat immediately for fear of becoming infected, and makes him long for his clean and bedbug-free bedroom. The bedroom, just like the house of his childhood, becomes the Bachelardian space where he imagines that he can still withdraw from the corrosive reality of urban life and maintain a wholesome existence where everything is stable and complete. However, as we have already seen, the centrifugal forces shaping the modern metropolis have already contaminated his home as well. The protagonist's home is not immune from the laws of the market that govern the city, nor is it free from sickness and suffering. Its wholeness is an illusion. The domestic serenity that characterized the protagonist's childhood spent in the patriarchal house in the country cannot subsist in the modern metropolis. Even his mother, as a representative of the organic feminine principle, loses her unifying role once she is faced with the harsh laws of the market economy: her ill health worsens once the family faces financial distress.

The sense of disorientation the protagonist experiences at this point of the narration is exposed thematically by imagining alternative existential possibilities expressed stylistically in disconnected fragments: he dreams of running away to exotic, violent places; he sees himself as a cynical journalist looking for the latest scoop or as an artist who has lost his inspiration; and finally, more realistically, he reflects on his role as a young contributor to *La Voce*. As such, he recognizes his own contradictions and inadequacies while expressing frustration at the narrow literary and philosophical interests of his Florentine friends: "I much prefer speaking with ordinary people and finding out what interests them. It could be that my whole life will amount to a vain search for humanity, but for me philosophy and art don't suffice, nor do they fill me with enough passion. Life is broader and richer than that" (47).

Here again, the protagonist seeks the mountain as a site of strength and rejuvenation. While his descent from Mount Kâl aimed at regenerating the morally weakened Trieste, his ascent to Mount Secchieta, east of Florence, is an attempt to counteract the intellectualism of *La Voce* in order to revitalize it and make it more relevant to the concerns of a wider humanity. Like his descent to Trieste in the first part of the narrative, his ascent of Mount Secchieta does not have the expected results. The strenuous climb through a frozen landscape and his final ascent to the summit does not give him access to the strength and power he imagined. In fact, the rhetoric of moral strength ascribed to the mountain is somewhat undermined by the fragment that follows. Through a sudden association of images, the protagonist finds himself unexpectedly immersed in the depths of the sea, described as a reassuring female principle where he can dreamingly lose himself, just as he did in the natural bucolic landscape that defined his childhood.[75] The unexpected change of topography, from the mountain in Tuscany back to the gulf of Trieste, coupled with the shift of linguistic register (from the harsh tone used during the ascent to the dream-like description of the protagonist drifting away in the immensity of the sea), point once again to Slataper's unresolved modernist angst: on the one hand his desire to engage in the complex cultural and social reality of the world he lived in; on the other hand his unquenchable sense of nostalgia for the organic world of a benign nature, where unity, coherence, and love are still possible.

The sense of homelessness that he perceived at the end of the first part of the narrative deepens in the final section of the text when he must come to terms with the suicide of his girlfriend, Anna Pulitzer. Anna, his "Little Joy" as he affectionally called her, the young woman who was his confidante and listened to the turmoil of his soul, killed herself after a failed rendezvous with the author in Florence. The note that she left him in which she stated, "this will be for your work [*opera*]. [...] be Scipio forever" (where *opera* might refer specifically to his literary

75 As Deborah Amberson noted, "this marine episode would not seem remotely out of place in the first part of the text" (14).

text *My Karst and My City*, the project he was working on at that time, or more generally his comprehensive life work) suggests that her final act was intended as a sacrifice to allow the writer to be always true to himself and pursue his intellectual and ethical dreams.[76] Moreover, as Thomas Harrison noted in his analysis of Anna's suicide, "by rejecting the limitations of life," her death became the "irrefutably dramatic, historical proof" (91) of the existential need to gain that sense of authenticity that many early-twentieth-century intellectuals were still desperately seeking and that Slataper himself was exploring and problematizing in the pages of his lyrical autobiography.[77] At the same time her suicide showed the shortcomings of such a way of thinking. If at the beginning of the twentieth century "suicide was not only accepted among the options of those who insisted on ruling their lives; it was often viewed as the most laudable of acts" (92), it also questioned the validity of a traditional system of beliefs that still embraced ontological and epistemological certainties.

After Anna's death, the narrator's belief that he could affirm the autonomy of the individual self as an absolute agent who could bring new life to a decadent society came to an end. Stylistically this change of perception is rendered through disconnected fragments in which he describes his movements throughout the city, his thoughts, and his fears. Thematically, this shift is expressed through the description of his loss of direction and an overwhelming sense of disorientation that accompanies his meandering through a nocturnal, lifeless Trieste and a dark, mysterious Karst. In these new, alienating surroundings the protagonist must recognize the absurdity of his previous self-perception as the strong individual whose words and actions could rejuvenate a decadent, weakened society. Now he can only admit to his own lack of direction and existential estrangement: "I don't know what will become of my life [...] and I look upon this unknown life like a stranger" (56).

76 The note, together with a detailed description of Anna's last attempt to see Scipio in Florence, is recounted by Stuparich in a footnote to his edition of Scipio Slataper, *Alle tre amiche* (503–4). Slataper never understood Anna's deep-seated unhappiness because he was too taken by his own intellectual aspirations to pay attention to her existential angst. Moreover, as he noted in a letter to the young woman, he was not interested in her as a full-fledged human being, but as inspirational, idealized muse: "You are not any woman: you are Anna. You understand that for Scipio to give himself completely [to you] it is necessary that Anna be Beatrice, Salome, Sappho, Juliet [...]" (*Alle tre amiche* 53).

77 Harrison, noting the similarities between Anna Pulitzer's suicide and the suicides of Irma Seidler (Lukács's fiancée) and Nadia Baraden (Michelstaedter's love interest), comments that the three deaths "reaffirm a principle to which the young Lukács, Michelstaedter and Slataper are absolutely attached: the autonomy of the single self, rejecting the effacements it risks in erotic fusion" (91).

Whereas earlier in the narrative the protagonist believed in his own power as a poet and a leader who could "destroy and remake the world" (31), now his journey does not promise a return to a familiar setting or a rewarding ending. Quite the opposite: "Where am I? My eyes are squinting in the heat, and I stroll along in a daze. I walk slowly and watch everything, like a stranger exhausted from travel who must still stay alert because someone is waiting for him, someone full of love and curiosity. But no one is waiting for me, and upon my return no one will sit with me, and ask with loving eyes: 'And so? How was the journey?' ... nowhere can I lay my great weariness down" (57). The narrator's endeavour is an apt illustration of the modern traveller, whose journey, as Magris put it, "becomes an avenue of no return, leading to the discovery that there is no, there can be no, and there must be no return" (7). Here we can only experience "a journey that moves in an ever forward direction [...] like a straight line lurching into space" (7–8).

The new condition of homelessness that the protagonist faces leads him at first to express his sense of alienation towards a world that appears to have lost its meaningful core: "The whole world is working in a great frenzy of self-obliterating pain. And it builds houses and closes itself within walls so that bodies can't see each other tossing sleeplessly between the sheets, and it weaves itself clothes so it can think that at least someone else's body is healthy and sound, and it issues millions of clocks so that the moment is whipped on perpetually through space, like one of the damned ceaselessly pushing ahead so as not to fall" (57). However, Slataper's vision of an existence centred solely on illusions and deceits (what Michelstaedter in the same years called "rhetoric") does not lead him to descend into a defeatist attitude towards life or to reclaim his earlier vision of stability and certainty centred in the world of his childhood or in the heights of the mountains.

Instead, facing the abyss of nothingness, he is now willing to question the traditional belief in a totality that can sublimate the multiplicity of existence: "And the whole: what is it? They've conditioned you to use the word. Maybe there is no whole, only fragments seeking fusion in vain" (68). Life must be accepted in all of its fragmentary and contradictory expressions. In this new, truly modern perception of life, a transcendental, absolute truth ceases to exist.

As a consequence, the emphasis of his writing process changes; rather than trying to give a unitary meaning to the various fragments that compose human existence, now he is compelled to grasp and record his urban experiences in their fleeting, splintered essence. It is in his aim to give poetic expression to the contingency and ambivalence of life that Slataper shows his modern sensibility. Slataper's notion of the task of the poet as well as his depiction of the reality that surrounds him has changed drastically. He has gone from the romantic belief in the poetic possibility of bringing order and clarity to a fragmented urban reality to the modern concept of the poet as a person who must express, in the words of Baudelaire, "the transient, the fleeting, the contingent" (403).

The new hero envisioned by Slataper at the end of his narrative is the individual who can overcome the absence of grounding traditional beliefs, not by recreating some transcendent synthesis and teleological aim, but by forging relations, and finding ways of constructing a shared destiny concretely and historically grounded in the reality of Trieste. The city is no longer perceived as a space of alienation or degeneration that needs to be revived by the young poet, but as an exciting and tangible expression of human creativity, energy, and work. His description of the city is now determined by careful observations of the early-morning activities, "full of movement and colour": gatekeepers opening warehouses, pilots preparing to depart, empty carts ready to be loaded with the goods that have just arrived, foremen efficiently selecting day workers. Moreover, the bustling activity of the city is not an end unto itself, but offers unforeseen experiences and possibilities:

> Our big steamers weigh anchor for Salonika and Bombay. And tomorrow locomotives will thunder across the iron bridge over the Vltava, then rush alongside the Elbe into Germany. [...] We will travel, uncertain and nostalgic, compelled by hopeful memories that we won't recognize anywhere as our own. Where did we come from? Our country is far away, the nest undone. But moved by love, we will return to our country, Trieste, and from here we will begin. (77–8)

The centrifugal force of the metropolis that propels its inhabitants to distant places, the mixture of nostalgia for the sense of home that has forever been shattered coupled with the thirst for novelty, action, and movement, render Trieste the symbol of the only possible homeland for the modern individual. As a home, Trieste offers all that is exciting and new without, however, bestowing the consolation of a traditional, romantic idea of fatherland as something that is defined by fixed, immutable beliefs.

As Slataper wrote to Gigetta Cariel, his future wife, conflating the destiny of his city with his own, Trieste has become the symbol of a new, modern vision of the world:

> Trieste is my country. Every day I find more of Trieste in myself. Trieste, which is the obstacle to victory, and could be its symbol. [...] The city contains,

> restless, the elements that disturb us moderns: we must truly reconcile them. I can try to convince myself that I'm calm, while I write in Italian and read German books, and I contemplate our nation with a human conscience, but unless I am able to realize and spread this balance of mine, it does not really exist. Also, if I am not able to encompass all the complexity of human life, witnessing and participating in all its apparently contradictory forms, commerce and literature, salon and tenement, Karst and pavement, Slovene and Italian, I am not a *poet.* [...] This is a man: this being who combines tragic opposites and gives a cry of joy. ("To Gigetta," in this volume, 168–9)

The city of Trieste becomes the symbol of a modern existence where differences and contradictions can coexist. As Slataper had already stated in his articles for *La Voce*, just as the city maintains its ethnic, linguistic, and cultural multiplicity, the poet must be able to give voice to the "tragic opposites" that make up modern individuals. Moreover, the lack of a unifying organic totality does not lead to a nostalgic longing for a romantic dwelling that is fixed and immutable. On the contrary, the metropolis, with its chaotic energy and centrifugal forces, becomes the true homeland of the city-dweller. It is here, not in the solitude of the Karst, that the individual can find his destiny: a destiny that no longer privileges the individual I but, as the sudden linguistic change from the "I" to the "we" of the final paragraphs suggests, embraces instead the plurality of a whole community. The powerful final pages of the narrative indicate Slataper's awareness that a solipsistic view of existence is no longer viable or desirable within the modern context of the metropolis. In this new environment where it is impossible to find a unifying meaning, where one cannot alleviate the existential angst of one's fellow human beings, it becomes necessary to accept the help of others and offer them the same humble sympathy that we expect in return. The sentence that concludes the text, "we yearn to love and work," suggests Slataper's intention to participate emotionally, intellectually, and practically in the life of his city, the only possible homeland for the protagonist of *My Karst and My City*.

Political Writings

Slataper's belief in a collective ethical commitment expressed at the end of *My Karst and My City* became the driving force of all his political writings. After the publication of his lyrical autobiography and the completion of his volume on *Ibsen*, he devoted his remaining years to reflecting on the evolving delicate political situation of Trieste, Italy, and Europe as they headed towards World War I. These texts show Slataper's ideological move from a form of cultural irredentism to the interventionist cause as the war approached. Although, as Ballinger has noted, Slataper's political views turned out to be "firmly Italian" (37) and revealed the limits of his political multicultural project, he strove to maintain a historical perspective of the events as they evolved. Following Machiavelli's political belief that it is "more fitting to go directly to the effectual truth of the thing than to the imagination of it" (61), Slataper acknowledged the ethical need to look with honesty at political events without deceiving oneself or others by blindly following a predetermined ideological perspective.[78]

His collaboration with *La Voce* and the publication in 1909 of his *Letters on Trieste* already indicated his commitment to analysing the cultural and political situation of Trieste without buying into the popular irredentist narrative that usually informed such discourses.[79] A couple of articles written in response to the reaction triggered by his *Letters* clearly showed his political acumen and his ethical commitment to always strive to report the "effectual truth," especially if such a truth would undermine preconceived political notions not based on facts. Slataper's intention, throughout all of his writings, was not to deny the Italian identity of his city, but to look at it as objectively as possible. Such an approach allowed him to separate himself from the conventional political and nationalist discourses that were taking shape in Trieste and in Italy. In a short piece published after the local elections of 1909, Slataper defended the choice of the Triestine socialist party to open its ranks to Slovenian nationals because this alliance allowed for a better understanding between the two ethnic groups while counteracting the popularity that the nationalist Slavic movement was gaining at that time (*Scritti politici* 338). Slataper was not a socialist

78 In a letter to Giani Stuparich, where he discussed a new editorial enterprise (the publication of *Trieste*, a new journal that addressed the political and cultural reality of Trieste), he noted the seriousness of such an endeavour and stressed how Machiavelli could become their maximum example of moral rectitude because the Florentine author never deceived himself: "politics (like 'morality') is so often immoral because one who is worthless believes he can do something by telling a few lies and cheating a couple of people. Machiavelli, on the other hand, is very moral: because his greatest aim is always to teach that those who deceive in order to achieve a certain purpose, [...] should never deceive themselves. This is for me the fundamental point: one should always be accountable" (*Epistolario* 162).

79 See also the short "Caricatures" that Slataper penned for *La Voce* in 1909: "The serious irredentist" and "the 'figs and raisins' irredentist" in which the author describes with irony two different attitudes towards irredentism – on the one hand, the serious young republican who believes blindly in the need for violent irredentism without understanding the contemporary political situation and, on the other, the typical Triestine trader, who poses as an irredentist, because that is the accepted norm, but is in reality more interested in his commerce of figs and raisins (*Scritti letterari* 12–13).

(notwithstanding his youthful sympathies for the party),[80] but he understood that it was absurd to ignore the increasing political influence held by the Slovenians living in Trieste. For this reason, it made much more sense for the party to embrace Slovenian members than to alienate them and thereby widen the divide between the two groups. The second article, in polemic against the newspaper *Il Piccolo*, which constantly minimized the importance of the Slovenian presence in the city, emphasized once again the fact that Trieste had indeed a large Slovenian population "with its own will and thoughts" and condemned with harsh words "the presumption of ethnic superiority that shrouds us [Italians] in a veil of disastrous ignorance" (343). The aim of a newspaper, he argued, should be to inform its readers both locally and abroad of the actual reality of the city, rectifying misrepresentations and errors. *Il Piccolo* had become instead an organ of disinformation in order to advance its political nationalist agenda: thus the paper had no qualms insisting that "Istria is almost completely Italian, [...] that Trieste as a whole wishes to be united with Italy, that the barbarian Slovenians live only in the outskirts of the city, but not in the city proper" (343). Slataper stated that false reporting, by sustaining a distorted image of reality, undermined any potential concrete solution to the ethnic and political complexity of the city.

For Slataper, speaking of irredentism without knowing the history and development of the city and without truly understanding its present situation was a useless and detrimental exercise. A year later, in order to put an end to the "disastrous ignorance" regarding Triestines' affairs, he edited two special numbers of *La Voce* dedicated to irredentism and nationalism, with articles by various intellectuals who explored irredentism from different ideological perspectives.[81] Slataper himself contributed two groundbreaking and well-researched articles, the first on the historical

80 Slataper's sympathies for an anti-bourgeois socialism were expressed in the short story "Il freno" (The break), published in 1907, when he was still a high school student in Trieste. However, he never adhered to the ideology of the party because he could not imagine an individual submitting to a collective will (*Appunti e note* 21). Years later, reflecting on his youthful attraction to socialism, he confessed to Elody: "I used to have sympathy only for the working class and for democratic principles, although I was always an aristocrat" (*Alle tre amiche*, 293).

81 In addition to two articles by Slataper, the two special issues included articles by Angelo Vivante, Ruggero Timeus, Giuseppe Prezzolini, Giuseppe Antonio Borgese, Alberto Spaini, Benito Mussolini, Giovanni Papini, Gaetano Salvemini, and Giuseppe Vidossich. Slataper's articles appeared on 8 and 15 December 1910, and are reprinted in *Scritti politici* 39–90. "Nothing had been published on the issue of irredentism that could be compared to these writings," Stuparich admiringly noted in his work dedicated to his late friend (245).

development of Triestine Italian identity and the second one on the city's current conditions. The articles were accompanied by an extensive bibliography dedicated "To the nationalists!" (84–90). Although Slataper did not add any comment to this dedication, the exclamation point at the end can be easily interpreted as an ironic exhortation to the nationalists to base their assertions on careful documentation, just as he did, by consulting not only articles and books but also the necessary archives in Trieste and in Rome. In his analysis of the irredentist phenomenon, Slataper strove to present the current situation in objective terms, refraining from nationalist ideology or rhetorical platitudes. In the first article, entitled "Un po' di storia" (A bit of history; 39–60), the critic described the specific realities of the various unredeemed territories (Trentino, eastern Friuli, Istria, Trieste), inserted their history into the wider Italian and European historical context, and provided an in-depth survey of European history, from the Napoleonic years to the Risorgimento uprisings to the Triple Entente. Here the author made two important points. He noted that Trieste's national identity was a very recent phenomenon that started only after Italy's unification and, second, he emphasized that the newly created Italian state had very little political or economic interest in those geographical areas. Even the pages dedicated to Oberdan, the major hero and martyr of the irredentist cause, were filtered by Slataper's desire to maintain his historical objectivity.[82] While he gave a heartfelt description of Oberdan's personality and ideals and showed his admiration for Oberdan's resolution to participate actively in the political and historical arena no matter the consequences, he also noted the political uselessness of his gesture: "His sacrifice was unsuccessful, like any individual attempt that tries to oppose the historical raison d'etre of a city. Trieste has continued on its way, without stopping to meditate in front of the tomb of Oberdan. Thus, instead of igniting [the irredentist movement], it was the proof that clearly showed Trieste's anti-irredentism" (56). Trieste's irredentism was, in his view, a rhetorical pose void of any political significance.[83]

The political absurdity of pursuing a nationalist campaign is further developed in the second article dedicated to irredentism. After

---

82 Guglielmo Oberdan, born Wilhelm Oberdank (1858–82), was a Triestine irredentist who plotted the assassination of Austrian emperor Franz Joseph in 1882, when the emperor was visiting Trieste on the occasion of the city's celebrations for the five-hundred-year anniversary of its annexation to Austria. The plot was discovered, and Oberdan was arrested and hanged. He became the most important martyr to the irredentist cause and a symbol of the oppression of the Italians under Austrian rule.

83 See also Tommasini 226.

providing a detailed historical background of the development of the political situation in Italy and in Trieste, Slataper in the following article, entitled "Oggi" ("Irredentism Today," in this volume), directed his attention to the present situation. With the same historical lucidity, he noted the need for the still young and weak Italian nation to submit to the will of the great European powers. Therefore, he recognized the strategic necessity for Italy to sign the Triple Alliance with Germany and Austria in 1882. Indeed, although such an alliance with Austria could be seen as the ultimate betrayal of the Risorgimento ideals, Slataper noted its inevitability. He acknowledged that the Triple Alliance was "a harsh necessity" for Italy as it entered the European political arena ("Irredentism Today," in this volume, 125), but he added that it was also a fact that the popular anti-Austrian sentiments one witnessed in Italy at that time had not yet been elaborated into actual political consciousness. This lack of a clear political agenda, he continued, was due to the chaotic and disorganized proliferation of many contradictory forms of irredentism that coexisted in Trieste and in Italy. Slataper distinguished and described in detail five types of irredentism: republican, masonic, imperialist, moral, and cultural. The only valid kind of irredentism in the present situation, he concluded, was the cultural one, which he had already discussed in his *Letters on Trieste.* This type of irredentism did not concern itself with political borders, but instead advocated the creation of cultural relationships among all Italians, on both sides of the border. It did not aim to achieve a politically unified Italy, but it claimed the importance of an ideal, transnational cultural homeland where Italian values and identity could thrive. One of the objectives of this type of irredentism was to inform all Italians living in Italy and in Austria about the present reality with historical clarity. What was needed, he felt, was not an irredentist war dictated by imperialistic aspirations, which Slataper rejected *tout court.* Instead he advocated the need to embark on a programmatic path towards cultural, political, and military preparedness for any future eventuality.[84]

After analysing the political power that Austria and Germany exerted over Europe, Slataper noted that, in order to defeat the German-Austria coalition, Italy should be willing, if necessary, to pursue a philo-Slavic

84 In the article "L'Università Italiana a Trieste" (The Italian university in Trieste), published in 1911 in *Il Giornalino della Domenica,* Slataper asserted the need of an Italian university in Trieste that could forge the basis for a national cultural identity: "Only when we are able to study in our own language will we be able to become a nation. We will be able to know who we are. Today we do not. Today we shout and trade" (*Scritti politici* 321). See also note 26.

alliance with all the Balkan states. However, this meant that Italy should "renounce Trieste, Istria, and its aspirations in the Balkans" (139). It is not difficult to imagine the reaction that such a statement produced in the local papers. Once again, *Il Piccolo* accused Slataper of endorsing anti-Italian, philo-Slavic positions. The author defended himself by stressing, once again, the need for a true, disinterested analysis of the present conditions. The true enemy of Trieste, he concluded, was not the Slavs or the Austrian government, but the Italian irredentists who, blinded by lies and moved by purely dogmatic stances, were unwilling to look at the current reality and therefore resisted any rational attempt to become better equipped to handle the present and future political life of the city (*Scritti politici* 366–8).[85]

Slataper returned to the political reality of Trieste in his 1912 essay "L'avvenire nazionale e politico di Trieste" ("The National and Political Future of Trieste," in this volume, 140). The long and complex article marked an important passage in Slataper's political views. While he continued to reject the nationalist irredentism of many Triestines, he also questioned the internationalist views embraced by the Austro-Marxist socialists. Furthermore, he started to reflect on the intrinsic value of the nation state, embracing Hegel's conception of history as the manifestation and unfolding of the *Weltgeist.* The point of departure for this article was Angelo Vivante's recently published book *Irredentismo adriatico* (Adriatic irredentism, 1912). Vivante, the director of the socialist paper *Il Lavoratore,* analysed Trieste's political situation from a strictly economic perspective. For Vivante the ethnic tensions present in the city could not be divorced from the city's financial identity. Like Slataper, Vivante recognized that Trieste's commercial strength derived from its port, and that such a privileged position would cease to exist once Trieste became Italian. While Austria would move its commerce to another port in the Austrian littoral, Italy, which already had other thriving ports, would have no reason to invest in Trieste, and the city would quickly decline.[86]

Vivante was deeply influenced by the internationalist socialism known as Austro-Marxism, theorized, among others, by Otto Bauer in his important volume *The Question of Nationalities and Social Democracy.* Bauer

85 The article, entitled "I nostri due numeri sull'irredentismo" (Our two volumes on irredentism), appeared in *La Voce,* 2 February 1911.

86 On Vivante's thought, see Apih, "La genesi di 'Irredentismo adriatico'" 265–313, and Millo, *Storia di una borghesia* 142–216. On Vivante and Slataper, see also Cella 21–7 and Pertici 635–59. On Angelo Vivante and Austro-Marxism, see Cangiano 117–30. For a summary of the political discourses in Trieste at that time, see Cattaruzza, *Italy and Its Eastern Borders* 30–50. On the development of the socialist party in Trieste, see Cattaruzza, *Socialismo adriatico.*

recognized that the socialist movement, before addressing the issues of the proletarian masses, should come to terms with the nationalist problem, which in a multinational state like the Austrian Empire was of pivotal importance. Bauer never questioned the legitimacy of the Austro-Hungarian Empire (357). For him and other Austro-Marxist theorists, the empire should continue to exist as "a federal state that regulates matters relevant to all nations and that safeguards the interests shared by all nations" (259). Within this federalist structure each national group would maintain the political autonomy necessary to develop its own cultural institutions and foster its own national identity.[87] Vivante applied Bauer's lesson to the ethnic reality of Trieste. He noted that the growth of Trieste's population, in terms of both Slavic and Italian elements, was a direct consequence of its commercial and financial development, and that it would have been anachronistic and detrimental to the well-being of the city to ostracize a large part of its inhabitants in the name of nationalist ideologies. Furthermore, the ethnically mixed working class was more interested in its daily struggles for better living conditions than in irredentist and nationalist alliances (Vivante 204–5). He concluded his work by envisioning an ethnically peaceful Trieste, perceived as "a vehicle and a link between different ethnic and economic currents, in a necessarily neutral and autonomous administration. [...] Here the two ethnic groups [Slovenian and Italian] would find the foundations of a peaceful national coexistence, facilitated by the existence of shared economic concerns that need to be protected" (259).

Slataper appreciated Vivante's analysis and accepted Vivante's view that "the historical mission of Trieste is to serve as a crucible and source of civilization – of three civilizations" ("National and Political Future," in

87 Bauer elaborated the idea of "the personality principle": "In its pure form, the aim of the personality principle is to constitute the nation not as a territorial corporation, but as an association of persons. The national bodies regulated by public law would thus constitute territorial bodies only insofar as their efficacy could not extend, of course, beyond the borders of the empire. Within the state, however, power would not be given to the Germans in one region and the Czechs in another; rather, each nation, wherever its members resided, would form a body that independently administered its own affairs. It would very often be the case that two or more nations would construct their own national administrative bodies within the one city, erect national educational institutions side by side, but undisturbed by one another – in exactly the same way as Catholics, Protestants, and Jews independently attend to their religious affairs side by side within the one city. The realization of the personality principle would require the division of the population according to nationality. However, the state would not be able to decide who was to be regarded as a German and who as a Czech; rather, it would be the mature citizen who was accorded the right to determine to which nationality he wished to belong" (281).

this volume, 157). He also admitted that being able "to choose a clear position between these two mindsets [the nationalist and the socialist]" was not an easy task and that managing to do so "would mean resolving the anxiety and uncertainty around ideas of nationality, country, moral and practical action, and much else besides all this" (151). Indeed, Slataper's article did not offer a univocal interpretation of the national issue but showed instead his own intellectual and ideological struggles and contradictions. He disagreed with Vivante's internationalist thesis because it ignored the national sentiments that motivated and inspired every ethnic group to belong to a single nation state. Following Mazzini's ideal of a republican nation, Slataper noted that it was only when the people belonged to a nation state that they could participate in its historical process and therefore fulfil their ethical responsibility. However, Slataper did not believe in Mazzini's universal ideal of nationality.[88] While Mazzini could still aspire to an alliance with "the southern Slavs and all the other populations ruled either by the Austrian or the Turkish Empire" (Mazzini 148), Slataper recognized that Mazzini's romantic principle did not hold in the present historical situation. He disagreed also with Herder's position "that all people are equal in history" (*Scritti politici* 107). Instead, noting Italy's recent success in the war in Libya, he asserted that a stronger Italy could pursue, if necessary through war, its own national identity. Yet, although he posited that "the conflict between nations is natural and good" (107) and perceived Italy as a political and cultural force that could eventually absorb Trieste and its mixed population into a unified Italian nation, he also emphasized that a nation's superiority could never be taken for granted; it must always be questioned and revisited, and most of all, it should lead to the betterment of society as a whole. Ultimately, he concluded, only history could demonstrate if men's undertakings were just and morally correct. Slataper's theoretical stance was certainly informed by a sense of cultural superiority, and by a questionable Hegelian perspective that made him assert that "the concepts of [military] force and justice coincide" (108).[89] At the

88 "May Italy ally itself with the peoples who are forcibly kept under Austria's yoke; with the peoples who also want to vindicate their liberty and independence. May our war be a war of Nations. Let us raise up high our flag, not in the name of local interests but rather in the name of a principle; the principle that for more than half a century has inspired and led every European popular movement. Let us write on our flag these sacred words: "For our own sake and for yours" (Mazzini 148). Giuseppe Mazzini (1805–72) founded the secret society Giovane Italia (Young Italy), whose aim was to free and unify Italy.

89 M.A.R. Habib noted the intrinsic imperialistic and expansionistic characteristics that underlie Hegel's dialectics: "[Hegel's] dialectic can be characterized as intrinsically

same time he rejected the intolerant views of irredentists such as Fauro Timeus, who denied the Slovenians the right to their own culture and education.[90] On the contrary, following Vivante and Bauer, whose work Slataper knew well (*Epistolario* 160), he emphasized the importance of a cultural irredentism, which would protect the cultural development of any ethnic group living within a single state: "but when the Italian nation [...] in our own provinces [...] denies *the means*, the schools, the right of national existence to the Slavs, it denies the principle upon which it bases its own existence: not just absolute justice, not merely 'the principle of nationality,' but the recognition of the humanity, of the very same virtues by which it enriches itself through the cultures of other peoples" (*Scritti politici* 110, italics in the original). After reiterating the importance of cultural irredentism, he reaffirmed the political necessity for Italy to maintain its alliance with Austria and admitted that at this point in time irredentism was not a viable solution. He exhorted his fellow citizens to continue to work for the future of their city, even if it was impossible to know exactly what that future would hold.

Slataper's political analysis did not offer a clear, univocal solution to the Triestine problem. As critics have already noted, it remained contradictory and vague because it lacked a clear historical methodological approach.[91] Yet we should also keep in mind that Slataper was not a

---

expansive and imperialistic, since it negates whatever is immediately given in the world, and ultimately integrates all forms of otherness into our equally expansive subjectivity, which in this way progressively 'conquers' the world beyond it, absorbing it into its own self. Indeed, Hegel sees this dialectical movement as characterizing history itself, where the principle of earlier civilizations gives way to the principle of more advanced cultures" (6).

90 Ruggero Fauro Timeus was one of the most vocal proponents of a racist and imperialist irredentism based on strong anti-Slavic sentiments. In addition to claiming Trieste for Italy, Timeus advocated Italy's imperialist role within Europe: "We do not accept the possibility of Trieste as an autonomous entity within the Austrian Empire. We shove our dream of an empire in everybody's face. We want to conquer: we do not care about national justice, international treaties or moral conveniences. [...] We launch a new act of faith and a new challenge that does not debate, does not doubt, does not compromise [...]. Italy should become the ruler of peoples, if not, the sea should swallow it" (210–11). In his vision, Trieste's importance did not reside in being a commercial hub, or a point of entrance for foreigners, but as a strategic point of departure "for [Italy's] future conquests" (198). Slataper never embraced these imperialistic positions. Reflecting on the issue of political supremacy, he wrote to Giani Stuparich: "For me, this is the main issue: we must be for intransigence, but against intolerance; we must fight, but not deny others the means to fight back" (*Epistolario* 155). On the imperialist nationalism of Timeus, see Diego Redivo.

91 Mutterle (150) and Damiani (54–8) criticized his historical superficiality and his lack of a serious methodological and scientific approach to the events, while Benevento

historian, but a journalist whose aim was to pose questions and inform his readers of the geopolitical complexity of his city. Moreover, his temporal and geographical closeness to the events did not allow him, in spite of his striving to do so, to gain a comprehensive view of the historical problems he witnessed. Although Slataper's complex and contradictory approach might frustrate historians, it also foregrounds his modernist spirit, a spirit that is suspicious of facile certainties and simple answers, and offers instead only doubts, questions, and ambiguities.[92]

After defending his thesis on Ibsen in 1912, Slataper received a post as a lecturer at the Kolonial-Institut in Hamburg, where he remained until the declaration of war in 1914. Here he continued to record and comment on the political situation of Italy and Europe in private letters to his close friends in Florence and Trieste. As in the articles written thus far, these letters expressed both his commitment to understanding the historical events as they were quickly unfolding, and his constant concerns about the ethical responsibility of single individuals as well as nations. On this topic he wrote a particularly interesting letter to Elody on 17 May 1913, in which he described an afternoon spent at the Hagenbeck Park, the famous Hamburg Zoo, where he observed the ethnographic exhibition of a small Burmese village. Watching a Burmese couple intent on making paper flowers for European children who gathered around their hut to observe them, Slataper expressed his deep embarrassment "for Europe that was watching them so shamelessly as if they too were not human beings" (*Alle tre amiche* 285). The exhibit also inspired him to reflect on Europe's cultural and political influence on the rest of the world: "Just think how terrible this Europe is, which penetrates, reduces, changes, corrupts, and destroys everything, so that she can conquer, take possession, exploit everything [...] for eternity" (286). For the critic, the colonial conquests of the present were comparable to the wars of religious intolerance of the past: if the latter fought to impose Christendom on the rest of the world, the former were violent attempts to impose Western values of labour and production. Faced with two opposing civilizations, Slataper wondered if "our winning civilization *is right*, and not the one that is oppressed?" (286, italics in original). The answer to his question revealed his vision of history: "And here there is no other solution than the one offered by the great Hegel: everything that happens,

(128–9) and Tommasini praised his historical commitment. On the complexity of Slataper's political thought and on Vivante's influence on Slataper, see Lunzer 21–35.

92 Moliterni recently noted the conflictual, constantly *in fieri* approach of Slataper's political analysis, which, for the critic, never led to a synthetic, ideologically comprehensive answer to the political situation of his time (63–77).

happens only because it is right: the real is the ideal. Hegel in this sense is the philosopher who explains and directs our entire era. [...] And yet, this way of thinking leaves us sometimes dissatisfied" (286–7). Although Slataper was unable to offer an alternative to Hegel's *Weltgeist*, and seemed to accept history as the manifestation of an absolute spirit that inexorably followed its course, he also recognized how such a view did not take into account the ethical responsibility of Europe towards its victims and could therefore not satisfy him completely. For this reason, he felt that it was his moral duty to record historical events as they were evolving, to try to understand them and, most importantly, to communicate them to a wider public.

Thus, in a letter to Giovanni Amendola written in the summer of 1913, he lamented his physical distance from Italy and his journalistic inactivity, and asserted his desire to deepen his knowledge of history by living for a couple of years in Vienna or Belgrade as a foreign correspondent for some Italian paper: "History above all attracts me more and more: and I realize that you cannot make history if you do not gain an in-depth knowledge of people and movements for a precise purpose and objective" (*Epistolario* 292).[93] The choice of Belgrade as a place where Slataper, burdened by his new academic post, wished to go to is particularly telling, and it demonstrates his understanding that although the city was still "a small provincial town, just starting to pave its main streets" (MacMillan 467), as the capital of Serbia it was becoming one of the hot places where the destiny of the Balkan states and of the whole empire was being decided. Slataper never had a chance to report from Belgrade, but in his letters to Amendola he continued to emphasize the need to keep the Italian public informed of the delicate situation of the Italian citizens living in Austria at this time: he described in detail the consequences of the Balkan wars for Trieste, noting how while the strengthening of Serbia and the South Slavs had unveiled the inefficiency of the Austro-Hungarian monarchy, they had also revealed the fragile state of Trieste's

93 His interest in history was also expressed in an unpublished article about the institute Revoltella (Trieste's school of commerce), where he emphasized the educational value of cultural history even for students interested in business: "All schools of commerce [...] had to convince themselves that the focus of their multiform activities could only be historical, [...] not a chronological or dynastic history, but [a history] of the abilities and movements of people. [...] We must raise a generation of educated young people who are less interested perhaps, in Foscolo, Petrarch, Schiller, or what not, but much more in the whole history of Germany, Italy, etc. Even literature professors (nice title!) should realize that literature does not exist detached from the living history of all the endeavours of a people" (*Scritti politici 1914–1915*, 125–7).

maritime power in the Adriatic.[94] In March 1914, just a few months before his return to Italy, he wrote to Amendola again, this time explaining why the current European situation required a different political approach.

While previously he had asserted that Italy should renounce the Adriatic provinces and allow the formation of small Slavic states that could limit Austrian power on the Adriatic, now he acknowledged that the newly formed Greater Serbia was not just threatening the existence of Austria-Hungary ("I believe that if one understands well the significance of the most recent events [...] one can predict finis Austriae," he noted with historical acumen [*Epistolario* 296]), but was a political power that Italy could use, in the event of war, to reshape the current political situation and establish control over the Adriatic Sea.[95] Thus,

> Italy [...] must support the South Slavs, but on specific terms: Trieste, all Istria, Fiume, and at least some Italian-Croatian islands of the Quarnaro (Lošinj for instance), and if it were possible also Lissa should go to Italy. This would now be the definitive solution: an eastern coast divided between Greece, Albania, the South Slavs, Italy, and watched over by Italy from Pula, Lissa, and Otranto. (*Epistolario* 295)

Aware of the power that nationalist and irredentist forces would wield against Italy in some of the other territories with a strong Slavic population, Slataper emphasized the need for Italy to treat the new subjects well, affording them the ability to continue to pursue their cultural identity by maintaining their schools and cultural centres.[96] He also stressed the need to help the South Slavs in a war against Austria. This possible war, he concluded, would mean the rebirth of the Slavic nations against the combined powers of Austria and Germany, and could escalate into a

94 For an overview of Italian and European foreign policy towards the Adriatic region and the creation of a Slavic nation, see Klabjan.

95 The events Slataper referred to are, other than the Balkan wars and the creation of a powerful Greater Serbia, the defeat of the Ottoman Empire in Europe and the diplomatic interferences of Russia and Austria-Hungary in the Balkan states. For a recent account of these events see MacMillan 465–543.

96 See also his article "The Eastern Borders" where, addressing the problem of diverse ethnic groups living within a state, he wrote: "If we desire assimilation to take place and spread as much as possible, we must not do anything artificial to promote it." Again, he affirms the necessity of creating bi- or trilingual schools, where Italian is taught together with German and/or Slovenian: "school is sacred, and therefore it is also the most tremendous political weapon. [...] We will have to allow all Slavic and German cultural manifestations, perhaps even encourage them. But we should prevent any political revolt from the very beginning with decisive serenity" (*Scritti politici* 300).

full-fledged European war, in which Italy would also be involved. Slataper could clearly see the possibility of this conflict, and therefore he urged Italy to start preparing for the eventual war by developing diplomatic relationships with Russia and France and, if pressed, to renew its adherence to the Triple Alliance, but only for a limited time (*Epistolario* 298).

Just a few months after Slataper's letter to Amendola, on 28 June, Archduke Franz Ferdinand, heir to the Austro-Hungarian monarchy, was killed in Sarajevo and Slataper's predictions became reality, confirming Slataper's understanding of the current historical moment. After Austria-Hungary declared war on Serbia on 28 July, Slataper, who had already highlighted the strength of Serbia and the inherent weakness of Austria-Hungary, embraced the interventionist cause. From Trieste, where he had returned after the proclamation of war, he wrote again to his friend in Florence, uncertain, however, if his letter would ever reach him because of the strong censorship imposed by the Austrian government. In agitated tones he described the dramatic situation of the city, which was then completely isolated from the rest of the world. While the Triestine regiment had been sent to fight in Galicia, on the eastern front, the Austrian government had moved all its offices, archives, and money to the city of Gorizia, leaving Trieste in administrative and financial chaos.[97] In the meantime, the Triestines were unable to receive news of what was happening abroad and were fed only Austrian propaganda. They did not know what to expect, and waited, disoriented, to see Italy's next move. Many of them, lamented Slataper, moved by their distrust and hate for the Slavs, were still willing to support Austria, while others hoped that England would quickly occupy the city and in this way end its state of uncertainty. Slataper concluded his letter by proclaiming his frustration at Italy's neutrality and noted that only by participating in the war on the side of the Entente and supporting the South Slavs would Italy be able to claim its unredeemed lands and become a player in European politics.

In September 1914, in order to avoid conscription into the Austrian army and to fulfil his mission to continue to write and analyse the evolving political situation, Slataper crossed the border into Italy with his wife Gigetta Curiel and settled in Rome, where he joined other Triestine exiles, among whom were his close friends Carlo and Giani Stuparich

97 There are some interesting journals and memoirs produced by Triestine women writers who described in detail the dramatic situation of Trieste after the declaration of war. See Haydée; Haydée and Astori; Rossi Timeus; and Cesari.

and Elody Oblath.[98] Here, together with many other Italian intellectuals, he participated in the interventionist campaign by collaborating with the newspaper *Il Resto del Carlino.*[99] The aim of his articles was twofold: to further the interventionist cause by presenting the dramatic destiny of Trieste, waiting to be liberated by the Italian army, and at the same time to continue to offer his interpretation of the events as they were unfolding. The first article published for *Il Resto del Carlino* is a good example of Slataper's convincing rhetoric. With an emotional appeal to his audience, he described the absurd and cruel situation of the Triestines who by wishing the defeat of the Austrian army are de facto wishing the death of their own children, Austrian subjects fighting against Russia on the Eastern Front (*Scritti politici* 152). He then explained to the Italian public how the Triestines had changed their mind about the war. Because Trieste had financially benefited from being part of Austria-Hungary, and had always looked at the Slavs with suspicion, it was at first indifferent to or against the war. However, after England declared war against Austria, Trieste realized that this "was truly a European war [...] against pan-Germanism" (156). Slataper's message was clear: just as Trieste changed

98 Elody Oblath recalled the sense of exaltation for the interventionist cause that moved her and her Triestine friends in Rome: "We thought we knew the horrors of war for having imagined them with our brain and our hearts, but in reality, we only knew our exaltation. Still, we knew with conscious certainty that whatever these horrors were, none of us would have retreated. [...] For it [the war], I am sure, each of us would have gone willingly to the gallows, just as we consciously instigated and helped all our friends (the best part of ourselves) to go to die. Days of foolish illusions, faith in a better humanity that made us exult and ask for the death of millions of men!" (32).

99 The majority of Italian intellectuals embraced the war as a means to rejuvenate a stagnant Italian state, finalize its national borders, and gain political credibility in the international arena. Antonio Gibelli summarizes how the Italian intellectuals saw the war: "Many expected from the war a restoration of order, of the principle of authority, of moral unity and of social discipline, which were all threatened by the ascent and insubordination of the subaltern classes, the fights among political parties and the crisis of [current sociopolitical] institutions. To others the war appeared instead as the instrument for the disintegration of the status quo that would have allowed the eruption of new forces and the elimination of the old and mediocre world of parliamentary democracy; it appeared as the opportunity for an outburst of healthy vitalism [*una esplosione vitalistica salutare*]. The intellectuals' motivations and their ways of elaborating the myth of war are the most varied, but they all share the common element of war as an inevitable necessity, a fatal attraction, and a political, cultural, and above all existential opportunity not to be missed" (32). On the failure of European intellectuals to take a critical stance towards the war, see also Isnenghi, *Il mito della grande guerra* and "La letteratura italiana." On the role of the propaganda machine, see Prochasson; on Italian nationalist political thinkers on the eve of the war, see Mondini 17–57; and see Ungari.

its mind about the conflict, so should Italy. Italians should stop engaging in theoretical debates on Italy's new borders and instead join the fight, because, as the title of one of his articles clearly stated, "national rights are affirmed with war" (in this volume, 158). Only "through victory in war" (161) would Italy be able to demonstrate its political worth. Another rhetorical device used by Slataper to encourage his compatriots to embrace the war was to diminish the image of the Austrian Empire as a great power. In more than one article he depicted it as an anachronistic political entity, nothing more than a bureaucratic apparatus that had allowed its multiple lands to develop financially without, however, developing a common cultural identity that would sustain its existence in case of war. There was no such a thing as an Austrian citizen, claimed Slataper, and as a consequence, it was also impossible to talk about an Austrian soldier (*Scritti politici 1914–1915* 76). The image that he wished to conjure was that of a weak monarchy defended by an unreliable army. Although Slataper was correct in pointing out the lack of a unifying cultural identity for the subjects of the Dual Monarchy, it is also true that its soldiers, including the many Triestine soldiers who were in its ranks, rarely questioned their loyalty to Austria-Hungary.[100] At this point, however, Slataper was no longer interested in presenting an accurate image of the Austrian Empire, but in persuading Italian public opinion, which was still against the war, to join the interventionist cause.

As time passed his articles emphasized more and more the political necessity for Italy to join the conflict on the side of the Entente. The active support of interventionism, he noted, was not just the task of the intellectual class, but the moral duty of the whole country. Everyone should participate in the practical preparation of the war effort: "If you act, you do not have any time left to waver and debate. As the soldier who is part of his military squadron loses his anarchist tendencies, so does each one of us, and the whole nation must find little by little its war character" (*Scritti politici 1914–1915* 119). The time of doubting and debating, in which he participated during the previous years, was over. Now he felt that it was time for action.

The articles he produced in 1915, while Italy was still neutral, stressed over and over again the political urgency of the situation. However, even as the propaganda machine became more and more emphatic and violent, Slataper never embraced the imperialist demagogy of

100 For a recent analysis of the complex relationship between imperial loyalty and nationalist patriotism, see Cole. On the Triestine soldiers fighting for the Dual Monarchy, see Di Michele 47–54. As the latter noted, more than one hundred thousand soldiers from Trento, Trieste, and the coastal areas fought with the Austrian army.

some of his fellow journalists. He believed that intervening in the war was Italy's opportunity to consolidate its power in the Adriatic and to defend itself against the creation of a strong Slavic state in the area after Austria-Hungary's defeat. Thus, the war should not be viewed as expansionistic, nor just as an irredentist conflict that would fulfil the nationalist dreams of Trento and Trieste: "today we must not want war on our own initiative, but because others have imposed it on us. [...] Right now we should not think about the unredeemed lands, but to redeem ourselves from this great menace. Our war will not be sentimental or imperialistic, although sentiment and imperialism will also demand it and rekindle it: it will be a war to defend ourselves. Trieste counts, but Italy counts much more" (*Scritti politici* 193). Thus, as he noted in an article probably meant for the *Resto del Carlino* but never published, the war must be accepted with a "quiet spiritual resignation." He explained: "There is no propaganda that can persuade a people to war. War is an imposition and a heroic resignation. War is a command. The order will come. And the nation will become an army. [...] Then, perhaps carrying with us, each on his own, our little cowardice and worries, we will all align ourselves, Germanophiles and democrats, supporters of the clergy [*clericali*] and artists, peasants and socialists" (190–1). As Mutterle noted in his study, Slataper's reflections on the imminent war and his interventionist agenda, coupled with his more insightful and introspective pages, revealed the tragic position of an author "who, like few others at that time, was able to grasp and underline the contradictions of his whole world, including the political ones" (179), but was unable to find alternative solutions that would have helped to maintain the peace.

On 23 May 1915 Italy declared war on Austria. Shortly after, Slataper, who was a citizen of the Dual Monarchy, enlisted as a volunteer in the Italian army. The letters he wrote to his wife and his few journal articles from the following seven months underscored the "sacred cooperation" that existed among his fellow soldiers, which "allows us to go beyond our human condition" (*Appunti e note* 264). The perception of the war as a "collective effort," where the single individual was part of a larger community of fellow soldiers united by a cause that superseded any single individual, becomes a recurrent theme in his letters: "I see that we are all men, that war demands more than human strength, that it has in it something higher and far more frightening than one single man can, by himself, offer or bear. But it is the community of men that succeeds, it is the collective effort of mutual help, of support, of cooperation that brings out our love for each other, and this is the real war" ("To Gigetta," in this volume, 171).

Slataper here gave voice to the same sentiments that informed the end of *My Karst and My City*, where the author finally recognized the need to overcome the self-centred view of himself as the strong, super-heroic individual who could endow the world with absolute meaning, and accepted instead his destiny among his fellow human beings in a quest for "work and love." With irony, Slataper told Gigetta that now that his beloved Karst had become the theatre of war, his novel had gained much popularity among the soldiers. Yet he felt very distant from the book he had completed only a few years earlier. "To you," he told his wife, "I will dedicate another book, if I will be able to write it. If not, [I dedicate to you] my life, as it is, in all honesty" (*Alle tre amiche* 483). But Slataper would never write a book dedicated to his wife. He died on the front only a few days later, on 3 December 1915. To us, he left his reflections, his contradictions, his attempt to find answers and to give voice, "in all honesty," to the complex reality in which he lived.

Works Cited

Amberson, Deborah. "Temporalities of Stone in Scipio Slataper's *Il Mio Carso*." *Italian Culture*, vol. 36, no. 1, Jan. 2018, pp. 1–17, https://doi.org/10.1080/01614622.2017.1350017.

Amendola, Giovanni. "Il convegno nazionalista." *La Voce 1908–1913: Cronaca, antologia e fortuna di una rivista*, edited by Giuseppe Prezzolini, Rusconi, 1974, pp. 685–9.

– *La volontà è il bene: Etica e religione*. Libreria Editrice Romana, 1911.

Angelucci, Malcolm. *Words against Words: On the Rhetoric of Carlo Michelstaedter*. Troubador Publishing, 2011.

Apih, Elio. "La genesi di 'Irredentismo adriatico.'" *Irredentismo adriatico*, by Vivante, Edizioni Italo Svevo, 1984, pp. 263–332.

– *Trieste*. Laterza, 1988.

Ara, Angelo, and Claudio Magris. *Trieste: Un'identità di frontiera*. 2nd ed., Einaudi, 1983.

Bachelard, Gaston. *The Poetics of Space*. Beacon Press, 1994.

Ballinger, Pamela. *History in Exile: Memory and Identity at the Borders of the Balkans*. Princeton UP, 2003.

Baudelaire, Charles. "The Painter of Modern Life." *Selected Writings on Literature*, translated by P.E. Charvet, Penguin Books, 1992, pp. 390–435.

Bauer, Otto. *The Question of Nationalities and Social Democracy*. U of Minnesota P, 2000.

Bazlen, Roberto. *Scritti*. Adelphi, 1984.

Benco, Silvio. *Trieste*. Maylander, 1910.

Benevento, Aurelio. *Saggi di letteratura triestina*. Minerva Scuola, 1977.

Biagi, Daria. "Nel cantiere del romanzo: Il Wilhelm Meister della 'Voce.'" *La letteratura tedesca in Italia: Un'introduzione (1900–1920)*, Quodlibet Studio, 2016, pp. 143–67, https://doi.org.10.2307/j.ctv1142j7.

Billiani, Francesca. "Political and Aesthetic Transgressions: Florentine Reviews à la Mode." *The Oxford Critical and Cultural History of Modernist Magazines*, edited by Peter Brooker and Andrew Thacker, vol. 3, part 1, Oxford UP, 2013, pp. 445–68.

Bini, Daniela. *Carlo Michelstaedter and the Failure of Language*. UP of Florida, 1992.

Boccardi, Alberto. *La donna nell'opera di Henrik Ibsen*. M. Kantorowicz, 1893.

Bond, Emma. "'Intoxicated Geographies': Sites of Refraction and Fragmentation in Scipio Slataper's *Il Mio Carso* and Hermann Hesse's *Der Steppenwolf*." *Modern Language Review*, vol. 111, no. 1, 2016, pp. 1–16, https://doi.org/10.5699/modelangrevi.111.1.0001.

Camerino, Giuseppe Antonio. *La persuasione e i simboli: Michelstaedter e Slataper*. Rev. ed., Liguori, 2005.

Campailla, Sergio. "Michelstaedter lettore di Ibsen." *Lettere Italiane*, vol. 26, no. 1, 1974, pp. 46–63.

Cangiano, Mimmo. "'E slavificatore sarà il capitalismo': Angelo Vivante tra l'Internazionalismo, La Voce, e gli Austro-Marxisti." *Irredentismi: Politica, cultura e propaganda nell'Europa dei nazionalismi*, edited by L.G. Maneti and D. Paci, Unicopli, 2017, pp. 117–30.

Cary, Joseph. *A Ghost in Trieste*. U of Chicago P, 1993.

Cattaruzza, Marina. *Italy and Its Eastern Borders, 1866–2016*. Routledge, 2017.

– *La formazione del proletariato urbano: Immigrati, operai di mestiere, donne a Trieste dalla metà del secolo XIX all prima guerra mondiale*. Musolini, 1979.

– "Slovenes and Italians in Trieste, 1850–1914." *Comparative Studies on Governments and Non-Dominant Ethnic Groups in Europe, 1850–1940*, edited by Max Engman and European Science Foundation, Dartmouth, vol. 8, New York UP, 1992, pp. 189–219.

– *Socialismo adriatico: La socialdemocrazia di lingua italiana nei territori costieri della monarchia asburgica, 1888–1915*. 2nd ed., Lacaita, 2001.

– *Trieste nell'ottocento: Le trasformazioni di una società civile*. Del Bianco, 1995.

Cavaglion, Alberto. *Otto Weíninger in Italia*. Carucci, 1983.

Çelik, Zeynep, et al. *Streets: Critical Perspectives on Public Space*. U of California P, 1994.

Cella, Sergio. "Il pensiero politico di Slataper e Vivante." *Pagine Istriane*, Jan. 1956, pp. 21–7.

Cesari, Aurelia Reina. *Trieste, la guerra, una giovinezza*. Licinio Cappelli, 1938.

Chmiel, Piotr. "Un nuovo arrivato? L'immagine dello 'Slavo' negli scritti di autori triestini dell'inizio del novecento." *Treatises and Documents, Journal of Ethnic Studies*, vol. 63, Dec. 2010, pp. 104–23.

Claudel, Paul. *Partage de midi.* Gallimard, 1994.

Coceani, Bruno, and Cesare Pagnini. *Trieste della belle époque.* Libreria Universitas, 1971.

Coda, Elena. "The Representation of the Metropolis in Scipio Slataper's *Il Mio Carso.*" *MLN*, vol. 117, no. 1, 2002, pp. 153–73, https://www.jstor.org/stable/3251845.

– *Slataper.* Palumbo, 2007.

Cole, Laurence. *Military Culture and Popular Patriotism in Late Imperial Austria.* Oxford UP, 2014.

Cova, Ugo. *Commercio e navigazione a Trieste e nella monarchia asburgica da Maria Teresa al 1915.* Del Bianco, 1992.

Dal Co, Francesco. *Figures of Architecture and Thought: German Architecture Culture, 1880–1920.* Rizzoli, 1990.

Damiani, Roberto. "Introduzione a Scipio Slataper." *Scritti politici 1914–1915*, by Scipio Slataper, Lafanicola, 1977, pp. 9–58.

Della Venezia Sala, Licia. "La scuola triestina dall'Austria all'Italia." *Il movimento nazionale a Trieste nella Prima Guerra Mondiale*, edited by Giulio Cervani, Del Bianco, 1968, pp. 79–156.

Deleuze, Gilles, and Felix Guattari. *Kafka: Toward a Minor Literature.* U of Minnesota P, 1986.

De Sanctis, Francesco, et al. *Storia della letteratura italiana.* Einaudi-Gallimard, 1996.

Di Michele, Andrea. *Tra due divise: La Grande Guerra degli italiani.* Laterza, 2018.

Domokos, Lajos. *Trieste: I fatti di febbraio, la politica nazionale e il partito socialista.* Mongini, 1902.

Dubin, Lois C. *The Port Jews of Habsburg Trieste: Absolutist Politics and Enlightenment Culture.* Stanford UP, 1999.

Engels, Friedrich. "Democratic Pan-Slavism." *Karl Marx, Frederick Engels: Collected Works*, vol. 8, International Publisher, 1975, pp. 362–78.

Fauro Timeus, Ruggero. *Trieste.* Gaetano Garzoni Provenzani, 1914.

Felski, Rita. *The Gender of Modernity.* Harvard UP, 1995.

Frà Giordano. "L'università italiana in Austria." *Minerva*, edited by Federico Garlanda, vol. 27, Società Editrice Laziale, 1908, pp. 1217–19.

Freud, Sigmund. "The Uncanny." *The Standard Edition of the Complete Psychological Works of Sigmund Freud*, edited by Anna Freud and Carrie Lee Rothgeb, vol. 17, Hogarth Press, 1953, pp. 217–52.

Gayda, Virgilio. *L'italia d'oltre confine.* Fratelli Bocca, 1914.

Gentile, Emilio. *The Struggle for Modernity: Nationalism, Futurism, and Fascism.* Praeger, 2003.

Gibelli, Antonio. *La grande guerra degli italiani: 1915–1918.* Rizzoli, 2014.

Goethe, Johann W. *Le esperienze di Wilhelm Meister*, edited by R. Pisaneschi and A. Spaini, Laterza, 1913.

– *Wilhelm Meisters Lehrjahre.* Berlin and Weimar: Aufbau-Verlag, 1997.

– *Wilhelm Meisters Theatralische Sendung.* Rascher, 1910.

Gulddal, Jesper. *Anti-Americanism in European Literature.* 1st ed., Palgrave Macmillan, 2011.

Habib, M.A.R. *Hegel and Empire: From Postcolonialism to Globalism.* Palgrave Macmillan, 2017.

Hametz, Maura Elise. *Making Trieste Italian, 1918–1954.* Boydell, 2005.

Harrington, Austin. "Goethe and the Creative Life." *The Anthem Companion to Georg Simmel,* edited by Thomas Kemple and Olli Pyyhtinen, Anthem Press, 2016, pp. 185–90.

Harrison, Thomas J. *1910: The Emancipation of Dissonance.* U of California P, 1996.

Haydée. *Vita triestina avanti e durante la guerra.* Treves, 1916.

Haydée, and Bruno Astori. *La passione di Trieste: Diario di vita triestina: (luglio 1914 – novembre 1918).* Bemporad & Figlio, 1920.

Hebbel, Friedrich, and Marcello Loewy. *Judith.* Edizione Studio Tesi, 1983.

Hofmannsthal, Hugo von. *Hugo von Hofmannsthal and the Austrian Idea: Selected Essays and Addresses, 1906–1927.* Purdue UP, 2011.

Hortis, Attilio. *Per la università italiana di Trieste.* G. Caprini, 1902.

"Il veicolo del colera." *L'Indipendente,* 19 Feb. 1893, p. 3.

Ibsen, Henrik. *Brand: A Dramatic Poem.* J.M. Dent & Sons, 1915.

– *Peer Gynt: A Dramatic Poem.* J.M. Dent & Sons, 1921.

Isnenghi, Mario. *Il mito della grande guerra.* Laterza, 1970.

– "La letteratura italiana e la guerra: Appunti su Scipio Slataper." *Ateneo Veneto: Rivista di Scienze, Lettere ed Arti,* no. 1, 1965, pp. 95–122.

Klabjan, Borut. "'Scramble for Adria': Discourses of Appropriation of the Adriatic Space before and after World War I." *Austrian History Yearbook,* vol. 42, no. 42, 2011, pp. 16–32.

"Le disastrose condizioni sanitarie di Trieste." *Il Lavoratore,* 27 Aug. 1910, p. 4.

Lichtblau, Klaus. "Eros and Culture: Gender Theory in Simmel, Tönnies and Weber." *Telos: Critical Theory of the Contemporary,* vol. 82, 1989, pp. 89–110.

Lukács, Georg. *The Theory of the Novel.* Merlin Press, 1988.

Lunzer, Renate. "Interculturalismo, irredentismo e la lunga ombra di Angelo Vivante." *L'irredentismo armato: Gli irredentismi europei davanti alla guerra: Atti del convegno di studi, Gorizia, 25 maggio, Trieste, 26–27 maggio 2014,* edited by Fabio Todero, Istituto regionale per la storia del movimento di liberazione nel Friuli-Venezia Giulia, 2015, pp. 21–36.

Luzzatto Fegiz, P. *La popolazione di Trieste (1875–1928).* La editoriale libraria, 1929.

Machiavelli, Niccolò. *The Prince.* Translated by Harvey Mansfield, U of Chicago P, 1985.

MacMillan, Margaret. *The War That Ended Peace: The Road to 1914.* Random House, 2014.

Magris, Claudio. *Journeying*. Translated by Anne Milano Appel, Yale UP, 2018.
Mainati, Giuseppe. *Croniche ossia memorie storiche sacro-profane di Trieste cominciando dall'XI secolo sino ai nostri giorni: coll'aggiunta della relazione dei Vescovi dal primo sino al decimo secolo*. Vol. 4, Picotti, 1818.
Mantegazza, Paolo. *Il secolo nevrosico*. Edizioni Studio Tesi, 1995.
Marinetti, Filippo Tommaso. "The Founding and Manifesto of Futurism." *Futurism: An Anthology*, edited by Lawrence Rainey, Christine Poggi, and Laura Wittman, Yale UP, 2009, pp. 49–53.
Martignoni, Clelia. "Una lettera di Scipio Slataper a Emilio Cecchi." *Autografo: Quadrimestrale del Centro di ricerca sulla tradizione manoscritta di autori contemporanei/Università di Pavia*, vol. 13, 1988, pp. 103–8.
Martinuzzi, Giuseppina. *Giuseppina Martinuzzi: Documenti del periodo rivoluzionario 1896–1925*. Edited by Marija Cetina. Naučna biblioteka, 1970.
Mazzini, Giuseppe. *A Cosmopolitanism of Nations: Giuseppe Mazzini's Writings on Democracy, Nation Building, and International Relations*. Edited by Stefano Recchia and Nadia Urbinati, Princeton UP, 2009.
Michelstaedter, Carlo. *Opere: La persuasione e la rettorica, dialogo della salute, poesie, epistolario scelto, scritti vari*. Sansoni, 1958.
– *Persuasion and Rhetoric*. Yale UP, 2004.
Milanini, Claudio. "Scipio Slataper, il nido disfatto." *Belfagor: Rassegna di varia umanità*, vol. 48, no. 2, 1993, pp. 141–52.
Millo, Anna. *L'elite del potere a Trieste: Una biografia collettiva, 1891–1938*. F. Angeli, 1989.
– *Storia di una borghesia: La famiglia Vivante a Trieste dall'emporio alla guerra mondiale*. Libreria editrice goriziana, 1998.
Minca, Claudio. "Trieste orizzonte cosmopolita." *Processi territoriali e nuove filiere urbane*, edited by Marina Faccioli, Franco Angeli, 2009, pp. 155–73.
Minghelli, Giuliana. *In the Shadow of the Mammoth: Italo Svevo and the Emergence of Modernism*. U of Toronto P, 2002.
Moi, Toril. *Henrik Ibsen and the Birth of Modernism: Art, Theater, Philosophy*. Oxford UP, 2006.
Moliterni, Fabio. *Esuli, funzionari e patrioti: Studi sul Novecento degli intellettuali*. Pensa multimedia, 2014.
Mondini, Marco. *La guerra italiana: Partire, raccontare, tornare 1914–18*. Il Mulino, 2018.
Mutterle, Anco Marzio. *Scipio Slataper*. Mursia, 1965.
Nietzsche, Friedrich W. *Thus Spoke Zarathustra*. Cambridge UP, 2006.
Oblath Stuparich, Elody. *Confessioni e lettere a Scipio*. Edited by Giusi Criscione, 1st ed., Fògola, 1979.
Patruno, Maria L. *Il "chiarimento" di Slataper dalla "Voce" All'"Ibsen."* Lacaita, 1987.
Pertici, Roberto. *Intellettuali di frontiera: Triestini a Firenze (1900–1950): Atti del convegno (18–20 marzo 1983)*. L.S. Olschki, 1985.

Pittoni, Anita. *L'anima di Trieste: Lettere al Professore.* Vallecchi, 1968.
Pizzi, Katia. "A Modernist City Resisting Translation? Trieste between Slovenia and Italy." *Speaking Memory: How Translation Shapes City Life*, edited by Sherry Simon, McGill-Queen's UP, 2016, pp. 45–57.
Presidenza municipale di Trieste. *L'amministrazione comunale di Trieste nel triennio 1900–1902.* Il Municipio di Trieste editore Trieste/Stab. arti grafiche G. Caprin, 1903.
Prezzolini, Giuseppe. *Italia 1912: Dieci anni di vita intellettuale (1903–1912).* Vallecchi, 1984.
– "La nostra promessa." *La Voce*, no. 2, Dec. 1908, p. 5.
– *La Voce: 1908–1913: Cronaca, antologia e fortuna di una rivista.* 1st ed., Rusconi, 1974.
– "Parole di un uomo moderno" (1913). *La Voce 1908–1916*, Luciano Landi Editore, 1961, pp. 345–53.
– "Relazione del primo anno della Voce" (1909). *La Voce 1908–1916*, Luciano Landi Editore, 1961, pp. 133–7.
Prochasson, Christophe. "Intellectuals and Writers." *A Companion to World War I*, edited by John Horne, Wiley-Blackwell, 2010, pp. 323–37.
Rainey, Lawrence S., et al., editors. *Futurism: An Anthology.* Yale UP, 2009.
Redivo, Diego. *Ruggero Timeus: La via imperialista dell'irredentismo triestino.* Edizione Italo Svevo, 1996.
Rossi Timeus, Carmela. *Attendiamo le navi: Diario di una giovinetta triestina 1914–1918.* Cappelli, 1934.
Rozdolski, Roman. *Engels and the "Nonhistoric" Peoples: The National Question in the Revolution of 1848.* Critique Books, 1986.
Rutar, Sabine. "Internationalist Networking in a Multinational Setting: Social Democratic Cultural Associations in Austro-Hungarian Trieste, 1900–1914." *Civil Society, Associations and Urban Places*, edited by Graeme Morton, R.J. Morris, and B.M.A. Vries, Ashgate, 2006, pp. 87–102.
Saba, Umberto. *Tutte le prose.* Edited by Arrigo Stara, 2nd ed., Mondadori, 2002.
Scartabellati, Andrea. *Prometeo inquieto: Trieste 1855–1937: L'economia, la povertà e la modernità oltre l'immagine della città della letteratura.* Aracne, 2006.
Schächter, Elizabeth. *Origin and Identity: Essays on Svevo and Trieste.* Northern Universities Press, 2000.
Schneider, Erik Holmes. *Zois in Nighttown: Prostitution and Syphilis in the Trieste of James Joyce and Italo Svevo (1880–1920).* Ashgrove Publishing, 2014.
Sengoopta, Chandak. "The Unknown Weininger: Science, Philosophy, and Cultural Politics in Fin-de-Siècle Vienna." *Central European History*, vol. 29, no. 4, 1996, pp. 453–93.
Simmel, Georg. "Female Culture." *On Women, Sexuality and Love*, edited by Guy Oakes, Yale UP, 1984, pp. 65–101.
– *Goethe.* Klinkhardt & Biermann, 1913.

– "Goethe and Youth." *Theory, Culture & Society,* translated by Ulrich Teucher and Thomas Kemple, vol. 24, nos. 7–8, 2007, pp. 85–90.
– "The Metropolis and Mental Life." *Rethinking Architecture: A Reader in Cultural Theory,* edited by Neil Leach, Routledge, 2006, pp. 69–79.
– "On the Concept and Tragedy of Culture." *The Conflict in Modern Culture and Other Essays,* edited by Peter Etzkorn, Columbia UP, 1968, pp. 27–46.
– "The Relative and the Absolute in the Problem of the Sexes." *On Women, Sexuality and Love,* edited by Guy Oakes, Yale UP, 1984, pp. 102–32.
Slataper, Scipio. *Alle tre amiche.* Edited by Giani Stuparich, Mondadori, 1958.
– *Appunti e note di diario.* Edited by Giani Stuparich, Mondadori, 1953.
– *Epistolario.* Mondadori, 1950.
– *Ibsen.* Edited by Arturo Farinelli, Fratelli Bocca, 1916.
– *Il mio Carso.* Photomechanical reproduction of the 1st ed. (1912), della Libreria della Voce (Florence), with the support of the city of Trieste, 1989.
– "Il solidificatore del vuoto." *La Voce 1908–1913: Cronaca, antologia e fortuna di una rivista,* edited by Giuseppe Prezzolini, Emilio Gentile, and Vanni Scheiwiller, Rusconi, 1974, pp. 425–6.
– *Lettere triestine: Col seguito di altri scritti vociani di polemica su Trieste.* Edited by Elio Guagnini, Dedolibri, 1988.
– *Scritti letterari e critici.* Edited by Giani Stuparich, Mondadori, 1956.
– *Scritti politici.* Edited by Giani Stuparich, Alberto Stock, 1925.
– *Scritti politici 1914–1915.* Edited by G. Baroni, Lafanicola, 1977.
Soffici, Ardengo. "La ricetta di Ribi buffone." *Opere,* vol. 1, Vallecchi, 1959, pp. 597–8.
Sondel-Cedarmas, Joanna. "'Trieste o Nulla!': La richiesta dell'università italiana in Austria negli scritti degli irredentisti – Nazionalisti italiani (1903–1914)." *Per Rita Tolomeo, scritti di amici sulla Dalmazia e l'Europa Centro-Orientale,* vol. 2, La Musa Talia, 2014, pp. 21–36.
Stuparich, Giani. *Scipio Slataper.* Mondadori, 1950.
Summerfield, Giovanna, and Lisa Downward. *New Perspectives on the European Bildungsroman.* Continuum, 2010.
Svevo, Italo. *Zeno's Conscience.* Penguin Books, 2001.
Tobin, Robert Deam. *Doctor's Orders: Goethe and Enlightenment Thought.* Bucknell UP, 2001.
Todero, Fabio. "Percorsi: Giovani irredentisti del Litorale verso la Grande Guerra." *L'irredentismo armato: Gli irredentismi europei davanti alla guerra: Atti del convegno di studi, Gorizia, 25 maggio, Trieste, 26–27 maggio 2014,* edited by Fabio Todero, Istituto regionale per la storia del movimento di liberazione nel Friuli-Venezia Giulia, 2015, pp. 59–84.
Tommasini, Lorenzo. "Scipio Slataper alla guerra: Dall'irredentismo culturale all'interventismo militante." *La via della guerra: Il mondo adriatico-danubiano*

alla vigilia della Grande Guerra, edited by Gizella Nemeth and Adriano Papo, Luglio Editori, 2013, pp. 219–42.

Tönnies, Ferdinand. *Community and Civil Society*. Cambridge UP, 2005.

Ungari, Andrea. "New Italian Nationalism." *The New Nationalism and the First World War*, edited by L. Rosenthal and V. Rodic, Palgrave Macmillan, 2015, pp. 47–64.

Valdevit, Giampaolo. *Trieste: Storia di una periferia insicura*. B. Mondadori, 2004.

Vivante, Angelo. *Irredentismo adriatico*. Edizioni Italo Svevo, 1984.

Walker, Julia A. "Suez Modernism: Transportation, History, and Ibsen's Stylistic Shift." *Ibsen Studies*, vol. 14, no. 2, July 2014, pp. 136–66.

Weininger, Otto. *Sex and Character: An Investigation of Fundamental Principles*. Indiana UP, 2005.

– *Über Die Letzen Dinge*. Matthes und Seitz, 1997.

Witz, Anne. "Georg Simmel and the Masculinity of Modernity." *Journal of Classical Sociology*, vol. 1, no. 3, Nov. 2001, pp. 353–70.

A Note on the Translations

NICHOLAS BENSON AND ELENA CODA

This is the first time that a wide array of Slataper's work has been translated into English. Apart from *Il mio Carso,* translated here in its entirety, the volume also includes excerpts from his *Lettere triestine,* his political writings and critical essays. Overall, the aim of this volume is to present to an English-speaking audience the work of an author whose literary and political reflections open a window onto a unique geopolitical area and cultural milieu that is still relevant today as we reflect on issues of national and cultural identities and international economic influences.[1]

The translation itself is the result of a joint effort over several years of intensive translation, editing, and discussion on how to render a particular word, phrase, or in some instances whole paragraphs whose meaning was difficult to grasp. Working with shared documents and utilizing Skype, we were able to collaborate both long distance and in the moment. We soon realized that for us, translating Slataper involved using two different approaches, which better suited his novelistic and essayistic styles. We approached the challenge of rendering into English the often-winding sentences more typical of early-twentieth-century Italian prose, whether of the *critico* or the *romanziere,* in somewhat divergent ways according to genre. As we discovered, we were more likely to break down Slataper the critic's often convoluted style in order to convey

1 Recently the city of Trieste has been in the news both in Italy and abroad because the Italian government allowed China to invest money in the construction of a new pier in its port to facilitate the distribution of Chinese goods in Europe. As the *New York Times* reported on 18 March 2019, the new pier will allow "favorable custom conditions [for Chinese goods], a faster trade route to the heart of the Continent and direct access to railroads for moving [Chinese] goods into the European Union" (https://www.nytimes.com/2019/03/18/world/europe/italy-trieste-china-belt-road.html).

his point clearly, while seeking to preserve his account of his thinking process. Slataper *romanziere* more deliberately deploys a broad syntactical canvas, with dramatic shifts of language and style, in order to mirror an array of thoughts and emotions. As this complexity is an intrinsic part of the novel's texture, we tried to be as true to the original as possible, altering syntax only where necessary in the transformation from Italian to English. Slataper's aesthetic disposition towards a fragmented modernist style embraced by the *Vociani*, who distrusted traditional narrative modes of expression, is combined with the author's proclivity, especially in the first part of the text, to adopt a sensual and aestheticized prose reminiscent of D'Annunzio's work. Thus, along the way, the novel challenges the translator to mimic its sudden starts and stops, its propulsive energy and power to evoke sensation.

Another type of challenge is posed by the instances of Triestine dialect and diction, which occur when the young Scipio reports the words of his companions, and are accompanied in Italian editions by notes providing the standard Italian equivalents. We sought to maintain the playful spirit of these interjections, without introducing distracting cultural incongruencies. It is of course impossible to find an adequate equivalent for Triestine in English, or any other language; what wins out is the imperative to maintain a colloquial and idiomatic form of speech that renders the nuances of the original. Some of the flavour of the original is undoubtedly lost, but without an intruding dislocation. A further difficulty posed by Slataper's *Karst* is the author's propensity to switch suddenly from past tense to present in a way that often disorients the reader. We decided to keep the original inconsistency of Slataper's use of verb tenses, which underscores the complication or deliberate undermining of traditional linear temporal narrative. Laying bare the texture of time and memory in this way seems entirely appropriate to a text that resists genre and that Slataper and others struggled to categorize, alternately calling it a lyrical autobiography, memoir, or novel. Slataper himself first entitled his work *Carsina*; then *Vita e sentimenti di Giusto da Trieste*; next, *Il mio Carso e la mia città*; and finally, at the publisher's request, more simply *Il mio Carso*. We decided to go back to *My Karst and My City*, the title we prefer for our own edition, because it brings to the fore the tension between the nostalgic, bucolic, regenerative world of the Karstic plateau that surrounds the city, and the fragmented, cacophonous experience of the modern metropolis that Slataper chose to embrace at the end of his narrative and existential journey.

In translating the critical writings, we kept foremost our duty to convey Slataper's ideas as clearly as we could, preserving the complexity of the sentences when Slataper was intent on conveying a laborious thought process. Although adhering to the intellectual rhythm of the original may give the translation at times an antiquated flavour, we found this preferable to a modernization of Slataper's prose.

In the end we consider that (after Valéry) a translation is never finished, only abandoned when one has to settle on a version to publish. Although every effort has been made to sift through the volume you are now holding in your hand to ensure the absence of egregious mistakes, we recognize that improvements come with each successive translation. Slataper's writings were all published in a very short span of time, from 1909 to 1915. After all this time, just as we celebrated the one-hundred-year anniversary of the end of World War I, we propose his writings in the first scholarly edition in English. We hope that this edition will allow readers to engage with the work of this seminal Triestine author who offered us a window on local, national, and international conflicts as they were developing in Europe at the beginning of the twentieth century. Slataper's engagement with Triestine reality, his commitment to observe, critique, explain, and clarify to himself first of all, and then to others, the political tendencies and the cultural tensions he witnessed in his multi-ethnic city, was always guided by a desire to inform his public about the geopolitical complexity of his place and time without falling into any facile rhetoric popular at his time. He embodied the figure of the engaged intellectual who questioned traditional interventionist and nationalist positions, but at the same time was willing to change or reformulate his opinions as circumstances changed, and, most of all, took full responsibility for his writings and for his actions. As such, Slataper remains a remarkable figure worth reading and studying.

Citations and Texts

Elena Coda's notes to the translations facilitate the identification of peoples, places, and contexts that might not be familiar to the contemporary reader. In order to distinguish the editor's notes from the notes provided by the author, Coda's notes appear within brackets. Unless otherwise noted, the biographical and historical information was obtained from the *Enciclopedia Treccani* and the *Encyclopedia Britannica.*

The translations are based upon the following editions:

Slataper, Scipio. *Alle tre amiche.* Edited by Giani Stuparich, Mondadori, 1958.

– *Ibsen.* Edited by Arturo Farinelli, Fratelli Bocca, 1916.

– *Il mio Carso.* Photomechanical reproduction of the 1st ed. (1912), della Libreria della Voce (Florence), under the aegis of the city of Trieste, 1989.

- *Scritti letterari e critici.* Edited by Giani Stuparich, Mondadori, 1956. ("Ai giovani intelligenti d'Italia"; "Il futurismo"; "Perplessità crepuscolare")
- *Scritti politici.* Edited by Giani Stuparich, Alberto Stock, 1925. ("Trieste non ha tradizioni di cultura"; "La vita dello spirito"; "Oggi"; "L'avvenire nazionale e politico di Trieste"; "I diritti nazionali si affermano con la guerra")

MY KARST AND MY CITY

AND OTHER ESSAYS

PART ONE

My Karst and My City

For Gioietta

I

I would like to tell you that I was born in the Karst, in a hut with a thatched roof blackened by rain and smoke. There was a mangy, raucous dog, two geese with mud-spattered bellies, a spade, a hoe, and, from a dung-heap nearly without straw, brown rivulets that coloured the ground after every rain.

I'd like to tell you that I was born in Croatia, in a great oak forest. In winter everything was white with snow, the door would open only a crack, and at night I heard wolves howl. Mamma wrapped my swollen red hands in rags, and I threw myself onto the hearthstones, moaning from the cold.

I'd like to tell you that I was born on the Moravian plain and would run like a hare through the furrows, startling chattering crows into the air above. I threw myself onto the earth on my belly, pulled up a beet root, and nibbled its earthy flesh. Then I came here, tried to tame myself, learned Italian, made friends with the most sophisticated young people; but I'll have to return home soon because I'm miserable here.

I'd like to fool you, but you wouldn't believe me. You are cunning and wise. You'd understand right away that I'm a poor Italian trying to make his private preoccupations seem barbarian.[1] I should confess to being your brother, even if at times I watch you with a distant, abstracted eye,

1 [Throughout the text Slataper plays with the myth of his "barbarian" origins. Although he recognizes that his barbarism is a literary posturing to hide the fact that he is just "a poor Italian" from the provinces who must acclimatize to the more sophisticated Florentine cultural society, he also wants to stress his alterity vis-à-vis traditional Italian culture. As he noted in a letter: "I am a barbarian who dreams. I don't have anything but my sorrow, and the joy in possessing it. And everything that comes from inside me is good, because I suffer just like the earth that must sprout" (*Alle tre amiche* 171).]

made timid by your culture and your reasoning. Perhaps I'm afraid of you. Your arguments gradually cage me in as I listen, indifferent and content, unaware that at every moment you're revelling in your show of intelligence. Then I turn red and fall silent at a corner of the table, and I think of the consolation of the great trees at the mercy of the wind. I think longingly of the sun on the hills, of ample freedom, and of my real friends, who love me and greet me with a hand-clasp, with a calm and deep laugh. They are strong and good.

I think of my distant unknown origins, of my ancestors tilling the endless field with a plough pulled by four dappled draught horses, or in leather aprons bent over the furnace of molten glass, and of my enterprising grandfather, who came upon Trieste in the days of the Free Port;[2] of the great faded-green house where I was born and where, hardened by suffering, my grandmother still lives.

It was good to see her sitting on our broad terrace against the vast backdrop of mountains and sea, leathery and spry next to my other grandmother, the old Venetian, rosy and carefree – almost eighty, and you could still see her strong blue pulse rise and fall through her skin, which was tender as a leaf. She spoke to me of the siege of Venice, of the sack of potatoes in the centre of the cantina, of the bomb that shattered part of the house.[3] And she wore a white kerchief over her little remaining fine hair, and she was cheerful. When she came to eat at our place, my father always said: Blessed are the eyes that look upon her.

But I wasn't interested in her then. I was running off into the fields to play among the trees.

Our garden was full of trees. There was a big red horse chestnut we would climb, with forking limbs where I would always lose a shoe. From the highest branches I'd see the red tiles of our roof, full of sunlight and sparrows. There was some kind of evergreen, ancient, with a huge wisteria twining up it like a python, all wrinkles, furls, and twists, magnificent for speed-climbing when playing hide-and-seek. I often hid myself in that

2 [In 1719 the Habsburg emperor Charles VI declared Trieste a free, tax-exempt port. It maintained this status until 1891.]

3 [Reference to the Austrian siege of Venice in 1849. At that time Venice was part of the Lombardo-Venetian Kingdom under Austrian rule. In 1848 Daniele Manin, a Venetian political leader, led a revolt to free the city from Austrian rule. Although the Austrians were defeated, and Manin was able to proclaim a free Venetian republic, internal political dissent and lack of support from other Italian states led to an ultimate defeat. The Austrians besieged Venice and launched balloons carrying bombs into the city. The devastation wrought by the bombs coupled with the cholera that was raging in the city led to its capitulation in August 1849. See Jonathan Keates, *The Siege of Venice*, Pimlico, 2006.]

old cypress full of dense corners and brush, and in springtime, while I spied upon the wary step of the seeker from up high, I'd suck on fresh wisteria blossom, which brushed against my brow like a bunch of grapes. Wisteria blossoms have an unusual sweet-and-sour flavour, like the leaves of a peach tree, and a little like ether.

There were also many fruit trees – plums, greengages, and especially figs. As soon as the flowers lost their petals and the petioles began to swell, I was up there to taste them, not yet sour. The sour ones are good! The shell of the pit is still tender, like curdled milk, and inside there's a bit of clear, succulent water. Then, some days later, when Mamma's gone to visit our aunt again, it becomes a sweet gelatinous gum to be savoured with the tip of one's tongue. And how good is the pulp, so bitter. At first your teeth are afraid to touch it, and press on it warily, while the tongue moistens it well and tastes the sap through its tiny holes. Then you bite down on it. Your gums burn, your teeth grind together and become coarse and rough as stones, and your whole mouth fills with a rich juice.

But when summer comes, you'd have to be a dormouse to reach the few fruits remaining – to go where the birds have no fear of you, because they're not accustomed to finding you up so high. At the fork of the two highest branches I braced myself with one foot, then with my right extended for balance, I stretched out my left like a caterpillar over the dangling branch, holding my breath – until the branch started to bend, and little by little drew closer to my mouth. Sometimes I let it spring back, because Grandma was shouting, "Boys, you'll kill yourself up there in those trees!" Then I turned red and, saying nothing, slid swiftly down.

And against the wall along the street, there was also a worm-eaten yew whose bark I tore off easily in large strips, just to see it clean and red. It had, at the third-floor level, two limbs that formed a bed, and sometimes after lunch I slept there; or triumphantly I'd sit contemplating the street urchins scuffling over the berries I tossed down to them like a lord (I didn't eat them myself; I found them disgusting). Then, growing bolder, they'd start throwing rocks at me, and like a demon I would leap down and run to the gate, heave the iron deadbolt across, and plunge headlong down the streets, nearly to the centre of the city, in my blue-and-white striped sweater and shorts, my long blond curls flying, yelling "Bash 'em! Bash 'em!" And in the evening, I'd fall asleep stretched out on my bed while my mother peeled off my leggings, still full of bits of earth and gravel. My dear, sweet mother.

Those urchins! They fought battles with terrible rock fusillades at Sanza, a ruined old Triestine fortress next to our land. We heard them shouting, running, massacring each other. They were Italians and Africans. The Italians won. Once one of them came back with an injured neck, chanting over and over, "Anyway, I won! Anyway, I won!"

I followed the whole Abyssinian War on a great map that Papa had pinned up in our bedroom, in front of which, holding the latest edition of the *Piccolo* in his hand, he would explain just where the Italians were heading.[4] Underneath, on horseback, with plumed helmets and dark faces, were the emperor Menelik and Ras Alula: I punctured their noses with little flag pins. I was very happy that the Italians were winning.[5] I think I prayed for them.

At that time I believed in God, and prayed every evening: *Our Father, who art in Heaven,* and I'd shut my eyes tight and keep quiet and still, thinking only of the person I wanted God to love. That was how I prayed. I prayed for my beautiful Italy, which had a great battleship, the strongest in the world, called the *Duilio.*[6] Our country was over there, across the sea. Meanwhile, here, Mamma closed the shutters on the eve of the Austrian emperor's birthday celebration, because we never put a lit candle in our windows, and she was afraid someone would throw stones.

But Italy will win and come here to liberate us. Italy is extremely strong. You can't imagine how much the word "Bersaglieri" meant to me.[7]

Our house was stately and beautiful. The entry was like that of a temple, spacious and grand, around which wound the staircase, with its white banisters framed in shiny, yellow-brown wood. In winter the sun streaming through the big windows did its best to warm the shrunken cacti

---

4 [The Italo-Ethiopian War of 1895–6 was part of Italy's colonial enterprise at the turn of the twentieth century. The Italians suffered a terrible and humbling defeat at the hands of the Ethiopians at Adowa on 1 March 1896. *Il Piccolo* was the most popular Italian newspaper in Trieste. It embraced the irredentist cause and was politically close to the Liberal National Party.]

5 [Negus Menelik II was the Ethiopian emperor from 1889 to 1913. Ras Alula Engida was the Ethiopian general who defeated the Italian troops in the Battle of Dogali (1887) and in the battle of Adowa (1896).]

6 [The *Caio Duilio* ironclad battleship was built in the 1870s for the Royal Italian Navy and was considered one of the most powerful battleships of its time.]

7 [The Bersaglieri (marksmen) were an elite unit originally formed in 1836 as part of the Piedmontese army. They were the unit that in September 1870 stormed through the gate of Porta Pia and occupied the city of Rome, which was still politically separate from the rest of Italy. Because of their role during the Risorgimento (as the Italian unification wars are known), they became the most idealized military unit in the irredentist rhetoric of the time.]

planted by Uncle Daghelondai.[8] It was Grandfather's house, in which lived Grandfather's many children, and his many grandchildren.

On Sundays and holidays Grandfather sat at the head of the family table, at the other end. He had a commanding posture, a broad, kind face, and a great white beard. Contentedly, he watched his sons and their wives. So many dear relatives were seated around the table in the great dining room on Sundays! All of them were seated at their place, and when someone else came, another leaf was added to the table and a longer tablecloth was taken from the armoire. Our relatives were numerous, and they arrived from Zagreb, from Padua, from America, and they brought us cookies and toys.

At the table there was Uncle Boto, who painted pictures and told us the adventures of Saturnino Farandola;[9] and Aunt Tilde, with her large, gentle eyes the colour of the sea; and our little cousin Biancolina, who was always with my brother, so that I was mad to know their secrets; and Uncle Daghelondai, who was always saying to us in his growling voice: *Like a Turk at sermon, Daghelondai!*[10] And I'd laugh and my brother would jump around excitedly, stomping his feet; and there were Uncle Guido and Uncle Feliciano, and Aunt Mima, and Mario and Bruno, and Grandmother, Aunt Bice, Papa, Toci, Mamma, and Aunt Ciuta, buxom and matronly. Her gaze was kind, and things became simple and straightforward when she addressed them.

And when everyone had finished eating and were drinking coffee and smoking long Virginia cigars, the door was opened with a great effort and in you came, in your white smock with pretty pink tassels on your shoulders, sleepyhead Pipi.[11] You were healthy and handsome, with blond hair and bare legs, your young skin still warm from sleep. Your strange eyes, restless and joyful, gazed happily at the pretty white tablecloth left out just for you, and at the many plates Papa had covered with others so the food would stay warm.

And they fitted you with a large bib scented with lavender, and sat you down in front of tender rice in rich chicken broth; chicken thigh and wing, for your sharp teeth; loin chop spread with caper sauce; plump red

---

8 ["Daghelondai," the nickname of the uncle, probably from the Triestine dialect "Daghedai" meaning "running around." See C.L. Cergoly, *Inter pocula: Poesie segrete triestine*, G. e A. Kirchmayer, 1974, 47.]

9 [Uncle Boto is Alberto Slataper, a painter of landscapes and portraits. Saturnino Farandola is the protagonist of the children's book *Voyages très extraordinaires de Saturnin Farandoul* (The adventures of Saturnin Farandoula), a fantastic illustrated novel written in 1879 by Albert Robida. The novel was translated into Italian in 1884.]

10 [The saying is analogous to "It's all Greek to me."]

11 ["Pipi" is Scipio's nickname as a child.]

cherries in bunches, which you would hang from your ears, delighted by their coolness; and a big slice of cake, the biggest piece, which Grandpa always sliced especially for you. Quiet, methodical, and serious, you devoured everything without even asking what it was. But you liked everything, and it was all just what you needed for a run in the garden. You were healthy and strong; your friends named you their captain right away, because you won all the races and fights, and excelled at stone throwing. You were a fine young boy, and everyone liked you.

Steno, Gigetto, Toci, Oidecani, Eugenio, Vincenzo, Scarpa, Pipi, here we go, into the water, into the water! Today we're fighting for the honor of the Bash 'ems club!

The sea erupts in waves as the Bash 'ems plunge headlong from the wooden pilings. The flabby guy in the faded straw hat, who always bathes his brow and belly button very carefully before easing himself into the water, flees in fear of our splashing. So do all the peaceful bathers on the raft, and on the rope, and on the trampoline, because no one knows where the Bash 'ems have decided to camp out today, and no one knows what new trick the Bash 'ems will play as they dive laughing off the wooden pilings.

The sea erupts in joy and spray. The sea doesn't love the slow asthmatic pawing of the aged, or the anxious thrashing of beginners. The sea loves to be sliced and struck cleanly, to surrender to muscular legs and brown arms. It loves the serene restlessness of the young, who merge with it completely, laughing with it, drinking it, spurting it from their mouths in long jets. It loves fresh eyes held wide open between the algae and the deep.

Come on, young dolphins! Today we're fighting for the honor of the Bash 'ems! Because last Sunday the Bash 'ems threw themselves in ranks from the pilings, cheerfully spraying the naked bodies of the unamused German nobility, who wouldn't let them pass through that corner of the jetty. On shore they protested, and the director threatened to prohibit the Bash 'ems from swimming. Today is our day of revenge.

The tide is coming in from Salvore, making the battle fiercer and more turbulent.[12] The fine Germans are in the water, laughing ironically into their moustaches as they move forward. Ha! Ha! One of them is

12 [Punta Salvore, in Istria, marks the southern limit of the Gulf of Trieste. The German Holy Roman Emperor, Frederick I (aka Barbarossa) was defeated here by the Venetians in 1177. The children fighting in the water against the German tourists are re-enacting the battle. The ensuing Peace of Venice (1177) became a symbol of Italian strength against the Germans.]

wearing a net on his upper lip to maintain the shape of his moustache! Bash 'em! Bash 'em!

"In a semi-circle! Firm, strong splashes! Aim for the eyes!! Forward, close ranks!" And we responded to our chief: "Bash 'em!"[13]

So this is the German attack! Flaccid and limp as a Medusa jellyfish. But the attack of the Bash 'ems is straight and strong as the flick of a slingshot. Sharp salt in pale German eyes!

"Watch out! Close ranks!" The enraged enemy has set upon our vanguard and plunged them under. Bash 'em! Bash 'em!

Down! Along my neck I feel the angry scrape of a hairy German as below me the water parts. I touch bottom. Two legs keep me firmly under. The sea is raging. I curl myself up, grab hold of a leg, and down with you, swine! "Long live the Bash 'ems!"

Down again. Up again. Bash 'em, bash 'em!

"Out to sea!" Steno vanished after shouting the order. Then we find out why. One after another, the Germans suddenly plunge to the bottom, pulled in by some massive octopus. "It's Steno! Long live Steno! Bash 'em!"

Now we destroy them. Water by the ton pounds onto their gasping mouths. Their pale eyes no longer see. They turn and take flight. And we begin to beat their desperate retreat. Steno invented this game, because the Bash 'ems never give any quarter until the shore is reached.

Cool, calm, methodical beats against their retreat! The Germans are fleeing, but one by one we catch up to them, and churning up the water with our feet, we dive down and surround their chief. Stinging water explodes in their ears, eyes, mouths, and noses. The Germans come up to breathe. And *splash!* into the open mouths. And *splash!* into stinging eyes. Into deafened ears. Splash! Splash!

Long live the Bash 'ems!

Who could stand up to the Bash 'ems, friends of long ago? Who could stay underwater like Toci, when bearded Calligarichichichich attempted to drown him with ten, twenty dunkings, one after the other? He'd come up panting "chi chi chich!" in his face and disappear again. And who could deliver a sharper splash than Vincenzo? It was like the blow of a marine monster, a sea-blade that shot from the wedge of his hands. And Steno could swim underwater for a whole minute, and Pipi was a fierce little shark.

13 [We kept the original inconsistency of Slataper's use of verb tenses. See "A Note on the Translations."]

And if one of us ever failed in battle, for seven days he had to endure abuse from the others. Because the Bash 'ems were a society with strict rules, and no one dared disobey our chief.

Now Steno, our chief, is dead. He was a professor who became neurotic and killed himself.

I told fine stories to the little cousins who listened, gathered around me on the shady veranda by the sea. The sea was quiet, listening. The house next door, where Tartini once lived, had closed its shutters and was sleeping, white in the sun, along with all the uncles and other vacationers.[14] The large master bedrooms were silent on their big square beams.

It was the hour of heat and siesta. The earth expanded under the broad reach of the sun. The sky was closed and solemn. Not a sail was upon the sea. The wasps and bees were quiet. A fruit thudded down from its branch. It was the great silence of the heat, when the dove shuts its eyes beneath a wing, and the big ox chews its cud on the fresh straw.

At this hour only the kids rush into the fields like a flock of autumn starlings, raiding the fig trees and snapping off dry branches, because the landlord, master Vatta of the watchful eye, is sound asleep. Then they gather again on the shady veranda, pockets bulging, and Scipio tells a long, strange, beautiful story.

It's a story that he continues each day and is never done telling. In a little hut in the woods a hero is born, strong as a hundred lions and clever as a hundred foxes. His adventures make the listeners gape in astonishment and laugh with happiness. He's a handsome boy, kind and calm. He is what they all want to be.

And after two or three hours, Aunt Ciuta calls out that there's a letter for me, and happily brings me a letter from my mother. My dear mother. In the great heat of August, you were getting the crates ready for our move. We had to leave the house where your children were born. Yes, I remember that before we left, they were tearing up the walls and paths of the garden to install pipes for water and gas; stonemasons, mechanics, carpenters, glaziers, carpet layers, and tile layers were at work. I enjoyed watching them working. But we were moving out, because Grandfather had died and other, richer relatives were going to move in.

And having come back from Strugnano,[15] I was so happy to find myself in a countryside that was a hundred times more vast, with

14 [Giuseppe Tartini (1692–1770), famous Baroque composer and violinist, was a native of Piran (in Istria), which was part of the Venetian Republic.]

15 [Strugnano is a small town in Istria where the young Slataper lived for a while with some relatives.]

endless fruit trees and vines, and so many friends to play with. On the day that I arrived, the landlord's niece arrived too, in a red blouse and jockey's cap. Ucio, a bit excited, gazed at her through the vines of the gazebo.

Beautiful is the harvest. The rows of vines echo with shouts and laughter; the dogs bound from one group of pickers to another, crouching on their front paws, and scattered sparrows flutter about. The landlord urges us on: "Come on, let's get to work, let's go! Keep it up! Come on!" Lips and chin are sticky with sap-like juice, and hands, and sweaters, the handle of the billhook, leaves of the vines, the baskets and carts. Everything is covered in reddish gum. And we are bathed in it as we squelch the full bunches into the basket with our open hands.

The grapes are so good, bitten right off the stem, while our eyes drip with sweat and our hands ache from gripping the billhook. But there's still this row, this vine, this bunch! Over here with another basket! Hey!

And then when we've bounded back down, the bread and broth taste better than ever. We enjoy the lovely white tablecloth under the lamplight. Tomorrow we start again.

It was barely drizzling. Two yellow stripes of light lay across the muddy courtyard. I went down into the cellar.

"Good evening!" – "Ah! 'Evening!"

The cellar had a low ceiling. In its centre, on a small barrel, the reddish flame of a gas lamp was smoking. The landlord was sitting near the flame, a glass in his hand. His face reflected the purple colour of the bottoms of the empty wine casks.

All around were ranks of large brown casks and potbellied vats. All over the walls, in the corners, and between the iron bars of the window, there were thousands of cobwebs, torn and tangled with dust. A red cat sniffed lazily but anxiously at the rat smell that saturated the air under the casks.

One of the men, who was rolling up his trousers with difficulty because of his solid, heavily muscled thighs, raised his eyes, watching me.

Vila was over there, on her feet, standing on the squared trunks that held up the vats. She was straight and vibrant in her red blouse, and she smiled at me.

I was a shy boy. And she said to me softly, "Jump up here."

The lovely full bunches that we collected yesterday were being pressed in the tub. We just nibbled at the biggest ones, sick of grapes. She offered me a fat one, big as a nut and transparent.

"Look what hands I've got," she said.

They were small but calloused, full of little cuts at the tips, black from cooking, the nails bitten. Then she said: "You have such fine hands!" And she shouted: "Come on, Toni, let's get started!"[16]

Vila's uncle, the landlord, wiped a glass with the lining of his coat and offered me a drink. I drank it.

They stamped on the grapes, bending forward, gripping the edges of the vat, panting like woodcutters. Their hairy, red-stained legs pounded alternately in a kind of frenzy, and the vat trembled under the blows. The pulp, the skins and the juice squirted between their large toes. Vila stood upright, leaning against the vat. Her nails had turned bright red.

Then the legs of the crushers vanished up to the thighs into winey slush. Their double treads became methodical, like pistons. Heavy and equal.

Vila's uncle was drinking, wiping the juice from his bristly moustache with the back of his hand. His snout was all red.

The must boiled in the open casks, swarming with drunken gnats. I breathed in the hot suffocating odour. Now the men were getting drunk. They knocked over a vat full of must, and the wine splashed all over them and onto the wall, pouring off in gushing rivulets and staining the terrified cat. One of the men threw himself to the ground to lap up the winey slurry.

The landlord swore, laughed, and offered me a glass of must. It burned. The cellar was cramped and stained red.

"Vila, a bit of wood for the cask!"[17]

I ran ahead of her just to get out of there, but she caught up to me. It was raining. The night was dark and muddy. She seized my hand and kissed my bare arm as we ran, streaming with rainwater.

I said, "Vila!" amazed, my voice low.

Down in the cellar the men were trampling rhythmically, the landlord was drinking, the cat was licking its sodden fur.

I sat happily on the floor. I was running down a long sunlit highway. Running and running.

When the sun is high in July, anyone running through the fields has to stop because his lungs are full of a heat and a poison so sweet and strong that he just has to lie down in the sun and sleep. He closes his eyes, and his eyelids burn like a sky ablaze, and all around huge flames rise, swaying from tree to tree. The air trembles, restless in the heat.

But I jumped up in a rage and ran off into the fields, screaming like a young hawk leaving its nest for the first time.

---

16 [In the original, Vila's words are in the Triestine dialect.]

17 [In the Triestine dialect in the original.]

Her bedroom had plaster walls stamped with a reddish-grey pattern, a floor of cracked bricks, a piano covered with a cross-stitched throw, a bed, a cupboard topped with medicine bottles and a stuffed owl. One pane of the window was made of rusty tin, with a hole in it for the stove-pipe. As the hole had grown larger, in winter Vila stuck some rags around the pipe with scissor tips. Smoke leaked through.

The house where Vila lived wasn't pretty! I used to creep in like a clumsy thief, stuffing my switch in my pocket, that fine switch with a crack like steel, tiptoeing swiftly and holding my breath. The air smelled of mould, wine, and dust. Sometimes the door of the last room, next to Vila's, was open, and Vila would quickly shut it. It was a reeking jumble of rags, bottles, and boxes, with plaster walls peeling from the damp; here slept the old lady, the landlord's mother, gouty, rheumatic, and bloated, with a black moustache over swollen lips.

I used to see the old lady only on Sundays, when everyone was seated around the table in the parlour playing tombola, children, old ladies, and the landlord's brother, delighted if he could win a penny or two.[18] She herself couldn't move. She was seated in a wheelchair and held her right hand, swollen as a rotten pear, beside her card, over the pile of glass markers. When she had to buy her card, Vila would go up to her, put her hand behind the old woman's back, and draw out a fat bag of rough canvas fastened with string. The old woman had the eyes of a barn owl by daylight, steady and full of cunning. I tried to stay out of her sight. Sitting next to Vila, knee against knee, I was pretending to play. I knew that this old hag saw everything, even what the others didn't see, and that she hated us all, but couldn't get up. She really disgusted me, and I felt no pity when Vila told me one day that her uncle spat in his mother's face.

Everyone feared this uncle. He wasn't mean. But he drank rum, and when he was angry he would spit at people and always curse brutally – but I don't want to talk about those people! I love Vila! Vila is kind and beautiful. She has a scarlet blouse, a little jockey's cap, and high-heeled shoes, and when we play at bats, she leaps about with marvelous agility.

What sharp, clear cracks as we swung the bat in the forecourt of that big yellow house! When Scipio and Vila play, the tenants smile down from the windows, crying: "Bravo! Well played!" The ball flashes like a flame from me to her, her to me: bam-bam; bam-bam. Each blow says *I love you.* The next blow responds *I love you.* The sun is high in the sky. It's summer. It's love.

---

18 [Tombola is a parlour game that originated in southern Italy. It is a type of raffle.]

Precious days they were, full of love and glory. She was all mine, Vila, a young lady, loved by Ucio, courted by all the lads of the village. She used to get postcards from rich young men, from students at faraway universities; but she would laugh with me, and kiss me. She was mine. I alone would go with her through the fields, looking for drops of sap on the trunks of plum trees, and four-leaf clovers, and when it rained, I sheltered her in my arms.

She came with me on my thieving raids beyond the boundaries of our land, frightened when I clambered over unsteady stone walls that threatened to tumble down. Between my lips I'd bring her the juiciest pear, and she'd draw me onto her knees, kissing me greedily.

I was like a young lord. I was proud that she enjoyed my strength and boldness. I was only eleven, but not even the peasants could catch me when I ran, or when I climbed the poplar and the ailanthus, which everyone said couldn't be done. The landlord gave me five bottles of wine as a prize; Vila smiled anxiously from the window. It was sunset. At the foot of the tree, my friends exploded into cheers while I, exhausted, feared the wind like a bird without wings, and I looked down scornfully at the houses of the city, which began to burn with yellow points of light.

Ah, now that Vila is married and has two or three kids, perhaps already reading what I write for children – and is more beautiful, far more beautiful than in those days, happy young mother that she is, and doesn't even glance at me when, blushing, I pass close by – if only she would think back sometimes on our two carefree years together! And the times we hunted blackbirds and cats with our flobert rifle! There was that stuffed owl in your bedroom, wings folded and a little bent upon its twig, solemn as the most proper gentleman. It had yellow eyes of glass, glowing in the half-dark of the room, round as targets. And one day you secretly loaded the rifle and *crack*! One eye was shattered! Remember? And I gazed at you happily, rapt with admiration.

Then one day I said to you: "Vila, you're not the way you used to be."[19]

And it was over.

I was tired of her. She had strange foibles that took away my freedom. When we were all giving chase with sticks and pitchforks to a dog that had gone wild, Vila, without warning, scampered up a tree and cried out to me, "Come up here." I climbed to the top and looked down from the uppermost branches, swishing them angrily. "Come on, come on over!" And she began stroking my hair and neck, then she started kissing me; in

19 [In the original, Slataper's words are in the Triestine dialect.]

the distance, I heard the shouts of our companions, and the exhausted howling of the dog.

Perhaps, too, Vila didn't love me; had never loved me. I had some slight suspicions; one hot rush of blood, and they were gone. I don't know what came over me. Sometimes I threw myself on the ground, weary and miserable. I was restless, and I would have liked to be alone sometimes, except that I needed to feel her nearby. And so, once I had blurted out those strange words without even knowing why, I was angry with myself and thrust my hand right into a pricker bush. Vila was silent. I glared at some little objects on the ground: a broken twig with two withered, faded leaves; a ball of silky poplar-fluff, all unravelled in little silvery threads by the predatory attack of hundreds of ants. She lifted her eyes and gazed at me for a long time. I felt a silence that would never end, and that really irritated me.

Then I seized her firmly in my arms, and Vila forgave me. We were happy and full of love for the rest of the day.

But the next morning she ran away from me. Chasing her breathlessly, I circled round at a distance and burst out of a bush in front of her. I took her wrists and cried fiercely, "What's happening with you?" "This is how you wanted it."[20] And she broke free and went away. Then, when I ran into her a few weeks later, she took my hands and kissed them.

I was immediately relieved not to be with her anymore. But I was full of confused desires; nothing interested me. I was bored. Sometimes I would lie on the ground, my half-closed eyes caressing the young foliage. Then I'd suddenly start rolling around in the stiff grass of the fields.

Ucio is a tall, strong boy, with hair on his arms all the way up to his elbows, with thick lips and bleeding gums. In his garden he grows touch-me-nots, dahlias from Slovenia, and St. Anne chrysanthemums. He needed a base for a flower basket he'd been talking about for the past five Sundays; so he filched our washboard. But he used it without scraping off all the encrusted soap. He also needed some rose bushes, because we were always teasing him about his simple flowers, so he stole some from our garden, but left behind a brass clasp from his shirt. Next Sunday Papa said in front of lots of people, "I've found this button. Whose is it?" And Ucio shouted out, "It's mine! It's mine!"[21]

That's what Ucio is like, the big lug. His breath reeks of garlic and his hands are filthy. When he ransacks the fields, he returns with his shirt

20 [In the original, Slataper addresses her in dialect.]

21 [The exchange is in dialect.]

stuffed with unripe pears, plucked without their stems, just as they came to him, all rusty with the marks of his scratching and sweaty from his hairy belly. He can't tell the good from bad, munching beans and potatoes, and rumbling deeply, "So good, so good!"[22]

Ucio is in love with Vila. He says, "Vila is an angel."[23] And because her uncle has forcibly banished her from the estate, Ucio strides up and down the courtyard, then all of a sudden slumps down onto the bench and vows revenge.

I'm with him. Revenge is an excellent thing! To slip at night through the thorns of the hedge with a long stick in one hand and a pruning knife in your pocket! The night is deep and silent. By now everyone's asleep. The landlord's shutters are closed. Dogs are barking somewhere in the countryside.

Ucio belts out a laugh and turns savage. He grabs the first vine he finds and fells it with one stroke. He grabs a branch full of plums and tugs at it, feet planted against the trunk; then he crashes down to the ground along with it. He plops a huge stone onto the frogs croaking like crazy in the pond, making the putrid water splosh, drenching him. He shakes himself, brings down a dwarf pear tree with a single kick, and dashes onward, snorting like a rampaging satyr.

Long live revenge! But for myself I am quiet and full of malice. I silently open the pruning knife and cut the vine roots underground, so that they'll die and no one will know why. With one slice, I slash the top off the pear tree, then quickly crouch down, afraid the crack might have awakened someone.

Silence. The frogs. The distant dogs. A shooting star.

Ucio calls from the apple tree. He's munching and ripping away: with each fruit he snaps off a whole branch. One after another, I scrape deep gouges in all the big apples the landlord likes so much. I lick my fingernails.

Hey! Ucio! He sure ran her off, didn't he!

It was on a night like this. They were yelling over at the landlord's place. Our doorbell rang desperately. I spring upright in bed, Papa's bedroom door opens, he opens the front door. In her nightgown, Vila rushes in, crying, "He'll kill me, he'll kill me! He's after me with his gun!"

Papa bolted the door. Quietly he said, "No one can get in here. Calm down." Vila was trembling and wringing her hands.

22 [Ucio's comment is in dialect.]
23 [Ucio's comment is in dialect.]

"Let me go, let me go, I beg you. He won't do anything to me. I'm sorry. I didn't know who to turn to. Oh God, oh God!"

A bang at the door: "Vila!" Vila jumped up; Papa made her sit down and went to open it. No one was there. But Vila dashed out, going first to Ucio's family, then back down to her own place.

"Filthy whore! Get out of here! Go back to your bitch of a mother! Get out!"[24]

And her uncle threw her out into the night, with the maid and a bundle of clothes, threatening her from the window with his shotgun.

"Right? Ucio?!"

We remember and gleefully recount the whole drama, then coolly decide to renew the devastation. Ucio became as fierce as the hail and the bora.[25] I was already bored with the whole thing, and I munched on a bunch of grapes, thinking to myself: "You get to work, Ucio! Vila was mine all along."

Poor Ucio. I went on holiday to Italy, beyond the border, beyond the bridge over the Judrio;[26] in the meantime Ucio, for the sake of revenge, shot the headlight of the uncle's carriage with his flobert, leaving the pellet inside. His family was sent away from the estate. I wrote to him, "Dear Ucio, if there's only one 6-mm flobert in the whole village, after you shoot, you need to recover the pellet from the headlight." So in the end the landlord took a great liking to me, and when I was ill he often took me hunting.

I used to get terrible headaches. I had grown too fast, and had read and studied too much while recovering from typhoid fever. They took me to a doctor who examined me all over, then pushed up his spectacles and looked me in the eye.

It was a long look, a silent battle between us. I hated him, because he saw right through my sick act. He had no pity for me. Only then did I realize I'd always exaggerated my migraines. And I looked back at him as if to say: "I don't feel ill, I'm fine, I'm just lazy, that's all. I hate going to school." I felt the blood course more vigorously through my veins and lifted my slightly drooping head: suddenly I was full of energy and strength. He looked at me sceptically for a long time, severe and almost

24 [All the exchanges in this dialogue are in dialect.]

25 ["Bora" is the name of a violent and cold north-east wind that blows off the mountains towards the Adriatic Sea, usually occurring during the winter months. The gusts of wind often reach a velocity of one hundred kilometres per hour.]

26 [The river Judrio marked the border between Italy and the Austro-Hungarian Empire.]

malicious; then he forbade my going to school and prescribed a life outdoors for me. I had won.

You don't realize how much cunning one learns from watching how a bee enters a flower or how a spider traps a fly. You don't understand how, in obeying, a boy can make his parents do just what he wants. Our refined world is very naive. All you have to do is create a situation in which it's already established how everyone else should behave. If, for example, a student faints during the Greek exam, there isn't a professor with the audacity to disbelieve him, and to make him retake the exam right away or fail him. Everyone may think what they like, but I assure you, in the end they believe in doing what's considered socially acceptable for them. So four people carry the student into the principal's office, lay him down with his feet up on the arm of the sofa, and loosen his tie, while the old porter totters in with the first aid kit, and they take his pulse, and splash water on him. "But you couldn't even hold your breath for one minute. If a barbarian were to come among us, my friends, how easily he'd outwit us!"

But this is all about the past. In reality I was seriously ill with cerebral anemia and had to go and live for six months up on the Karst. And it was then that I discovered my Karst for the first time.

The earth where I spent my deepest nights got to know me, and so did the broad sky that resounded to my victorious shout when I leaped down the thrashing waters of the torrents, or darted from the hills in a burst of stone and earth, and in one step I would check my headlong flight to pluck a tiny, pale blue flower.

I ran with the wind expanding across the valleys, jumped joyfully over stone walls and juniper bushes, zooming through, like a stone whistling into space from a sling. Rebounding off logs and brush, I'd land on my feet amid trunks and earth, then charge off wildly and noisily through the forest like a stream carving its bed. And angrily tearing away the final obstructing branch, I'd burst forth, hair bristling with twigs and leaves, face full of scratches, but with my soul large and alive as the white scattering of doves frightened by my sharp cries of excitement.

And gasping, I flung myself headlong into the river to quench my burning flesh, filling my throat, nostrils, and eyes with water, gulping it down in great mouthfuls, swimming underwater with my mouth open like a pike. I fought my way upstream, clasping in my arms the turbulent water that burst foaming against my body, gripping the leaping current like a flowering tuft sticking out of the mountainside. And the current thrust me down and spun me, throwing me to the bottom and carrying me back up to the sunlight, dragging me a distance along its steep banks, along roots and rocks clutched at in vain. Then I sank down and, grasping at the riverbed, hoisted myself exhaustedly upstream.

The sun on my dripping body! The hot sun on my bare skin, deep in the prickly heather, thyme and mint, amid the buzzing of the golden bees! I threw my arms wide to embrace the whole earth, pierce it with my body to unite myself with it and rotate in its enormous whorl in the heavens – fixed there, like a mountain rooted at its heart by a frame of stone, like a lone high meadow vigilant in the August heat, a valley drowsing warmly in the heat's bosom, like a slope bolted by the pull of countless deep roots, its summit sprouting with a thousand restless, foolish flowers.

And at mid-month, at the hour when the moon emerges from the distant bushes and finds its way between the clouds, limpid and white as a patch of jonquils in the midst of a wood, I felt myself immersed in a gentle, mysterious vibration, as if in the tremor of a quiet, endless dream.

I came to know the terrain like the back of my hand. As I walked, I looked at everything around me with brotherly affection. The earth conceals a thousand secrets. Every step was a discovery. Wherever I was, I knew the thickest shade and the nearest cave that would shelter me from rain.

I love the heavy and violent rain. It comes down shearing off all the weaker leaves. Air and earth resound with rapid drumming, like a herd of stampeding bulls. Man feels as if he has cast off a yoke. At the first drops I jump to my feet, nostrils flared. Here comes the water, fresh water, our great release.

The water is good and fresh. It enters everywhere. The stone absorbs it, simmering. If you poke your finger in beside a plant stem, you can feel the roots sucking at it. All suffering lives breathe freely.

Because the earth is full of suffering. Every creature is burdened by a stone or a broken branch or a leaf that's too large or a molehill or the step of some animal. All trunks bear a scar or wound. I would lie down flat on the meadow and watch the dense thickets of grass, and at times I felt sad.

Sad for the lovely creatures of the earth. I knew them. My hands knew the deep summer cracks on the edge of which the insect stands probing with his long antennae, and a falling twig or gust of wind is enough to topple him in; and the little walls of sand that grandly bank even a little stream of water; I enticed an ant with a great burden onto a large sycamore leaf, so that I could carefully deposit it on the other side of the alp. Every creature was my brother. I loved the lovesick butterflies caught in the black mesh of the bramble, desperately beating their wings in a shower of white dust; the handsome velvety spider with his frail legs, who delicately spun a silver thread onto the prickly hairs of a leaf, then tried the thread with his tiny foot before casting himself outward and spinning his web. The fly caught in flight buzzed desperately in my fist; I stroked the smooth, fresh caterpillar that curled up like a dry leaf, and held the dazed dragonfly by its big, pale blue wings. I plunged my arm into the water to abruptly pluck out a toad with its yellowish-black belly; the wasp's abdomen laboured to deliver its stinger in my palm. I pelted snakes with stones.

I smiled at the erratic fluttering of the midges, cut short by the imperious blow of a bluebottle; at the whirling chatter of the swallows; at the clouds romping in the light and trembling shyly in the cold, curious fingers of the wind; at the leaf tumbling and darting through the air; and at stars budding in the sky when the evening breeze spreads gentle warmth over the earth, like the breath of spring.

Sliding through bushes, clutching the cliffs with two fingers inserted in a mossy cleft inside the rock, splashing and slapping at the edges of ponds with open palms, I spied upon the birth of spring. In the softest hiding place in the woods, a damp warm nest of withered twigs, warmed again and again by a sleeping hare, I searched out the first primrose, the first ray of sun! the dazed eye of tiny awakening spring! And I followed its delicate undulating motion, sniffing like a dog on the trail, amid swollen roots and delicate sprouts, beyond an airy puff of dewy grass, wet soil, earthworms, and gummy juices; an odour of vegetable milk, of bitter almonds – here it is, the rosy smile of the peach trees, hesitant as a winter dawn, how dear! And frantically I shake this trunk, then that one, then this, showering myself with petals and perfume. On the ground, little violet puddles of water splash here and there, as the young sparrow fans them with his wings, his beak open. Spring, my dear love!

Sometimes I stopped in the woods and lifted my head towards the tall line of trees. I heard leaves rustle, a juniper berry fall, birds chirping. Then all was silent. I was still.

I wanted to hurl myself against one of those tree trunks, embrace it, stay with it. But I was afraid of causing an uproar.

My eyes lazily searched for a butterfly, an insect. Nothing was moving. Something was hiding in the foliage, watching me, and I couldn't see it.

In the woods I learned to pray again. I said: "God, love me; God, love me." Once I threw myself on the ground, and for a long while I wept.

I jump up, and leap towards the patch of open sky. Under the sun, in the distance, my sweet memories glimmer and flare. Where am I going? My country is far away, the nest is shattered. But the wind wanders with me, full of desire, beyond the rocky edge of the Karst, and I am above the sea, in the broad path of wind and sun.

I was born on the broad flatland where the wind runs through tall grass, wetting its lips like a young fawn, and I followed it with hands outstretched and emerged, my face hot, under open sky. My country is far away; but the sea sparkles in the sunlight, and the world beyond the sea is without end.

And the fertility of the earth gushes up, pregnant with sap in its broad fleshy leaves, and lights with vermilion the full apples in the thickly growing trees, filling the soul of man with joy.

The golden harvest glows with heat, and the perfume of cedars and magnolias has overcome man in his weariness, so that he folds himself over the grain, and sleeps ensconced in the sun.

Pennadoro, newcomer, if you don't slumber, the land of the sun will be yours.[27]

27 ["Pennadoro" is the Italian translation from the Slovenian of the author's surname, "zlato pero." It is the equivalent of the English "golden pen."]

Mount Kâl is a heap of stones.[28] But I'm happy here. My coat clings to the rock like flesh to hot embers, and if I press down, it does not yield; my hands grip its ridges, which long to join with my bones. I am cold and bare like you, brother. I am barren and alone.

Brother, sunlight and pollen pass over you, but you don't blossom. Ice cuts your skin in sharp lines, but you don't bleed; and you don't produce a single plant to slow the springtime clouds that, brushing against you, pass through and away. But the air embraces and wraps you like a blanket on a man awaiting his lover in vain.

Motionless. The bora, sharp with stone splinters, lashes me and rips at my ears. My hair is like juniper needles, and my bloodshot eyes and parched lips widen into a laugh. The bora is a thing of beauty. It is your breath, gigantic brother. You blow your breath angrily into space and the tree trunks are ripped from the ground, while the sea, swelling from the deep, churns monstrously against the sky. When you unleash your raucous soul, the city screeches and swirls. Brother, I want to go down there with your mighty soul.

Forgive me if I jump up in a way you can't and abandon you. It's as though all of a sudden a spring were fertilizing you, bursting forth in your heart. A restless nostalgia bursts forth and gushes. I long to depart, brother. I long to possess broad fields of wheat and shady meadows. My country is down there. Mount Kâl, I must become brother to other creatures you do not know, whom I also do not know, but they live together down there, where clouds fall, heavy with rain.

Years of my youth, opening like crowns of violets trembling in the snow, where are you taking me with such joy? I raise and lower my arms wildly as though I had wings, as with every stroke, my teeth seem to grip material that is lighter, and so sheer that my soul expands to become the dawn of a new life. And I bound along, shaken by the same mountain that understands and helps me. I'm descending.

The bora strikes my back in waves, and I plunge on, like a torrent. The stones roll and tumble, thundering. Each step is new, because if my foot finds a track, it twists and turns. Down. My chest breaks through the air like a ram. And further down, sliding: flying to the next branch, to the next clump of grass that, with a finger grip, keeps me on my feet. The precarious rock tips over to toss me down, the ground splits open to

28 [Mount Kâl, in Italian Monte Calvo, is a small mountain located in the Karst, just to the north-east of Trieste.]

gather my shattered body; but my legs are strong and flexible. "Alboin came down this way."[29]

Lichen underfoot, squeaking, holding fast; yellow grass like dead leaves; a twisted oak, and now the little green pines that shake their heads like wary children. They grow thick and tight, entangling my feet, and as I stoop to find an opening, they prickle and scratch my cheeks. I keep going: I am among the giant pines. A peasant with a cowherd's whip stops and stares after me.

Mongol with hard, swollen cheekbones, like stones just covered with earth, dog with bluish eyes.[30] Why do you stare at me? You stand there dazed, while they steal your arid pastures, those who are afraid of your bora. You have a barbaric soul, but if the city spends a nickel on your milk you soften up, like your juniper thickets, if you rid them of rocks. Stuck in the woods, stunned, you await your destiny. What are you doing, dog! You'll become a putrid carcass to feed your barren Karst. Lime that breaks apart, shatters, and spreads, you are future soil. Tell me, Slovene! How many daffodils will you produce this spring for the ladies in the Caffè Specchi?[31]

S'ciavo, want to come with me?[32] I'll make you master of the broad fields of the sea. Our fields are far away, but the sea is handsome and bountiful. And you must become its master.

Because you're a Slav, son of the new race. You came to land no one could inhabit, and you farmed it. You took the net from the hands of the Venetian fisherman and made yourself a sailor: you, a son of the soil. You are loyal and frugal. You are strong and patient. For so many years they spat servitude in your face; but your hour too has come. It's time you became a master.

Because you're a Slav, son of the great future race. You're brother to the Russian peasant who will soon come to the worn-out cities to preach the new gospel of Christ; and you're brother to the Montenegrin fighter who liberated his country from the Ottomans; yours is the force that armed the galleys of Venice, and the grand, prosperous, rich Bohemia is

29 [King of the Lombards from 560–72, Alboin ruled most of the Italian peninsula after leading his people out of Pannonia and through the Julian Alps in 568.]

30 [Here Slataper addresses the Slovenian peasant as being a descendent of the Mongol tribes whose territory expanded from China to eastern Prussia and Bohemia. Their scouting patrols reached the vicinity of Vienna and Venice.]

31 [Caffè Specchi, located in Piazza Grande, today's Piazza Unità, in the beautiful Stratti palace, was one of the most elegant cafes of the city. It opened in 1839 and soon became a renowned meeting place for the Italian irredentists. It was also a favoured place of the Triestine upper class.]

32 ["*S'ciavo*" is the Triestine dialect word that denotes both "Slav" and "slave."]

yours. You are brother to Marko Kraljevic, Slovene peasant.[33] For many centuries Marko lay in his hillside tomb, and many of us believed him dead, forever dead. But now his sword has sprung forth again from the sea, and Marko has risen again. Trieste must become for you the new Venice. Set the woods on fire, and come with me.

The Slovene looks at me, annoyed. "Burn down woods the Italians, exhausted by twenty centuries of civilization, brought here so they could go and listen to Donna Paola speak, and enter the Stock Exchange to get away from the bora!"[34] The Slovene shoots me a scornful glance, cuts off a branch, takes from his pocket some old matches that burn with a slow violet flame, and patiently lights a fire. I'm provoking him, but he's just playing shepherd; I'm provoking him as though I were Slav myself.

O Italy, no, no! When the wood began to burn, I took fright and wanted to run for help. But he told me: "The firemen are far away!,"[35] smiled slyly, took up his whip, and went off, urging on his four cows.

I lay down, exhausted. "This is how Alboin came down!"

Weak Italian blood, blood of a house cat. There's no point in creeping along, crouching and pouncing with claws tensed for the prey; the prepared meal is sitting on the plate. You're sick with cerebral anemia, weak Italian blood, and your Karst won't regenerate your city any longer. Lie down on the stones of your streets and wait for the new century to run you over.

So I lay still as stagnant water. And the woods burned and pretty snapping flames coloured the sky blood-red.

At dawn I was reborn. I don't know how it happened. The sky was clear, and I gazed at the beautiful white city below and the ploughed earth. And with one leap, like one who has seen God, I threw myself upon it. Dream and nightmare had vanished: because I am greater than Alboin.

---

33 [Marko Kraljevic (1335–95) was a Serbian king and a vassal to the Turkish sultan. He became the hero of Serbian folklore, and many traditional popular songs and legends inspired by him were later anthologized and translated into Italian by the Italian-Dalmatian linguist Niccolò Tommaseo (1802–74).]

34 [Donna Paola is the nom de plume of Paola Baronchelli Grosson (1866–1954), a popular writer who addressed both political and social issues in her novels and articles. Her novel on the woman question, *Le confessioni di una figlia del secolo* (Confessions of a daughter of this century; Aliprandi, 1901), was a bestseller. On the eve of World War I she embraced the interventionist cause. In her book *La funzione della donna in tempo di guerra* (The duty of women in war time; Bemporad, 1915) she emphasized the role of women in the war effort.]

35 [In dialect in the original.]

Trembling, I dive into the furrow and cover myself with fertile earth, unsettling the seed. And I bite into this sliver of frozen soil as if it were bread. The roots vibrate underneath. And my soul actually expands, like water in a vast chamber, and I feel a distant tree startling in the wind as it compresses all the surrounding earth, and without doubt this idea born in me must be the first primrose in the fields.

On all fours I grope about, my eyes open wide, and the winter boughs thick with buds, the sapless twigs of vines, the gravel that presses against my trousered knees – everything trembles as I touch it, because I am the spring.

Roses, roses, roses. And, pricked all over, I pluck and fill my path with roses. One day she will pass by here and find me by following the red path. Ah beloved soul, today a poet is born unto the world, and he awaits you.

A poet is born who loves the beautiful creatures of the earth, because he must restore the purity of their turbid thoughts, like water drawn up by the sun. And he steals and snatches from the beautiful creatures of the earth because he is not merciful and only knows how to feed himself with living blood. Too many breasts full of milk in the world and the vital force is weak and wasted, and men lament their existence.

In my city, many were demonstrating for an Italian university in Trieste.[36] They walked arm in arm, eight to a row, shouting *Long live the Italian university in Trieste!* and dragging their feet to annoy the guards. So, I joined the front of the column, and I too dragged my feet. And so we moved down along Aqueduct.[37]

Suddenly the front ranks came to a halt and reeled back. From the direction of the Caffè Chiozza a broad double file of gendarmes marched towards us, bayonets fixed.[38] They marched as though they were on parade, their legs rigid, with long impervious strides. We all knew nothing could stop them. They would march on until the emperor cried *Halt!* Behind those gendarmes stood the entire Austro-Hungarian Empire. This was the force that held the world in its fist. This was the will of an enormous monarchy that extended from Poland to Greece, from Russia to Italy. It joined Charles V and Bismarck. Everyone knew this, and each of us bolted in fear, ashen-faced, pushing, shoving, scattering canes and hats.

I stood watching in amazement. They marched straight on without a smile, without a laugh. For them, there was no difference between the fleeing crowd and the compact column that marched to support the Italian university. I stood there watching them all, and I was arrested.

A gendarme seized me by the left wrist and off we went. It was a very strange thing. He continued at his fixed pace; I did my best to imitate him. The eyes of the passers-by, looking me up and down, were like cold drops of water on my spine, making me shudder; so the gendarme probably thought *Der Kerl hat Furcht.*[39] But maybe he wasn't thinking of anything, and was just striding along at his fixed pace. I remember vividly that a young man passing by extracted his right hand from his glove to stroke the right side of his moustache, then did the same with his left. I had turned my head to watch, so as the gendarme pulled ahead, I was wrenched forward. A woman wearing a fine feather boa looked at us curiously, but I could see that she was laughing. Why am I letting myself get pulled along by this imbecile?

He has broad epaulettes, black and yellow. Why not let him lead me along? Where we're going I don't know, but that's not important. He's the one leading me, he changes direction and ducks around a corner, as

36 [See Introduction, note 26.]

37 ["The Aqueduct" was the name of the most fashionable street in the centre of the city. Today it is called Viale XX Settembre.]

38 [The Caffé Chiozza, located on Aqueduct Street, was one of the many Triestine cafes frequented by Italian irredentists and artists.]

39 [German for "This guy's scared."]

my feet continually beat a parallel path. His bayonet shines brightly. Hey, is your rifle loaded?

Why doesn't he answer me? A butcher's boy stops short and hops over the sidewalk bench, his bloodstained apron rising and fluttering. As soon as we're past, he glares after us, and shouts, "Bash the gendarme!"[40] Then he vanishes.

I can clearly see this imbecile's jugular pulsing. And my fingers are very long, they're bony right to the tips. And no one's around. *Alboin …* But I am greater than Alboin. I am greater than Bismarck.[41] Gradually I slide my thumb inside my palm and turn my hand into a narrow extension of my wrist. Slowly I slip through his fingers, numbed by the cold. Meanwhile I start talking: "It's a sad life for you, isn't it? I understand you're just doing your duty. How long is your shift? Eight hours? In a row? And up there in the Karst, in all kinds of weather, even at night …" I feel some eternal words take shape in my throat that my fine old Venetian granny taught me: *Neither through error nor for good reason, never let them put you in prison.*[42] I look straight into the gendarme's eyes, tear my hand away, and I'm off! Long live liberty! I'm Italian!

He didn't even chase after me. And after a mad dash of two hundred metres, I felt bad seeing him rooted to the spot, in the distance. And then he took up his regular pace again, click, clack, in the opposite direction.

Click, clack. It seems as though he's getting closer, that he's here behind me, with his hand on my shoulder. I slip into a doorway; in the porter's hut there's a bald pate hedged around with a crown of hair fine as a child's, bent over a lady's shoe. I exit, pull my beret down more firmly on my head, wrap myself in my cloak, and stride off stomping the pavement as though there's a battle between it and my boots.

Then I ran down to the sea.

I washed my hands and face in the sea. I drank the salty water of our Adriatic. In the distance, in the sunset, the Italian Alps were red and gold, like the Dolomites. Above the Romagnolo trawlers the joyful tricolour flags were lowered, and polenta steamed on the galley hearth. Our sea.[43] I breathed freely and happily, as though after intense prayer.

---

40 [In Triestine dialect in the original.]

41 [Otto von Bismarck (1815–98) was a German politician and diplomat. He played a pivotal role in the unification of Germany. He served as prime minister in Prussia and later as chancellor of the newly established German Empire.]

42 [Italian proverb, in Venetian dialect in the original.]

43 [In the original "*Mare nostro.*" This is a deliberate echo of the Roman designation for the Mediterranean, *Mare Nostrum.* It became an irredentist and later a fascist imperialist slogan that claimed political supremacy over the eastern Adriatic coast.]

But later, I realized that people were watching me. My studded boots were dusty and my actions strange. I didn't look like those perfect gentlemen who walked up and down the promenade, not going anywhere in particular. They were people who gazed, and were gazed at. The young men had bell-shaped topcoats with long tails, like servants' jackets, and carried tall, light canes, that looked like branches freshly peeled of bark. Young ladies were accompanied by their mothers or fathers, and wore high-heeled boots as shiny as a beetle's back. The boots were much cleaner and clearer than their eyes. And cautiously, they also glanced at me; but when I returned their look, they turned their eyes away. They don't know how to return a man's gaze.

Now in all this coming and going, young men ducked between the ladies adeptly, brushing against them a little, but not enough to elicit a rebuke. Generally everybody smiled and tipped their hats every five steps, giving a slight bow. I watched them in amazement, then dived in among them, stunned by the rustle and whisper of that unthinking procession.

I moved slowly through the city, carried along in the leisurely flow. It's difficult to walk among people who are milling about. The person in front suddenly stops; another steps out of a shop with her head turned to thank the owner, who has freed her puffed sleeve from the doorknob; a third trails right behind a young lady. Finally I was so tired of dodging them that I stuck my hands into my pockets and strode along straight ahead, my boots clacking on the pavement. I tore someone's petticoat and they let me stride on, giving me a wide berth.

But even this way, you're not really free to walk in the city. In the city, your every step is observed by spies who pretend they're not watching. Porters at the front gates keep an eye on who's coming in; cafe idlers spend long hours admiring the legs of passers-by; a lady grips her purse tightly, glancing right and left lest anybody draw near. No one trusts anyone else, though they all greet each other.

And though I'm well covered by my cloak, these eyes, this covert surveillance oppresses me. The street lamps light up with a blinding red glow; the big rectangular houses press in. Why not just stretch out here, on the cobblestones? I'm exhausted.

I turn around abruptly. Up there is Mount Kâl. Why did I ever come down?

All right: you are here now. And here you must live. I thump my hands against my chest to feel if my body is still there, and it holds firm. And so, onward! I want to enter the filthiest tavern in the Old Town.[44]

---

44 [Old Town: in dialect in the original. This is the poorest part of the city. See Introduction, xii–xv.]

Stench and smoke. I'm suffocating. But I too light up a pipe, smoking within the smoke, and I spit. "Waiter! A shot of grappa!" I will drink grappa too, if others are drinking, and the glass is clean, if others put their lips to the glass and gulp it down. On the rim of this glass, invisible, agony for the rest of my days may be waiting; but I drink.[45] And I raise my eyes to look at my companions.

A coal hauler, his left shoulder swollen like an enormous tumour, spits black gobs. A woman with stiff hair above her lip, dusted with powder, wipes her mouth with fat fingers. Under the table, the shirtless man sitting opposite her coolly shoves his knee between her legs. In the greasy black hair of the matron of this dive, a rosy cyst glints in the gaslight. I look at her through the cloudy bottom of my glass.

"Waiter! Another shot!" And I thump the unsteady table with my fist. The others look my way, then resume their conversation.

Next to me, two figures in blue shirts with jackets slung over their shoulders are talking about a tin jug, about how it was stolen. Others are shouting and singing. Good. Nothing is odd here, everything is solid and sure, like the ridges of the Karst. If I punch that porter's face, he'll take two swings at me. If I start in about the evils of prostitution to that woman, she'll slap her ass in response. I'm among thieves and murderers; but if I leap onto a table and Christ inspires my words, I can destroy and remake the world with them. This is my city. I'm fine here.

45 [Slataper here refers to the fear of contracting an infectious disease by drinking from a glass in the tavern. Cholera, yellow fever, tuberculosis, and syphilis were very common in Trieste, and a major concern for both health officials and the public at large. See Introduction, xiii.]

II

And yet, in the city, even before I went to the Karst, I was quite bored. I think it over now, and I'd like to tell you about my school years, about my dear classmates, about the first people I met; but I'm not interested enough in doing it. I would just write you long, annoying pages. Instead, I enjoy recounting my dreams and adventures to you. I take pleasure in thinking back on my life.

The city is enjoyable too, even if it annoys me sometimes. I love the bustle, the noise, the rush and activity. No one wastes time, because everyone has to get somewhere promptly, and everyone has a purpose. From their expressions and their pace, you can tell immediately how people go about their business. If you watch carefully, soon you're involved in an exciting, industrious game, and your intelligence quickens, swiftly devising new strategies of cunning, culture, generosity, or revenge. A restless young animal is stirring within you, and you head into the streets full of its vitality, like someone whose blood is returning to gloved hands gone numb with cold. You walk happily through air dense with noise and the clash of wills, understanding that here – where the concerns of each passer-by overflow, and come together, and rush into each other, where one weaves among the jostling and the carts, instinctively reacting to the movements of others – here in the streets the future of the world is being decided.

I walk through the streets of Trieste and I'm pleased that the city is rich. I delight in the clamour of the wagons rushing past; the bulging grey bags of coffee beans; the swollen boxes where plump oranges are tucked between layers of thin paper; the sacks of rice leaking a narrow snowy trail from the customs stamp; the split-open barrels of Greek pitch; the tumbling bales of raw wool; the slick casks of oil – in all the beautiful, fine merchandise that passes through our hands from the Orient, from America, and from Italy, on its way to the Germans and the Bohemians.

If you come to Trieste I'll take you to the wharves, along jetties square and white in the sea, and I'll show you the three new breakwaters in the Muggia inlet, impassive in the waves, bulwark against storms, built on enormous blocks of cemented limestone.[1] To make the new port, we mined a whole mountain and blew it to fragments. Months and months of wild ripping that echoed to the horizon and shook the windows of all our houses like an earthquake. And little steam tugs, a mite proud of their pennants of smoke, drew potbellied barges in straight lines – and from the Napoleonic road one could see the loads of gleaming stone blazing in the sea.[2] This is the fourth port of Trieste. The history of Trieste is in its ports. We were a little cove of pirate fishermen who knew how to make use of Rome and of Austria, and how to resist and fight Venice until she went under. Now, the Adriatic is ours.

I should have been a trader. I would have liked negotiating and making deals more than studying books. What a fine living thing is man! His hands hidden in pockets to conceal their instinctive reaction to your words, his mysterious deep eyes that pierce yours and keep you from leaping away, as all the while, his fixed, subterranean idea attracts you to its vortex, and then spins you into an ironic swirl, turning you entirely around! A fine thing is man, and he makes you want to fight. From his way of talking you know what price to offer him. He gains time, smiles, polishes his glasses, lights a cigarette – but let's see, you too know your way around, all the steps. Oh! He's also just arrived, and he pretends not to notice you, but his whole body marvels at the discovery and joyously lets its guard down; and you are two men facing each other unmasked, each armed to prevent the other from fleeing back into the underbrush. But which of you can expose the other's inadequacies? Which of you can spin the other around, drain his blaze dry, burn it all to the ground? Tomorrow is another day: a day that could yield a thousand crowns to replace the hundred you were robbed of today. Just think of all the coffee in Brazil that's flowering badly this spring!

Spring, warm spring, my friends, a new sun on new grain, broad roads and arms laden with branches in flower – and we're walking to school with a satchel of books at our side. We walk amidst the people and carriages, dreamily following our desire to become traders, soldiers, or

1 [Muggia is a town situated on the southern coast of the inlet, only a few miles south of Trieste. The construction of its port started in 1901.]

2 [The Napoleonic road is a panoramic pathway on the Karst that stretches between the town of Opicina and the hamlet of Prosecco. It was erroneously attributed to the Napoleonic troops that occupied the area in 1797 and for this reason it was (and still is) known under this name, although its official name is Vicentina, from Giacomo Vicentini, the engineer who designed it in 1821.]

firemen; we rise every morning at seven, or seven plus a few minutes of sweet semi-consciousness in bed; every morning, because on Sundays there's Mass. Spring, glowing through green blinds. Grey, rainy winter. Apples and plump pears in the trees. Autumn come back again. Every morning. The carpenter planing; in the workshop black with glittering stains, some with their faces half-hidden by goggles, a hammer raised; workers in blue coveralls lifting paving stones, digging into solid ground, laying pipes for water or gas. How sad the pick and spade become in the worn-out dirt of the city! It's work with no prospect of planting anything.

Here's the drab schoolhouse. Eight class levels, in twenty parallel rooms. I passed nine years of my life inside this building.

A nice girl with a ripe body, and a sturdy, tall young man, melancholic at times. In eight years they'd be married. They're seated on a broad sofa, holding hands tightly and enjoying the warmth of their bodies.[3]

The mother loves her girl, and is a bit annoyed by the lengthy wait, and by the seriousness of the young man. She'll be content when they marry, if the young man doesn't take her daughter away, and if they stay together, happy and without troubles.

The aunt rushes around, popping up and down on her lame leg, preparing the roast for her pretty niece, who's promised her a kiss. The aunt is pleased that her niece behaves as the young man wishes, not going to dances, rarely to the theatre, reading the occasional book. This young man is the only one who will defend the aunt against her sister-in-law, and she's happy that his ideas are contrary to the mother's.

The father, seated at the table, unbuttons his vest and gestures at the super-abundant spread with a pudgy, greasy hand, saying in a satisfied voice: "If I were to die, my family wouldn't have a crust to eat."[4] He's content to have an ever greater weight on his shoulders, and he's always grumbling loudly so his family will realize how hard he works.

The young man well understands the little family of strangers, and even admires them. The girl is good, and when he reproves her or is saddened by some misunderstanding, she says to him: "Yes, yes, you're right, but you'll see, I'll study, I'll read, we're still so young. Come on, let's not be sad!"[5]

---

3 [Slataper here remembers his first love relationship with Maria, a young woman who, as Stuparich noted, loved him but did not understand his drive "to live an original life, away from bourgeois banalities" (Stuparich, *Scipio Slataper* 82). For this reason, Slataper left her but suffered a great deal for having broken his engagement and for hurting the young woman.]

4 [The father's comment is in Triestine dialect.]

5 [Maria's comment is in Triestine dialect.]

And the years go by, three years pass, and eventually each of us discovers our own path. So the young intruder left the girl disconsolate, bade the mother farewell, and went on his way, and for a while everybody suffered.

I was a member of the club "Young Trieste," I forget under what name, because Austrian secondary school regulations forbade membership in any society, "especially political." I dutifully paid my weekly ten-cent dues. I dutifully attended the meetings.[6]

The sound of a doorbell ringing, and a member came in, said, "Good evening," looked around for an acquaintance, had a bottle of beer brought to him by the porter – a nice little fellow with ears sticking out and a broad, long nose that would have looked just right in the starched collars of our grandfathers – then lit up a cigarette, read the papers, and conversed a little. No one ever did a thing, but we consoled ourselves thinking of what was in store. Everyone complained about "the Nation," the leadership of the Liberal Party, of which we formed the left wing; but before issuing one or another of our representatives a gentle rebuke, we would ask for permission from "the Nation." One evening, at a meeting, when the imperial commissioner had already left – because while he was there we bored ourselves totaling balance sheets and grinning over official memos – we inveighed with strong language against the submissive apathy of Attilio Hortis and our other representatives.[7] We voted in favour of a resounding order of the day; then, as though it were pro forma, the president asked who would come with him to see Venezian for permission.[8] I asked timidly from my seat: "But why ask Venezian for permission?" They were all shocked. A young man jumped up, his face pasty and atrophied, all pockmarked and pitted, smiling condescendingly through rotten teeth and spluttering all over. Finally, stammering a little, but like someone convinced he's on the winning side, he said: "You

6 [Young Trieste (La giovane Trieste) was a secret irredentist youth association affiliated with the Liberal National Party, established in 1902, whose main association was La Patria (The homeland). Young Trieste also produced a leaflet by the same name. The society remained active until 1909. See Tullia Catalan, "Le società segrete irredentiste e la massoneria italiana," *Storia d'italia, Annali 21: La Massoneria*, edited by Gian Mario Cazzaniga, Giulio Einaudi, 2006, 620.]

7 [Attilio Hortis (1850–1926) was a Triestine politician and intellectual. In 1873 he became the director of the civic library and maintained that appointment for fifty years, enriching the library with important collections. In 1897 and again in 1901 he was elected parliamentary deputy in the Austrian parliament, where he fought for the Italian university in Trieste.]

8 [Felice Venezian (1851–1908) was a lawyer and the head of the Liberal National Party of Trieste. He was considered the most important leader of Trieste's irredentist movement.]

can see this youngster has a lot of growing up to do!" Then he sat back down, very pleased with himself, and everyone laughed and applauded.

That was the only time I said anything at all at a meeting. Usually I just grumbled with the few other younger members around a chess table, plotting every evening how we would establish a revolutionary "mountain" at the heart of our club.[9] But nothing was ever decided on. And above all I listened to the discussions of the elders, to learn about politics, and to arm myself against my aunt, who disapproved of any involvement with irredentism. Usually they talked about pranks to be played on the imperial guards, about the latest pro-Austrian sycophantic ploy of the socialists, or the way their secretary-general took his seat and held his pen. One could learn how to make a stencil for the tricolour, painting the red, white, and green over the insignia of the imperial police; or find out that Franzca, the whore born in '41, had for some unknown reason moved to the brothel in Via del Solitario. A young man with a three-hair mole talked about the Domokos campaign, and about the feast given in Rome on the anniversary of the Statute of 1848.[10] Because the homeland was mixed up with *risotto alla Milanese* and with permanganate of potash.[11] Their feeling for the nation was like the newspapers' when they announced the death of Carducci amidst brief notices, just above and below, of a blizzard in Carinthia and of the French ambassador's visit.[12]

---

9 [The "mountain" is a clear reference to La Montagne, the leftist group led by Robespierre that sat on the highest benches of the National Assembly.]

10 [The Domokos campaign: in 1897 during the Turkish-Greek war, a battalion of Italian volunteers led by Ricciotti Garibaldi, son of Giuseppe Garibaldi, fought for Greek independence from the Ottomans. The 1848 Statute is the constitution granted by Charles Albert I (1798–1849), king of Piedmont and Sardinia. After Italy's unification in 1861, it became the basis for the constitution of the newly founded Kingdom of Italy. It remained in place until the monarchy was abolished in 1946.]

11 [Permanganate of potash: used at the time to treat the effects of venereal disease.]

12 [Giosuè Carducci (1835–1907) was an Italian poet and recipient of the Nobel Prize for literature in 1906. His patriotic poems helped forge the myth of the Risorgimento. He was particularly loved in Trieste, where his poems were banned by the Austrian government. Stuparich, in his *Trieste nei miei ricordi* (Il ramo d'oro, 2004), remembered the infatuation that Italian students had for the poet, reading avidly all his writings and poems. When Carducci visited Trieste in 1878 he was greeted as a hero of the irredentist cause. The visit inspired the poem "Saluto italico" that was first published in 1879 in the leaflet "La giovane Trieste" with the title "Canto di Giosuè Carducci a Trieste e a Trento." In 1905 the city of Trieste presented the old poet with a gold medal in recognition of his commitment to the irredentist cause. See Chiara Tognarelli, "Martiri dell'idea: Carducci e l'irredentismo Triestino," *La letteratura italiana e le arti,* Atti del XX Congresso dell'ADI – Associazione degli Italianisti, 7–10 Sept. 2016, edited by L. Battistini et al., Adi editore, 2018, 1–9.]

I was amazed. I felt the nation to be singular, and sacred. My breast trembled as I read about Oberdank.[13] I would have liked to die the same way.

And I followed the campaigns of Garibaldi on the map, deeply moved by these heroes. To me Garibaldi was like a revered friend and a god.[14] Even today, when I hear people speak of him as a historical figure, my heart rises in revolt. I'm still like a boy who would like to battle under his command.

But we were born to another generation. We would sing in the streets:

To arms, to arms! The yellow and black
banners still wave.
In God's name, fire on the barbarians,
fire on the German ranks!

We'd escape the security guards, come together again a little ways off, and continue to sing:

We won't lay our swords down
as long as a single corner
of Italy is enslaved.
We won't lay our swords down
until over the Julian Alps
the tricolour brightly waves.[15]

And at home we'd find Mamma in tears, breathless with worry. We would kiss her and go to bed, quite satisfied with ourselves.

---

13 [See Introduction, note 81.]

14 [Giuseppe Garibaldi (1807–82) was an Italian general and patriot who fought in the wars of the Risorgimento for Italy's unification under the House of Savoy. He was a charismatic revolutionary leader with republican aspirations, and he quickly gained strong popular support. However, he did not have the political skills and network to create an alternative option to Cavour's more conservative plan for a unified Italy.]

15 [The lyrics belong to "Suona la tromba" (Play the trumpet), the patriotic hymn written by Goffredo Mameli (1827–49) for Giuseppe Verdi at Giuseppe Mazzini's request. Here it is slightly modified: the last three verses are adapted to the particular situation of Trieste and the Julian provinces. The original reads: "We won't lay our swords down / until Italy is one / from the Alps to the sea." The hymn is reprinted in its entirety in Mauro Stramacci, *Goffredo Mameli, tra un inno e una battaglia*, Mediterranee, 1991, 86–8. Mameli was also the author of "Il Canto degli Italiani" (The song of the Italians), which would become Italy's national anthem; he died in 1849, as a national hero at age twenty-one, of wounds suffered fighting for Italy's independence.]

I had a Garibaldino uncle who, at the age of four, sent a piece of bread he was served at boarding school to his father, so he could taste the kind of stuff they gave him to eat; and at the age of thirteen he escaped, at night, shouting "Long live Italy!" and walking, not a penny in his pocket, all the way from Fiume to Venice to join up with Garibaldi. They wouldn't take him, because he was too young; but they offered him a lira a day so he could get by. He took the lira coin and threw it into the canal: he wouldn't accept money from those who had less than him. A relative found him sitting on the bank of a canal chewing a piece of bread, completely content. He started fighting when he was a young man.

He was a good merchant, resourceful and full of initiative. At first he was poor, then obscenely rich, then nearly destitute again, and then finally well off. Once somebody came to Uncle's desk saying he owed him fifty florins. Uncle replied that he'd already repaid the debt. The other guy disagreed. Uncle drew a ten florin note from his pocket, laid it on the table, struck a match, lit a candle and, taking the banknote delicately by the corner, held it over the flame until it was all burned up.

"That's to show you ten florins mean nothing to me; but to you, I don't owe a single penny. Good day!"[16]

He married whom he wanted, against the wishes of all his relatives; he learned Croatian in three months and went off with his woman into the forests of Croatia to sell timber. So for most of his relatives he remained a renegade, an enigma to be held at a distance, a man both arrogant and lacking in judgment. Annoyed, they kept out of his way; and if they ever had to converse with him out of propriety, they listened to him as one listens to the same old tales of an old country priest, keeping a wary eye on him to divine what new trick he was inventing. And yet he was a steady, reliable fellow, even if he was given to strong passions. He was tall and barrel-chested, with broad, somewhat rough features; but he had Mamma's eyes, and a pale blonde smoke-darkened beard. He strode along like a mountain guide. He spoke slowly, his voice low and deep, his eyes twinkling almost with a schoolboy's delight in what he was saying. But it was a delight tinged with sadness and desperation. He had no one but his family; and now his wife was dead, one daughter had killed herself, and the other had left her husband to become a cabaret singer. He never wept; but seated among us, whenever he coughed, the deepest chord in Mamma's harp gave a long, terrible vibration. He was tired, almost worn out. Mamma would say to him: "Courage now, you're still as fit as a young man." And he would smile: "Yes, I'm still strong; but ..." and he

16 [In Triestine dialect in the original.]

would hoist his right arm as though to rest a gun barrel on it, and his arm trembled although he hoped he could hold it still. "But my legs are still good,"[17] he finished. And at fifty years old he lifted himself up again for the third or fourth time, and went hunting, and started building a little house in the Karst, close to Gropada, on a limestone terrace dominating a broad sweep of stones and sky.[18] I remember him with an iron-pointed walking stick, tracing for us the outline of his future house.

He was intelligent, and who knows how much of what preoccupies us now, which people are only beginning to discuss, he had already spoken of with clarity, like someone so far removed from conventional values and thinking that it was natural and obvious for him to see things as they really were, marvelling that other people didn't share his ideas.

He was always in the Karst, and the peasants called him "the boss." His acquaintances would ask, just for the sake of saying something: "But doesn't being alone with just those brute Slavs frighten you?"

"But they wouldn't hurt a fly! They're as gentle as children. Anyway, it's only human! If one of those bow-legged Triestine Jews comes to sing in their ears 'In the country of Rossetti we only speak Italian,' well, they're in their own home, so they just give him a good hiding, of course. How else should they react?"[19] And he continued: "But I go right through the fields, across the pastures, and no one ever says a word to me. Only once, when I was about to flush a partridge and was trampling the grass, a peasant called out: 'Who's going to pay me for that grass, mister?' But he was a distance away and didn't want to risk coming closer. I took a good look at him. And I said to him quite calmly: 'Why don't you come over here, so we can count the blades of grass I've stepped on together? Then

17 [The exchange is in Triestine dialect.]

18 [Gropada is a small village on the Karst plateau, just above Trieste.]

19 ["In the country of Rossetti we only speak Italian" is a verse of the popular irredentist song "Al putel apena nato" (To the just born child) composed in the Triestine dialect by Giulio Piazza in 1890, and dedicated to Domenico Rossetti (1774–1842), an important Triestine intellectual and Italian patriot, founder of the Minerva Society, a cultural circle that hosted important speakers and intellectuals. James Joyce was invited repeatedly to lecture there. See John McCourt, *The Years of Bloom,* U of Wisconsin P, 2000, 192. Piazza's song was an instant success and became popular throughout the irredentist provinces, in spite of the Austrian police prohibition on its public performance. See Risa Sodi, *Narrative and Imperative: The First Fifty Years of Italian Holocaust Writing (1944–1994),* Peter Lang, 2007, 89–90. "Bow-legged Triestine Jews" in the text both offers a stereotypical anti-Semitic physical image of Jews, as lacking a powerful and healthy physique, and draws attention to the fact that the large Jewish community living in Trieste at this time embraced the irredentist cause, a cause that antagonized the Slovenian population living in and around Trieste. It should also be noted that Giulio Piazza was himself Jewish.]

I can repay you.' But I'd said it to him in such a tone … he scurried off like a hare." He concluded: "it's only human; and it's never a bad idea to carry a rifle. But try going over to Italy, into Friuli, into the countryside, and tell me what happens then! They're really too easy on us here, us scoundrels from the city."

He detested shallow, judgmental people, though he himself was passionate in his own judgments. He couldn't stand the incessant talk of Venezian and his cohort: "… the Roman heritage … twenty centuries of civilization … and just look at their fat bellies! What sons of bitches! I'd like to see them in a real battle. They'd shit their pants."[20] But I never heard him speak of Garibaldi, not even once.

I'm so glad he was my uncle. I grow more and more fond of him, and sometimes regret I was just a kid when he was around, so I couldn't really get to know him. Now some evenings I rest my head on Mamma's knees and get her to tell me stories about him.

She told me that once I had been ambushed by ten little ruffians, and the whole family was comforting me because of the large bruise on my cheek; but my uncle rolled his eyes almost playfully, and said to me: "I hope you don't still owe them something?"

I think not, Uncle.

Mamma is ill. I'm lying on the edge of the bed beside her, patting her forehead and her hands. And so several hours pass.

She looks at me every now and then and asks: "Do you think I'll get better?" I scold her like a child and talk about how things will be when she's well again.

I want to protect her from illness and keep her spirits up. Mamma is so good. She has suffered quite enough in life, crying silently, always trying to justify those who have mistreated her. She never said a mean word, but shut herself in with her children, like a poor beaten creature. I don't forgive those who have hurt her. I want Mamma to be proud of us, and to know we're better than all the others.

"When you're well, you'll come spend a month with me in Florence, would you like that? There are hills and olive groves, and we'll be at peace. Three months have passed now, one more will soon pass, and then we'll have a big party. I'll throw my hat in the air and yell out 'Mamma is all better!' Would you like that?"

She is quiet, trembling with joy. And I talk to her and tell her lots of nice things, but I'm tired of this sad, dark bedroom, the stale air, the

20 [All the direct quotes are in Triestine dialect in the original.]

ceaseless ticking of the clock. I'd like to hunker down at my desk and work, write a happy poem, head into the countryside alone, with just the sun and fresh air. I'm almost angry at her illness, at the darkness that has fallen upon our house for so many years.

We live in fear of awakening in others things that are always present within us; we live with lowered voices, furtively looking at each other after something has made us laugh. Many days we swallow our soup and meat without exchanging a single word, forcing ourselves to take an interest in the little ones, who tell us stories about school. We've lived like this for many years. And Mamma gazes into our eyes, which lower themselves guiltily, and she can't do anything to help her children. She kisses our foreheads, and silently asks our forgiveness.

One day she was putting some clothes by the stove to dry, and she was crying. I asked her: "Mamma, what's the matter?" I asked her once more – and she kept on crying and fending me off, trying to hold back her tears, and she looked exhausted. "What is it, Mamma? Why are you crying?" "My son, it's nothing, Father's business is not going well."

And one day Father returned from a journey, another one without result, and there was nothing to be done. We were sitting around the table having dinner. He came in, greeted us, and took his seat. We were quiet. He lifted his fork and swallowed some food. He said to us: "So then, let's eat!" His voice was calm.

I've never seen Father cry. His eyes sink into his brow, his forehead swells, and he stands fast, head up. He is a man, he does not complain, and he holds firm. Father taught me to stay quiet, and to disdain sorrow.

And so the months and years passed. I began to love my family, and I was comforted knowing they believed in me. And one evening, Mamma leaned against my chest, and said to me: "My son, I'm tired, but you must push on."

I love my brothers and parents because our life has been full of suffering, but we have always been self-reliant. I go forward with them, and never give in. We too want what's ours. They have done us great harm. Some have been good to us, but they haven't understood us. We want to be ourselves, with all our faults and virtues, free to breathe the air that is ours. I'm happy to have had a poor family. I grew up with a duty and a purpose. They love me deeply, and we share one name.

The clock ticks on impassively, the bedroom is narrow and dark. What will become of us if Mamma doesn't get well? Her brow is all perspiring, her face is pale and full of bitterness.

I want the room dark. No sunlight should filter through the blinds. I'm stretched out face down on the bed, motionless, not thinking of anything.

I'm not suffering. Through the darkness, an infinite boredom spreads, and I'm oblivious, glimpsing with disgust the shelves of books on the opposite wall.

I've read, I've gazed out the window, I've had a smoke; no point in trying again. I don't want anything, and the room is cold.

I hear kids yelling in the street, and the shadows of carriages flicker rapidly across the wall. Soon it will be night, finally extinguishing even that bright sunbeam illuminating the bouquet of flowers painted above my head.

Meanwhile the men are returning from work and greeting one another in the street. And the earth proceeds on its unchangeable course.

I've been all over the city this night of Mardi Gras, bored and disgusted for no reason. Maybe I was remembering the year before, when I was with her, in a cafe. I looked for her in all the cafes, afraid I'd run into someone. I thought I had completely ruined her evening. The poor girl.

Up near Aqueduct I bumped into a fellow student, Nando Baul, who convinced me to go into The Cats.[21] It was the first time I'd entered a cabaret. I looked at all the flabby flesh and the people looking on. The conductor had a horrendous nose, and the singers were just fooling around. Nando was having a good time, showing off like he'd been there many times. Nando's eyes were shining. He said some nights it was better. Right. Cheers.

I went all over the streets of the Old Town, hoping to find some dirty fun along the way. I'm still pure, but like a virgin who always dreams of debauchery, to paraphrase Nietzsche.[22] I've stayed physically pure, from fear of contagion. Or maybe that's not it. Anyway, it's not important. I've been learning through books and expert friends, and now here I am, anxiously nosing around. I would have liked some kind of action, but

---

21 ["Nando Baul," a nickname and a popular Triestine caricature, whose last name means "dummy" in Triestine dialect. The Cats ("Alle gatte" in the original) was the first cabaret to open in Trieste, on the Aqueduct. It showcased singers and comedians from all over Italy, notably the renowned comedic actor Nicola Maldacea and the singer Pina Ciotti. See Lino Monaco, *Atlante della Storia: Trieste,* Demetra, 1998, 121.]

22 [See Nietzsche's "Propriety and Honesty" in *Human, All Too Human*: "Those girls who mean to trust exclusively to their youthful charms for their provision in life, and whose cunning is further prompted by worldly mothers, have just the same aims as courtesans, only they are wiser and less honest." Friedrich Wilhelm Nietzsche, *The Complete Works of Friedrich Nietzsche: A Book for Free Spirits,* vol. 7, pt. 1, *Human, All-Too-Human,* edited by Oscar Levy and translated by Helen Zimmern, Allen & Unwin, 1909, 300. See also Roberto Damiani's introduction to Slataper's *Il mio Carso,* Biblioteca Universale Rizzoli, 1989, 117.]

nothing's going on. The stench of piss. I don't have the courage to lift my head and look through a window as I pass.

Down here, the usual eight or nine are waddling back and forth like geese, all bundled up over their blouses. The rouge extends only so far, then the purple rash from the cold takes over. As I pass, they touch my arm. "Want to go upstairs, boy?" I blush and press on without responding. They disgust me.

They disgust me terribly. That's why. Especially their hair and hands. I smell a kind of musky oil that I can't stand. If not for that, it wouldn't mean a thing. I understand it well, I don't have romantic illusions. It's I give you this, you give me that. It's clean. It's society that's dirty, and cleanses itself by giving this the name … love. (That's not my ellipsis; society puts it there. I never use ellipses.)

A band of bearded brutes dressed as women bursts from the cafe where I drank grappa the evening of my descent from the Karst; there are women with naked bellies, and other riff-raff, and all are shouting and leaping about, brandishing lanterns and clubs. I move aside. I'm happy that I have a clean, white bed at home, without bugs.

But a woman, a real woman, all for me, to roll in bed with, to squeeze and bite, to make her scream! No, this bed is too big. It's too soft. Anyway, it's better to sleep on the floor under only a blanket.

I went to see if Credit would hire me.[23] As soon as I'd gone up the wide staircase, so full of decorations and extravagant candelabras, the silence of the work brought me up short, and I held still as though I might disturb, at its heart, the pulse of a mysterious world.

They told me it would be impossible to hire me because I'd gone to the Lycée rather than the Commercial Academy, and I couldn't speak German well enough.

As soon as I left the place and saw the wonderful bright green of the gardens below the castle, childish fantasies from Salgari's adventures came back to my mind.[24] I saw the glorious mounted adventurers I would meet at every turn in my life, who always bid me well, dazzling my eyes

---

23 [The Creditanstalt, founded by the Rothschild family in 1855 in Vienna, was one of the most powerful Austrian banks. It opened its branch in Trieste in 1907. The imposing palace that housed the bank was designed by the Triestine architect Federico Nordio, who had studied architecture at the Academy of Fine Arts in Vienna. The bank was located in the centre of the city on Piazza Nuova, now Piazza della Repubblica.]

24 [Emilio Salgari (1862–1911) was a popular and prolific writer of adventure novels that took place in exotic and faraway places. He became a beloved writer of many generations of Italian children and young adults.]

with their gleaming rifles, loaded and polished. Polished at the table, the candle alongside; and Mamma's sleeping breaths are so laboured that my hand, furiously polishing back and forth, slows to match that rhythm, while my soul begins to ponder our troubles – and fills with doubt, as rainwater fills holes in the earth left by a tent that's just been struck. Again I see the brownish tent, streaming with dew in the first light of dawn, and I stoop to crawl out of the narrow opening, cautiously looking around, observing the squelchy grass straightening up again.

A flatbed drawn by two draught horses, loaded with iron rods, was rushing headlong, deafening the city. The coachman, legs planted astride two long wooden planks that formed the bumper, whipped and urged his horses on. In the face of that infernal cart, all dreams disappeared. I was on the Corso, surrounded by people wrapped in fur coats, and by automobiles.

I went home, dazed.

I thought: I'll knock on every door. Maybe a big company will send me to the Indies, to Rangoon, like Ucio. A Chinese slave will move an enormous red fan into my bedroom, so the malarial mosquitoes don't land on my skin. I'll write nothing but phrases like this one, in English: "In reference to your esteemed letter dated ..." I'll swindle everyone in such astute ways, merchants can't equal them even now. In my pocket, a revolver.

I laughed out loud at myself. Why India? And why a revolver, shining like an explorer's carbine? Kid, you're an intellectual. And an intellectual you'll remain, no matter how much ocean separates your first step and your last. Even in Rangoon, even on Crusoe's island, to you the red fan will seem to show – how to put it – the power of action over ideas; one of your exaggerated notions to rile up people or to make them swoon. And you'll write such things in your business letters that the typist won't be able to copy them down without the supervisor thinking you've gone mad.

I went out, feeling depressed. I touched the leaves of trees damp with rain, forcing myself not to compare them with anything. A tactile sense of wet and cold – that's all. I wanted them to feel unpleasant. I walked for a long time, trying not to think. And then I decided it: I'm leaving.

I went to the station to buy a third-class ticket. "Where to?" asked the ticket clerk. I stared at him. I'd imagined travelling without a destination; travelling in hopes of a railway collision that would crumple two engines and many carriages, from which I save myself by holding tight between two luggage racks, which protect me from the impact. Then I escape by smashing the window of the upturned carriage and crawling away on all fours; without rescuing anyone, I dash to the next station to calmly report what's happened. "Your hand is bleeding," the stationmaster says, looking concerned. I glance at my hand, take out my handkerchief, and bind it up. Then I politely ask the stationmaster if I might telegraph my newspaper.

"Where to?" the ticket clerk, out of patience, asked again.

"To Milan." I was thinking, I'll present myself to the *Corriere della Sera*.

Smirking, the clerk told me the train was headed to Vienna. So I returned home, determined to make myself into a journalist.

The *Piccolo* hired me at a salary of a hundred crowns a month: my hours were from midday to 4 p.m., and from 8 p.m. to 3 in the morning.

The first time I interviewed an actress – I no longer remember who, Bellincioni or Tina di Lorenzo[25] – as I hooked my thumbs in the armholes of my white gilé, I was thinking: the premiere of something unfamiliar and new; an interview between the acts; some black coffee and a cigar; back to the newsroom: and the hour strikes. I put the broad green pages in order and number them. I have to write two articles, a review of the new play and an interview, within an hour and a half. (I could just write up the interview the next morning, but I enjoyed writing under pressure.) Good. What to say about her? She's stunning. And the *Piccolo* is the most widely read paper in Trieste; and I am, at this moment, its theatre critic.

A flock of images, like swallows returning: is that me standing beside an autumn wood, the bora in full blast, gold and purple leaves swirling all around? Certainly, in my soul there was turmoil, a mad dash, a hopping and darting about, as in a pond when a child throws in a crumb of bread. But her tinted red lips and puff of golden hair seemed to parody mine, and I was frightened, as though I'd glimpsed myself in a funhouse mirror. I wrote a terrible review of the comedy that I'd actually liked, for revenge, because I too needed to do violence to the reality of others. But the editor had the proofs brought to him before they could go to press, sent for me, scolded me sharply, and tore up the article.

As I left the newsroom, dawn attacked my tired eyes.

One night a few years afterwards, a night of intense work because the pope had just died, I was gazing fixedly at the gas lamp on my desk. I heard movements, a muttering, a rustling of pages and rumbling all

25 [Gemma Bellincioni (1864–1950) was one of the most famous sopranos at the turn of the twentieth century; Tina di Lorenzo (1872–1930) was a renowned stage actress who also worked in silent films.]

around me, then getting farther and farther away, and – who knows why – I was thinking about Cain and Abel. I told God he'd been very unfair with Cain: why couldn't you accept the smoke of his sacrificial fire? Weren't those fruit-laden branches and all that fodder equal to Abel's lamb? What wrong had he done you, before he killed Abel? Why? The Bible doesn't say anything. I thought this could be the central problem of a tragedy, and began laughing maliciously. I had killed Abel already.

Abel had tied a rope between the horns of a buffalo I had just shot, and he was singing. I had killed him. But now the leaves that scratched against me were hard and bitter with poison, like thorns. Ardently I pleaded: "O Abel, Abel, if you were only still singing within me, in this hour of utmost weariness! I want to see the stars in heaven, and sing a great song."[26]

But I laughed at myself.

My soul was already thick with the trickling away of a life turned negative, bitter, and angry, etching my face with wrinkles, carving my eyes deep.

I no longer saw things clearly, and I crashed right into sharp corners without even taking notice, so that others thought I was a hero. I walked along well-trodden streets, disgusted with myself, hoping someone would set upon me and beat me to death.

Once I even thought of doing myself in, but I couldn't kill the malign, ironic being returning my stare in the mirror. The woman who loved me didn't turn her face away, she clung to my neck anxiously and strove with all her soul to kiss me; but her lips never reached mine.[27]

Now I'm calm, and always take the express train.

But no, my life was not really like that, but all the same I felt anxious and out of place. I found companions and friends,[28] and I worked alongside them, but I'm not as intelligent as they are. I can say nothing to persuade

---

26 [Reference to a drama that Slataper outlined but never completed, entitled "Caino e Abele" (Cain and Abel). The drama, set in modern days, explored one of Slataper's key intellectual concerns: the conflict between an active and a contemplative existence. After the killing of Abel, a scene that is particularly interesting for its strong expressionistic elements, Cain is condemned to homeless wandering and meaningless toiling, void of any ethical and aesthetic values. The outline of the play is recorded in his *Appunti e note di diario,* edited by Giani Stuparich, Mondadori, 1953, 108–9.]

27 [Clear reference to Anna Pulitzer (nicknamed Gioietta, 1891–1910), who killed herself on 3 May 1910, leaving Slataper with unanswered questions and a deep sense of guilt for not having understood the emotional and psychological turmoil of his beloved. The whole novel is dedicated to her.]

28 [The companions and friends are the other contributors to *La Voce.*]

them. They on the other hand know how to argue and demonstrate the strength of some conviction or the other. I am unsure and inconsistent. Better to stay quiet and get ready.

But why are they so down and despairing sometimes? We who want to reform others no longer have the right to weakness. We must stride forward unbowed. We must welcome life with love, even when it's a burden. We must obey our duty. They are more intelligent, more civilized, and more exhausted.

Maybe it's just that I'm from a young city, and the junipers of the Karst are my past. I'm not sad; I'm just bored sometimes, and then I throw myself down to sleep, like a beast in need of rest. I don't brood. I have faith in myself and in life's laws. I love life.

But discussions about art and literature bore me. I'm somewhat outside that world, and I suffer because of it, but it can't be helped. I much prefer speaking with ordinary people and finding out about what interests them. It could be that my whole life will amount to a vain search for humanity, but for me philosophy and art don't suffice, nor do they fill me with enough passion. Life is broader and richer than that. I want to know other lands and other men. Because I'm not at all superior to others, and literature is a sad and solitary vocation.

All right, let's get that article written. I've been quiet for a long while; time to get back into it. Red pencil: 1, 2, 3, 4, 5 ... the pages are numbered and ready. Light a cigarette. Bend over the desk and worship the thought that surges up and, mixed with ink, on down through the pen.

The development of a soul in Trieste. I begin to write; and tear it up; and again, one more shredding. Cigarettes. The room fills with smoke, thoughts close up like petals at vespers. No chance of fooling myself: I have nothing to say. I'm empty as a reed.

"What are you doing here, at this desk, in this seedy rented room? Even if you stick your mug right into this green branch stuck in a bottle, where your tired eyes, weary of the dingy stencilled wallpaper, seek respite, you still can't breathe. Now, even Shakespeare is just a stack of books that wall off part of the horizon. Beyond, Mount Incontro is rosy with the dawn, and if you look out the window, to your left Fiesole is bright as ambered crystal. There's snow on Mount Secchieta. Let's climb Secchieta!"[29]

Ankles taped; torso wrapped in layers; a block of chocolate in my pocket; and while I stamp hard on the city pavement to speed the flow

29 [Mount Secchieta, located not far from Florence, in eastern Tuscany, is the highest peak of the Pratomagno Massif.]

of warmth to my head, I'm thinking: "What does this sudden excursion have to do with the life of the spirit? There's an obstruction in you, a little more challenging than Secchieta; and, instead of confronting it head on and bashing it in, you prefer to go around it, thinking that's how you'll draw closer to the sun, which will shine on everything for your benefit alone. You're tired already? Just yesterday you were flinging yourself down from the vineyards, along the crumbling stone walls held together by ivy that entangled your feet, and *plop!* you went, your nose in the turf, a beaten stag; and your fellow hunters, belting out cries of victory, bound your legs with reeds, while they dragged you home – their faces red with excitement and exultation. You guzzled litres of water, your mouth, nose, and eyes plunged into the bucket of the well, as you snorted and gurgled away without a break; your nostrils bore two deep holes in the water. And you're tired now?"[30]

Here on the train that's bringing me to Sant'Ellero, there are some peasants who fell asleep as soon as they came on board, their heads lolling on the wooden backs of the seats. I walk up and down the central aisle of the car. Am I tired? I can't tell anything anymore. I know I'm no longer in the city. I no longer need to find a reason for doing this or that. I am an irrational beast. Escapade or excursion, flight or folly, lunacy or lark: I don't know. I know that I'm climbing Secchieta, where there's snow. I get off the train, and breathe deeply.

Up through the winding alleys of the coal men, which here and there open onto a blackened clearing. Which way to go? The hillside is hiding Vallambrosa. Fine, if I don't lose my way; and if I do, so much the better. I tap on the trunks of old chestnuts without sap or flesh; the black hellebore is in bloom. Maybe between the dark leaves and the moss, my eyes will find the first primrose, beside a patch of snow.

Slow your step: the soul grows by plundering Nature. Everything is flowering with images around you. Stretch out your hand! You're not touching the thorny bramble, or the tenacious broom, or the stones of the earth: you're soothed and pricked by your own spirit, which has flown from you to create your own world. It has pitched itself against the shapeless dark, and set root there straight away; and there the wind

30 [Slataper's rhetoric clearly borrows from Petrarch's "Ascent of Mount Ventoux": "What, then, is holding you back? Nothing, surely, except that you take a path which seems at first sight easier leading through low and wordly pleasures. Nevertheless, in the end, after long wanderings, you will have to climb up the steeper path under the burden of labors long deferred to its blessed culmination or lie down in the valley of your sins." Petrarch, *Selections from the Canzoniere and Other Works*, translated and edited by Mark Musa, Oxford UP, 1985, 14.]

shakes it, winter branches grown big like fists that grow bigger the more they tense; and your boots stamp the earth wet with the sap that the sun drew up to itself in a thousand shapes; and your vision widens in the brotherly divine circle of green-black hills, under the limpid, weightless sky that seems to lift – it's the light – up above the air. Walk lovingly through your wondrous realm.

The houses of Saltino. The first snow in the ditches beside the cog railway. Plunge in, legs! It's hard and it cracks, like a bone in a dog's jaw. There are a few trees full of buds covered in silvery down, like strange flowers. From open stall doors, the mouth of a cow bellows, and licks its wide nostrils. *Royal Telephone*: fifty cents, and I'm in Florence. And yet I walk on, shouting across the snow, and there's no one to stop and stare at the madman. Everything is wonderful. I fully understand the reform of the middle schools, just as I fully understand the cypress tree snapped under the weight of snow, stuck lying across my path, forcing me to hop over jauntily, holding the flaps of my cloak to my chest. And wonderful are the salami, butter, tea, and the week-old bread at the Vallambrosa inn.

It's impossible this place has ever witnessed ladies trailing long skirts over the well-groomed and trimmed fields, or ministers playing tennis in collarless shirts: in time, plenty of hotels could open their doors here; but I doubt it will happen. Still, I could sling stones to take down those two eagles wrapped in yellow rags, roosting atop the pillars of a gated entranceway.

But up we go, because on Secchieta the snow is completely untouched. Not a track on the spine of the mountain: where are all the young Italians? They're waiting for winter outings to be organized, with skiing and skating and girls. With the point of my alpenstock, I write the letters VOCE in the snow. I propose that the *Voce*'s celebration take the form of an annual ascent, in February, of Secchieta. The Lupercalia festival.[31] Aha, at this moment someone is leaving the newsroom of a daily and heading home to rest! Come drink in the dawn upon the peaks!

And this is enough: everything below disappears. There is only one thing, up high, out of sight, that has to be reached. This is not an illustration. The branches are tense, and they whack you in the face if you let them out of your grip. Dig your heels into the snow to create a step, and then another higher up. Drive in your alpenstock. And if it plunges in entirely, that's your warning that the snow is as tall as you, so don't meander; push straight on.

31 [The Lupercalia was an ancient Roman festival, celebrated every year on 15 February.]

There is no regular, easy impulse, around which ideas might gather and grow to become mine, fruit of my deep soul. Instead everything is the sensation of obstacles that must be overcome: there is the mountain, and me; nothing else. And I need to be nothing else but me, right at the peak.

You're stopping to admire the view? So tired already that you turn poet, my good friend? If your calves are burning and your back aches, and with every inch you conquer, your face or chest is whacked by a branch, and then another, and who knows how many more await you, and they're hard, frozen solid, and deceivingly glazed with grains of snow like almond branches in bloom, and the icicles break against your neck or your eyes, which are dazzled by the eternal white glare; and your beret slipping down forces you to step back, and the alpenstock gets stuck between branch and trunk, so that all these essential things are trying to keep you from doing what you have to do – then just grit your teeth to keep your tongue from cursing, and keep on walking. And if the snow, softened by the sun, slides underfoot so that you're tempted to lie down gently and have a rest, don't surrender to that pillowy abundance, don't take light steps; slam your boots down, sink in, pull yourself out, and push on upwards. Upwards – you don't know exactly where to, because perhaps you're not climbing towards the real summit, the one on the map – and your summit might even be shrouded in mist; so that once you've reached it, heart thumping in your chest, you may not be able to see the Apennines turning copper like young flesh in the sun, or see the immense snowfield you've conquered blaze with colour, or see Florence far below in the distance. But, my friend, you pried yourself from your desk to climb Secchieta; and even if everything people say, which has come through the window and penetrated your ears, along with the jangling of the carriages and the filthy songs of jug wine; even if the lives of all the others are even now in your ears, trying, like a dusty wind, to twist you back to what you've already overcome, to make you pause in admiration, to kneel your weary legs down between the heights and the depths; even if the whole city with all its exhaustion remains within you, without release – it doesn't matter: you are climbing to the top. Only that is true. You must; only that is beautiful.

A snowy ledge prevents me from zig-zagging around; I attack it three or four times with my fingernails. And! –

On the top of Secchieta there is a low chapel with a frescoed Madonna. I light a match, afraid a wolf might be in there. Squeezing through a narrow aperture in the snow-packed door frame, I tumble down beneath the Madonna.

I comb my outspread fingers through seawater as through a woman's soft, resistant hair; and I flip over on the surface to rest. Little ripples murmur at my ears, like a woman's heart beating against her lover lying upon her.

I lift my gaze: the sea is rippling in the sunlight. Its soul is quiet and serene, and it spreads over the soft sand and rocks itself, babbling little words; and with a child's fingers it searches for little shells and crabs in the pebbles of the shore.

I rest on the sea. White clouds meander across the sky. If I raise my head a little I can see the olive trees of Muggia trembling; nothing else. The repose is vast, and infinite.

A boat slowly unfurls its sails, lists slightly, and pauses. Then it sets off, gathering up the light wind. I remain, borne along by the slow shifting of the rippling waves.

And the sea carries me into the distance, where I see nothing but sea and sky, where everything is silence and peace. I open my mouth, salt water rushes between my teeth, and my body lets itself sink slowly in the sea.

I'm here on the earth like a dog in pain, my nerves are swelling from the need to love, and I stretch out my head as though a harness were growing ever tighter around my neck. Then I leap to my feet and look up at the night. Where are you, beautiful creature who must one day love me? Are you also looking at the night? The air sparkles like a mirror under the stars, and we see each other.

Lively creature, in your soul all is refreshing hope for life, like a forest under the sun. The spindly grass caresses the rough trunk, trembling with anticipation. The earth murmurs, water close by. And here's the water, the cool water. And you are here in my arms, my creature.

I can kiss you because I've kept myself pure. I have suffered and wept for you. Now it's August, and the branches burst with sap and extend with longing. I want to hold you fiercely and feel your untouched flesh squirm under my fingers, here on earth as hot as my blood, because you must be mine.

Oh beautiful creature, I don't know what colour your eyes are, but they must be blue, because the great air above us is blue. I don't know where you are, but you look on from above and brighten everything again like the sun. You are in all things, because I love them all: in the white bell-flower of the meadow, and in the river that reflects you and traverses the broad valley, holding you in its heart.

Oh new creature, I don't know who you are, but I feel you within me like a seed setting root in my soul. And I'm a child climbing a green slope, hopping about and picking flowers, suddenly finding before him the valley and its villages, and the distant city, full of hazy light.

You must be smiling, because the stars are shining so brightly tonight. I feel your smile on my face like a breath of wind in a tuft of grass. Ah, dear one! All my thoughts gather around you like bees around a sweet flower. They whirl around and around you, my creature.

All things have their truth; some have their time now, others in the future. And if on this sad winter night I tell you of a fairy who comes carrying fragrant flowers in her lap, you have to believe me, o my poor soul.

I want airy things
carried on a swallow's wing,
brushing against my ear. The sun is warm
as an adolescent cheek.
Walking easily along,
towards apple trees in blossom.

Along the lane
an olive branch
grazes my face.
Fresh things! Roses
brimming with dew;
grass on a riverbank.
Ah! if I could only
kiss your lips!

The night-time dreams of flowers vanish as soon as the dew of first light touches them. And yet, I'd love to feel your lips on my eyes in the morning as I think this so tenderly.

We walk across pathless meadows, because today a warm sun soothes our eyelids. We walk for a long time, basking in the winter sun and the little violets poking up amidst ivy spreading over the ground.

It's a day when the soul is borne up by its own breath. When we breathe, we leave white vapour trails of ourselves in the air.

Let's go on ahead a little, to where the sun warms the trunk of a white plane tree, and gently lean our foreheads there. Fresh spears of grass rustle underfoot as we walk, holding hands and looking through our eyelashes.

III

I rediscovered my Karst in a period of my life when I needed to get far away.[1] I often went for walks, slowly strolling along the wharf, watching people departing. I studied the schedule of the Lloyd ferries, and if I'd only had a few hundred crowns, I'd have gone off to Dalmatia, to Kotor, and trekked as far as Cetinje, and from there, who knows?[2] Into the interior of Croatia, where there are immense forests and you have to ride long hours to reach a cabin of fading timber. In the old style, the paterfamilias is still the old-fashioned host. At night, when you can't sleep, you're lulled by a sad song that soothes you to sleep. Or maybe I would have sailed for the East.

I was watching the Chioggian fishing trawlers, swollen with cargo, as they were thrust from the quayside with a great heave.[3] The ship's captain stripped off his shirt so as not to stain it with sweat, clambered up the mast, and bracing himself against the rope ladder, unfurled the sail, yellowed and stained brick-red. They'd dashed across the Adriatic all night long before a stiff breeze, and then another day, then another under full

1 [The third part of the *Karst* is greatly influenced by the suicide of Anna Pulitzer.]

2 [The Austrian Lloyd was the most powerful Austro-Hungarian shipping company based in Trieste. Founded in 1833, by the end of the nineteenth century it had established trading routes not just in the Mediterranean, but also in East Asia. See Lawrence Sondhaus, *The Naval Policy of Austria-Hungary, 1867–1918: Navalism, Industrial Development, and the Politics of Dualism*, Purdue UP, 1994, 148–9. Dalmatia is a coastal region on the eastern shore of the Adriatic Sea extending from the Island of Rab to the Bay of Kotor in the south. The Republic of Venice controlled this region from the fifteenth century to 1797, when the republic ceased to exist. In 1814 the region became part of the Austro-Hungarian Empire. Cetinje was the capital of Montenegro.]

3 [Chioggia is a town at the southern end of the Venetian lagoon, a few miles south of Venice. Fishing was its main source of livelihood.]

sun. I especially longed for that marine utter calm that comes when the breeze suddenly drops.

I felt a need to be alone. I walked the least frequented streets, in the shadows of tall, rectangular tenement blocks, and I looked around, watching the faces of passers-by from a distance. I was afraid of being recognized, of being hailed and having to reply. A friend sent me a postcard: why hadn't I written to him? *Since you don't want me to, I won't come. But it's unkind of you to be so rude and selfish in your grief. Now is when you have the greatest need of friendship.* All good, kind people; but I needed distance.

I kept to myself, in my little room, and every evening I heard the slow striking of nine, then nine-thirty, then ten, then ten-thirty ... Time meandered along as one moves on a Sunday afternoon, burdened by the ennui of all humanity. And every night I heard a carriage pass in the street, then the voices of those out late, shouting to their wives or mothers to throw them the key.

All right – I thought – now I'll start reading, and taking notes, and studying. But I lay my head down on my arm – and couldn't cry.

I couldn't sleep. I was weighed down by a deep despair. And so one leaves the house at night and walks with weary steps. I dreamed of a long night with the bora blowing, when the few passers-by walk leaning into the wind, without thinking. I dreamed most of all of cedars fixed in the bottom of the sea, petrifying little by little. I needed stone, and sterility. And I remembered the Karst, and within me I felt a little cry of joy, as when someone has found his country again.

How many stories I told myself that night! I stretched out on the mattress, my head resting on my right arm, and I was a child again, waiting with wide eyes for a glimmer of light in the doorway, and for my mother to come in: "Not asleep yet? Come on now, it's late. Go to sleep, and I'll tell you a story."

I felt sorry for myself and treated myself gently. And I told myself aloud a story of the Karst: "Many years before our time, a woman from the Karst with blonde hair gave birth to a boy who shivered even under a bear pelt. Then, because her breath wasn't enough to keep him warm, she lit a fire for the first time. So the boy grew, but not once did he go hunting. He ate roasted meat, and on winter nights, when he awoke suddenly and didn't see the fire, the darkness and cold entered into him, and he would have strange thoughts, and shiver. From high in the cave's vaulted roof, the drops kept falling, more slowly than the beating of his pulse, and as they fell upon his straw bedding, he heard someone walking outside the cave. But quite far away; who knew where, or who, he was?

He brought the goats out to pasture; he plunged into a bush and looked through its branches at the sky. A stag passed, sniffing around, and a bird sang out; and these sounds entered into him and mingled together. Then he slept for a little while. At sunset, he returned and recounted everything in words as clear as leaves after rain. And his family listened, rapt.

One day while he was talking some men with chests like boulders chiselled by ice came to the cave; they massacred the family, stole the fire, and took him away as their slave."

And I told myself other stories. Then I was tired, but still I couldn't sleep. My head brimmed with shattered thoughts that were born and fluttered off every which way, taking me to a thousand places all at the same time. I was sweating all over. I leapt suddenly to my feet, dressed in a fury, pocketed my jackknife, and headed out. There were still a couple of lovers in Via Chiadino, the woman playing with the man's fingers as he held her close against him. I thought: "That woman could die on him this very night." Stray dogs howled. Once I got up towards Kluč,[4] beyond the yellow-and-black striped customs barrier, I was by myself, and could breathe freely. I kept on walking, not a thought in my head.

The sun rose even on this morning. And as always, the bricklayers made their way down the silent street in their heavy boots. I saw a woman throw open her shutters opposite my window and call out to her son that it was time for school.

Within us nausea and disgust accumulates, until one day it pours out and poisons the air we breathe. It's odious to get dressed, to eat, to rise from a chair, it's all meaningless; but it's best not to disrupt our habits, to go on putting one foot ahead of another, because we were taught to walk that way. Just don't obstruct boredom, because then thoughts become turbulent and make you suffer; otherwise, life proceeds calmly, without accident or alarm.

Silence and peace. You pass through the streets without making a sound. No need to wake up anybody. People are sleeping, badly or well, but they're sleeping. No one has the right to disrupt the sleep of anyone else. A few night owls stroll by, and a security guard strides past. Near lampposts you can hear gas hissing through the spout. A well-lit stretch; your shadow walks ahead of you, then wavers a moment; a second begins following you; it becomes smaller, draws close; now it's your size. You

4 [Village on the Karst, near Trieste.]

can stop, lie down on top of it, right on the city sidewalk, and go to sleep yourself. But you can also keep on going, and turn right or left, it makes no difference. Now you're amidst a stink of burning oil; then as that zone recedes, a hot greasy blast from a hotel kitchen begins. You can walk till dawn through the silent city, while the dust sifts slowly down to earth.

It's raining. The day is long. The doorbell rings: Guido enters, drops his umbrella in the umbrella stand, goes to his room, throws down his books, and goes off to have something to eat.[5] Mother passes by my door softly, because she hopes I'm asleep.

The day grows longer, infinite and without variation.

A cart lumbers slowly down the street. I hear a pinging of iron. Doves coo in the gables of the house. I don't know what will become of my life.

Two men pass by and greet one another, tipping their hats. One has a triangular face, all bones, with tired, wandering eyes; the other walks with little, deft steps, entirely satisfied. Satisfied with his appetite. Satisfied with his house, with the young wife who's waiting for him at the window. He has the *Piccolo* folded in his pocket, and he's carrying a little bag of cherries for lunch. – Why did they greet each other? What kind of relationship could there be between these two men? All of life is interwoven so absurdly. No one understands anyone else, but everyone puts on an act of loving or hating. Why? Somebody does something, and everyone else says he's done something good, or he's done something bad. In whose name?

I pass by others, and let others pass by me, and I look upon this unknown life like a stranger. I am here because at this moment I'm walking along this street, and I see a watchmaker bent over his bench removing a watch spring with a little steel screwdriver. His eye grips a tubular loupe tightly and naturally, not a muscle wrinkled in effort. In the shop a thousand pendulums swing rhythmically, a thousand hands indicate the identical hour and the identical minute. The girls of the lycée flock home, all dressed in dark blue, gossiping and stealing glances at the boys who are there waiting for them.

A young man sprays water over the cobblestones in front of a shop, goes back in, comes out with a broom and sweeps dust into the street. A coachman sleeps, huddled in his cab on rumpled cushions, and his horse, muzzle in feedbag, chews his fodder. The pigeons of the Piazza Grande rise every now and then in a great flock, turn in great circles, then descend again and strut around between the puddles.[6] The Bos-

5 [Guido is Scipio Slataper's youngest brother, born in 1898.]
6 [Piazza Grande, now Piazza dell'Unità d'Italia, is the major town square in Trieste.]

nian soldier posted before the governor's palace marches with heavy strides, in three movements turns about, and marches back again.

Where am I? My eyes are squinting in the heat, and I stroll along in a daze. I walk slowly and watch everything, like a stranger exhausted from travel who must still stay alert because someone is waiting up for him, someone full of love and curiosity. But no one is waiting for me, and upon my return no one will sit with me, and ask with loving eyes: "And so? How was the journey?"

I am tired and alone. I can go back or I can stay. I can stay here in the middle of the piazza until the sun makes me stagger and fall to the ground; or I can walk between the rumbling carts, just as I can walk in the silence of night; because nowhere can I lay my great weariness down.

And the coal haulers filling the bunkers of the *Baron Gautsch* with coal from the barge watch me with their sunken, reddened eyes, wondering at my attention.[7]

One of them coughs, spits, the breeze blows long threads of mucus back onto his half-naked torso plastered with coal dust and sweat, and perhaps he's angrily thinking that I feel sorry for him.

But no: I am indifferent. The thing is, I don't understand it. I can see that everyone around me is working. A Greek vessel is taking on heavy timber; two fishermen are raising a dark, sopping-wet mainsail; an ice cream vendor is crying his wares; someone in dark glasses marks in a ledger the number of sacks of cement; a porter pushes onward with his red cart; puffing steam, the Grado ferry is approaching; an ox is pulling a wagon loaded with bales of cardboard. On the wagon is the script: *Troppau. Trieste-Rozzol-Assling.*[8] Now a train is puffing its way up the hill to Opicina; another is arriving in Pola, and another rumbles over the bridge across the Po. The air resounds with clangour. Movement swells. The earth is at work. The whole world is working in a great frenzy of self-obliterating pain. And it builds houses and closes itself within walls so that bodies can't see each other tossing sleeplessly between the sheets, and it weaves itself clothes so it can think that at least someone else's body is healthy and sound, and it issues millions of clocks so that the moment is whipped on perpetually through space, like one of the damned ceaselessly pushing ahead so as not to fall. Don't stop even for a minute, O labouring earth!

---

7 [The *Baron Gautsch* was a steamship of the Austrian Lloyd, launched in Dundee, Scotland, in 1907.]

8 [Troppau, the train's destination, is now Opava, in the eastern part of the Czech Republic. Rozzol is now Rosenbach, Austria, and Assling is now Jesenice, Slovenia.]

That's how I felt; and I was transfixed, as though at the centre of the earth. I would have liked to ask the coal haulers to let me work with them; but I laughed with scorn, and thought: Yes, sure, you work. Yet there is always some mystery within you, like a little knot that won't unravel. You carry it around with you in everything you do, and it's quiet and behaves, until suddenly it scratches you. Eat your bread and drink your wine; increase and multiply; because your mystery is feeding itself on the bread you eat and the wine you drink, and it's the only certain truth your children will bequeath to their children. Let your hands grow calloused and your spirit penetrate the tightest weave, let it be so clear as to become its own reflection. Torture every part of your body with all the instruments of work, and also, if you so desire, throw yourself onto a comfortable bed and exhaust your spirit. You can't break down the mystery. In which part of you is that little mystery hidden away? You can smash yourself to bits, but you won't even get a glimpse of it. You can even look for it on a starry night, between seams of iron ore, or down in the darkness, among forest roots. You can even kill yourself, if you like; but the bullet that penetrates your temple won't graze it, and it will live in you eternally even after you're gone, that little unknown thing that has created this fine expanse of sea, and has created us, and has made us build these red-and-black steamships.

I was practically laughing out loud. Then I realized they were all staring at me. I was disgusted with myself. I stood up straight and firm. Every part of me was infected. It seemed to me that a single word of mine could contaminate the world. I gazed at the vast, pure sea and felt an impulse to pray. But no: all my sorrow is my own, all my anguish is mine alone. And I gripped my chest with my hands, a spasm of pain twisted on itself. I felt that I could die, because my secret was avidly burning my blood, red like the cursed sun setting on the sea.

Why don't you work? Remember that someone believed in you. She's waiting, and she isn't happy. Every minute you plead for is an offence. Bang your head against the desk, but get to work, blessing her. That she died is just; because you're a coward.

I sat at the desk, took the pen, and started making marks on the paper, doodling her name. Suddenly I was frightened, and ran over to the mirror. I stared hard into my eyes and asked myself: "Are they really shining? But Vedrani says you can't tell by external signs if a person is crazy.[9] I'm

9 [Alberto Vedrani (1872–1963), prominent psychiatrist in Lucca, and an acquaintance of Slataper's since 1910. He collaborated with *La Voce*, and published articles on psychiatry in the Florentine journal. In 1916 he published one of the first articles

not crazy. Stay calm, Scipio." I looked at the objects reflected in the mirror. The things reflected in a mirror – according to the laws of physics – are as distant from the eye as they are from the mirror reflecting them. I tried to figure out whether I was seeing things this way too. "If I hit myself, I should feel pain. But crazy people also feel pain. How can I get objective proof that I'm not crazy?" The carpet in the mirror was at an angle to the real carpet. I saw things as though for the first time, like a child. Long red threads, long blue threads. I ran into the dining room; Vanda was there, busy doing something. – Now, I'll talk! – But I couldn't. I was scared to hear my own voice. I paced back and forth. What if my voice is strange, and Vanda looks at me in fear?[10]

"Is Mamma at home?" But no, no: I'd asked in a normal and simple manner. I returned to my room. I threw myself on the floor, gripping my head tightly; I called out to her, then again, three times, four, a fifth … and I said her name again and again, for a long while, quietly, and gradually more softly. After a while I began to sing a lullaby: *Din, don, campanon – Tre putele xe sul balcon – Una la fila, l'altra canta, – L'altra la fa putei de pasta – Una la prega Sior Idio – che'l ghe mandi un bel mario …* [11]

I don't remember anything after that. I was overcome by exhaustion. After a few minutes I got up and felt more calm. I don't know what it was I lived through. But many times I prayed for madness or for death.

I'd like to become a forester in Croatia. I love leafy oaks and the axe. I would walk to work leaning a little to my right from the habit of chopping wood, and the long handle of the axe fixed in my belt would bump against my thigh.

The boss gives me a slap on the back, laughing between brown teeth. The boss is strong and proficient, and we obey him with gratitude. We like having orders. The boss drinks grappa like water and never staggers, but with feet firmly planted monitors the work from dawn to dusk – and he roams the forest like a big hungry animal. If you're not working,

---

commemorating Slataper's work and life. See Alberto Vedrani, "Due morti: G. Perusini e S. Slataper," in *Critica Sociale*, 15 February 1916.]

10 [Vanda is the next-to-youngest of the five Slataper children.]

11 [This is a popular Triestine nursery rhyme, which translates as: "Ding dong bell / Three girls on the balcony / One spins, another sings / Another shapes babes out of pastry / One prays the good Lord / Will bring her a fine husband …" The three girls are an echo of Slataper's "three friends," the three young women with whom he developed a close friendship: Anna Pulitzer, Elody Oblath, and Luisa Carniel (Gigetta). As mentioned above, Anna, his beloved, killed herself. Elody Oblath, the most intellectual of the three women, loved Slataper and helped him in many projects. Luisa Carniel became Slataper's wife in 1913.]

straight away you'll hear the snap of branches behind your back, an angry cackle of laughter, and a kick right to your spine.

But the boss is a good man, and he says to me: Hey, Pennadoro! I've found a tree for you. It's hardened over a hundred years. How's that axe? Chop! Chop! Its teeth are just coming in. Strike the first blow here. Feel that flesh!

My axe is handsome, with a long handle of oak and a square eye. It laughs coldly, like ice. It's tired and sluggish, full of disdain. It loves to rest deep in the damp grass and to contemplate the sky. Sometimes it amuses itself by toying with the tips of shrubs or the splaying fronds of an ash. Then it smiles like a little girl with bitter saliva flecking her cheeks. But more often it's sad and gloomy.

Ah, but when it's warm, how it cuts! It cuts like a beast in heat. It plunges, small and bright and without respite, and whack! like a bolt of thunder, it's deep in the flesh of the tree. The air all around vibrates, and the chaffinches break off their song. It slides itself free to savour the wound, dangles on a straight wing for an instant, and whack! straight to the bone. The oak starts up straight and unyielding, and with its lower branches caresses the little saplings all around it, so that they won't be frightened, as though only a gentle breeze from the sea were making it shake. The great oak is silent, like a mother that's dying.

But the axe sings. The axe rises, falls, and sings. Glinting and red, it laughs. It seems to have gone mad. I fear it. I see nothing but a flashing in front of me that whistles and roars. Whack! Whack! I can no longer feel my hands. The flashing throws me against the tree, then back again! Whack! Little hand of steel, let's destroy the forest!

Why then were we lifted from the earth? We were sleeping quietly in the humid warmth of the roots. We were deeper still: we were the dark hard heart of the earth. One surge of light came down, split us open, and lifted us to the sun.

All right then: now we're alive. Now we want sunlight on the earth. The great desert sun. A sun that splits your forehead open. Let's destroy the forest!

The blows sing out relentlessly, amid the crackling of shredding wood. Ah, how good it is to reach the heart of the old oak! The blows are deafening. And down it goes! A great crash: the echoes resound into the distance.

Now the cutters and planers will have work for a week.

Children have come to see her lying dead on the ground, and they carve her lichened bark with red-handled jackknives. They are happy. They give me strawberries and raspberries. I scrape sweat from my eyebrows with my index finger and gaze at them.

Maybe I'd rather be the overseer of a coffee plantation in Brazil. Today I spoke with one of the merchants here; he said that if I knew Spanish, I could do the job quite well. You just need to be firm. Make sure they're hard at work.

A touch of the whip does no harm. I'd enjoy letting the broad shoulders of the mulattoes have a taste. It's odd that people don't think I could be a slave driver. People don't believe that I'm really cold and calm, that their misery simply leaves me bored.

. . . .

And I?

I'm the same as you, you can be sure. The hands of the young barbarian have become the pale and weak hands of a girl. It's time to dream now: the trees are down, the backs flogged, and many things besides. So many other powerful things.

Mamma said to me timidly, it's no wonder you can't sleep, pacing back and forth all day long in your airless little room! – Just like a condemned man: five paces up and five paces down, between two shelves of books all read and read again, and a white wall on which these words were written long ago: *All things are true; but some have their time now, others in the future. And if this sad winter night I tell you of a fairy who comes carrying fragrant flowers in her lap, you have to believe me, o my poor soul.* – So much time has passed. Now the little psalm is scratched by a fingernail. And also written there, in red pencil: "Look well at me: for I am, I really am Beatrice."[12]

Up and down, up and down. Then sit at this little desk, then stretch out on the floor. In the street countless children are yelling and screaming and throwing stones at the covered cart of the herb vendor. With a great crashing sound, the carriages of a brewery return to their depot. The grey house opposite ours is horrible. When it rains, it drips with yellowish sweat. The light invades stifling rooms, the corners of big peeling armoires, a rag on the floor, a fat woman pulling off her stockings. At all hours of the day the windows are piled high with sheets and faded blankets. All day there's an ugly, toothless hag, half-dressed, who bawls down to her boy: "Hey, you pig! Where are you, you little son of a bitch? You brat, just wait till I catch you! Run, Paulin! May God curse your soul, you filthy brat! Just wait and see what happens to you when you come in for supper!"[13] All day long. At seven thirty a wife raises her window shade and, with a baby at her neck, waits for her husband, who's approaching with little steps, playing with his walking stick. Every evening. At night groups of youths pass by, singing the anthem of the League of the Workers.[14] At dawn the masons walk along with their wooden soles slapping, and the woman opens the shutters and wakes her son, as it's time for school.

Let's go somewhere, it's not possible to stay here a moment longer. I've entered the woods of Melara.[15] I've crossed meadows and enjoyed brushing my feet through grass already grown tall, walking slowly and bending slightly forward, my head bare in the full sun, like someone tracking something that is cautiously moving away through little signs and noises.

12 ["*Guardami ben: ben son, ben son Beatrice*": a slightly inexact quotation of Dante, *Purgatorio* XXX, 73. The words, written by Anna on the wall of Slataper's bedroom, portray her as the spiritual guide who could have led Slataper to salvation.]

13 [In dialect in the original.]

14 [The anthem of the League of Workers is the "Internationale."]

15 [Melara, a wooded area on the Karst east of the city.]

All the fleshy pea flowers are blooming red, yellow, and freckled. The oak leaves become heavy with juice, and the junipers have more berries than thorns: greenish, smooth berries, fresh as drops of seawater. The trunks of the plane trees are peeling, and at their knots the first branches are swollen with rippling muscles like the arms of powerful creatures. Meadow grass spreads right onto the main road.

The first gentle stirrings of summer, when everything is alive. Around me I feel the wonderful assurance of everlasting life. Spring yields gently, with a shower of blood-red and white petals on the humid breeze, while calyxes grow broad and strong, butterflies break their stringy cocoons, and the sheaths of new buds fold back, faded and dry. Some rubbery and reddish boughs are still quivering, and curled amidst the exuberance of the grass there are still a few violets, growing pale in their damp hideaways: the gentle babble words of infancy returning to the lips of a woman who has just given birth.

I lie under an oak tree and watch thousands of blue-red insects wheel about amidst its leaves, in love. All the air above my head is filled with their abrupt flights. One falls, totally spent, clings to a blade of bending grass, and raises its antennae, stupefied. Along the gnarled trunk, a double caravan of ants marches up and down; tiny black dots jump like miniature cicadas out of the grass and onto my clothes. I stretch deeper into this thriving, flowering grass, and I am full of sorrow and death.

Be still. The sky is clear, as after a rainstorm. Your gaze rests calmly on the deep blue of the sky, as upon the expanse of sea. A white cirrus cloud glides across tremulously. The edges of leaves glow silver against the sun. Rest. Wind from far away brings you a beautiful dream, if you stay still and let yourself doze. Rest your head on the ground. Now the peaceful sound of tolling bells reaches you. Your country is nearby.

No, I can't sleep. My arms sleep, abandoned at my side; my eyes sleep; my entire body and soul yearn for sleep's relief; but one thing, just one thing is still awake that no mother's lullaby can soothe, that the water falling drop by drop nearby cannot appease, that the wind can't carry along with the flowers it bears away. Nature! There's just one thing: I can't sleep. The dry stubble of this grass prods me like this thought that gives me no peace even in my dreams and won't be dissolved by all the noble virtues of the earth, and is harsh and torments me everywhere. I can't sleep. A horrible disgust at all this joyful life around me twists my face. What have I done that keeps me from becoming one with this time of warmth, in which a divine certainty of love vibrates from every leaf, trunk, and flower, from each bird, from the sun? I plunge my fingers into tufts of grass like someone searching for the white brow of his beloved, and her eyes would gaze into mine and arrest infinity between our eyes. Where is your mouth, my darling, for me to kiss? Where have you gone?

You've left me here all alone. And I could travel every road and mountain and every sea of this great earth, and I wouldn't find you anywhere. The ways of the wind are endless and broad, full of foam and crashing waves; but you are even farther away. And even if the sun clears my weary eyes, I can no longer see you, you've gone so far away. When the night is alive with stars, I search for you in the immensity of space; but the infinite is without you, because I can no longer hold you in my arms, my darling.

You were youthful and fragrant as the dawn. You were a sapling in spring. When you held my hand in your lovely long one, I walked with confidence, with a firm stride. I would look into your restless eyes curiously searching out fresh shoots under the dry leaves, and they would suddenly widen in amazement or grow deep as sorrow, and I would smile at you. You sang with a voice soft and clear as a thread of water among the grass. Sweet thing! And when you rested your head on my shoulder, I would hold your chin in my hand, stroke your cheeks and fine hair, and a trembling tenderness would take hold of me, unable to comprehend that you were mine. Oh girl, my girl! Why have you given me this sadness?

You've left me alone here, after I kissed you.

And my soul, now there can be no more peace, not anywhere. Where can we bury our bitterness? Let us rise and walk at our slow daily pace, searching out our solitude.

The Karst is a land of limestone and juniper. A terrible cry turned to stone. Boulders grey with rain and lichen, twisted, fractured, sharp. Dry juniper.

Long hours of limestone and juniper. The grass is bristly. Bora. Sunlight.

The earth is without peace, without continuity. It has no field where it can stretch itself out. Every attempt it makes is fractured and riven.

Cold, dark caves. Water drops, bearing all the soil it has stolen, steadily, mysteriously, for a hundred thousand years, and another hundred thousand still.

But if a word must be born from you – kiss the wild thyme that squeezes life from the rock! Here all is death and stone. But when a gentian succeeds in lifting its head, and blooms, it gathers in itself the entire deep sky of spring.

Press your mouth to the earth, and don't speak.

NIGHT: stars slowly fading; the hot sun; evening tremor of the boughs. Night. I am walking.
GOD SAID: let even sorrow have its peace.
GOD SAID: let even sorrow have its silence. Let even man have his solitude. Karst, my country, may you be blessed.

But one night, sorrow was almost stronger than me. I could feel it gathering itself drop by drop, and my soul shut in on itself, dry and indifferent, trying not to give it a grip. I understand fear. There's nothing but this: at this moment that man is coming to kill me. I can't budge. I can't run. Can't even start yelling. I must stare straight at him.

That's the state I was in. I walked trembling over the flaking rock, cracking like sheet metal under my feet, between shrubs and young pines. The sound of my footsteps didn't frighten me; but it unnerved me, and made me sweat, how flakes of rock plunged interminably down, crashing against others, smashing amidst brush and leaves. My soul was tired and didn't want to suffer any more. It wanted to stay quiet and alone. It murmured prayers that sorrow and suffering would not come, that it would be allowed to stay quiet and alone. But prayer brought no peace; I could not hear my own self. I was entirely, mournfully tense, anticipating a sudden collapse, a flash of lightning, a rifle shot, a great roar. A thing terrible and foreseen that could snatch me up here, right out of this dark brush, behind this little wall, here it is! – I ran, fleeing the sorrow that followed me into the rustling thicket, into the open sky, where you can see all around, by the light of the starry horizon.

But in the infinite night I was more alone and without defences. Alone, with just my sorrow, my sole companion, my good companion, to lean my head upon and weep. I wept like a lost child. The whitest moon hung in the sky, suffusing stones and trees, and dampening my lips, a coolness I could touch with my hand. The sea beneath lifted up like a silver road, spinning broad coils. In the immense dawn light, the distant horizon watched over everything, indifferently penetrated every object. And I wept alone, a tall black shadow, empty and exposed.

I crouched down among the rocks high above the sea, hiding my face in my hands, ashamed. I don't believe in God! I don't believe in God. But maybe she is here above me, in this inescapable light, in this sky, in this earth. You are here with me too. Maybe you too are suffering. Help me, my darling. If I could hear your voice say just one syllable, and feel your hand on my brow; because all is solitude and silence here, there is no one to disturb us. All around, not a single thing breathes. The earth could split open and give back her prey. The heavens could meet again to recreate her form. The soul is diffuse in all things; but I want to have you here again, my love. I can bring you back to life. If I believe, that is enough. I believe you can be born again. You are not yet dead. You are waiting for me to return. I wrote you that we'd be happy together. Can't you see, when I'm with you life is so simple and lovely. We'll see each other soon, my love. Expect me soon. I'll head back in July. – And yet, when I wrote those words to you, you were already dead. But now I've come back, and I'll wait for you until dawn, because you are still mine, and it's not possible that you're dead. You couldn't have abandoned me! Stay with me, my little one. I beg you. My darling – I didn't even look up, not to disturb your will. Just believe, stay calm, and believe. – Something brushes my hair. Maybe it was the wind. The earth is brilliant under the moon. Because you are eternally dead.

She is dead. The word is incomprehensible. No one will ever see her again. No one will hear her voice any more. She is dead. I don't understand death. I don't know anything. I stand before death and stare at it spellbound, the way I stare at this rock splitting under my feet. But I don't want to die, because I don't know what death is. She is in a tomb, within smooth stone, in a coffin, tightened with screws. How do they manage it, when they tighten the screws? She lies with her hands by her sides. On the outside there's a name and two dates. That stone should be flung aside. All the juniper of the Karst should be brought to her tomb. I'll bring a great boulder; and the branches of a young oak, so that you'll be among the coolness of leaves, and buds, and the daffodils, all of them, so much that flowers will never grow on the Karst again. The flowers of the Karst are withering on her grave, my good people! Go ahead, go and take a look if you're brave! I've brought them all here, and now I'm going down to bring her back up with me, and we'll be at peace. It will take every pine in the woods to burn her white body.

Let's rest. Just rest. She is dead; it's hopeless. A person lives among us. For years and years. Nursed by one woman, learned to write from another, and taught another to write. I was a torment to her, and you suffered for her. Yes, because she had many friends, and when they were far from her, she barely seemed alive. She spoke with thousands of people. Every act and every word of hers is interwoven with our acts and our words, forming one single entity: not hers, not ours, but belonging to us, to us all. Then nothing intervenes. A mere nothing, an act of will: just an instant, and that person is never with us again. – How is it possible that one person can die, while the rest go on living? I'm not asking how one person can die, I'm asking how the others can go on living. That person dies, that person only. The next morning, the others see the sun rise. The name is printed in the papers. The trains are running as always. You can already read the name in the obituaries of a newspaper purchased at a commuter station. I'm not suffering. Even this woman sitting opposite me is reading her name, in the same newspaper I'm holding in my hand. Thirty thousand copies. I am going to view her dead body. But this doesn't matter; here's my question: if someone, mourned by us and loved by us, if this person could die alone, while our lives go on – then what of all our hatred, and love, and understanding?

No one can enter into another person, loving them so perfectly that they're bound together, body upon body. A person can die solely because no one else understands them; within each individual there's a secret all their own, that neither lover nor teacher can touch. And the individual is eternally separated from other individuals, yet aspires to be whole, from the tips of his fingers to his innermost belief, all one invisible secret that others cannot find, silent and alone; he aspires to his own individual peace, where his form won't be disturbed by others; where it will become entirely his own. And as long as he's on his way there, he is suffering: and this search is life. The individual longs to die away from the others. And naturally we cannot comprehend that death.

Already from infancy, regret exists within man. Even then we already feel the lack of something we once enjoyed and now is gone, and we weep; and all of mankind together, all the history of man can't console the little child who is crying for something. This is the humanity I have believed in. Work is a vain attempt to restore what has been lost. Everyone searches for it, dishonestly, savagely, in the body of a woman, in the hand of a friend, in faith, in God. Everyone, in vain. I alone, up here, by myself, am honest; but even solitude and honesty aren't enough. It's not enough to know. I think in words that others also use. What's necessary is to die. But this only is indispensable: being.

But how can the individual still exist, once he has attained solitude and there are no more obstacles in his way? And if he dies imperfect: how could he have perfected himself without means, method, purpose, or practice? He dies, human still. What happens to the individual spirit that dies, so that it can change its human character so deeply? Is it then the final moment of life that makes the individual whole? In that instant it is perfect, and as a human, enjoys its divine perfection, because nothing human can die before it has attained its deserved measure of divinity.

But who has decreed all this? What truth asserts that in order to die one must be perfect? This could be the illusion on which you've sustained your feeble life. Who can show that individual perfection exists? One can die just as well in imperfection, leaving one's finest qualities unrealized, unrealized for all time, with no possibility of a future. In an eternal, unchanging anguish. Death does not bring peace. Death is a horrible torment. But does one feel it? Does individual consciousness persist? With the horrible torment of the whole passing through you. Or does the whole go on suffering, without relief?

And the whole: what is it? They've conditioned you to use the word. Maybe there is no whole, only fragments seeking fusion in vain. What god revealed to you that death should be alone? That could be just your anguished thought. It could be that not even your harshest torment touches the truth. It isn't written anywhere that there is one truth. Why should there be? And even if there is, sorrow is not granted the particular grace of clairvoyance. This is the rhetoric of visionary sorrow. Why should sorrow be more profound than joy? What everyone believes isn't necessarily true. For example, what is it that people say about perishing into cosmic harmony, about the organic transformation that gives birth to particular form?

But it could also be true, who denies it? Only your pride, refusing to find any benefit in what others say. And what is your pride worth, before the mystery? You're someone who doesn't even understand why this plant is dying, now that you've pulled it from the ground. It was a thyme plant. You came here, attracted by its perfume. You caressed it. You were already fond of it. It was a tender thyme plant. Slender, softly fringed, fragrant. But you pulled it up because you didn't understand what it was. You didn't understand because you're an intellectual. You could have planted it more deeply in the earth, and no one would have been able to pull it up again. You could have been its god. Now it's rotting. New life will sprout from it. Life? Are a thousand worms and a thousand weeds worthy of this thyme plant, whose death is your own doing? God, why do you take the good, why also the good? Does life really require that loved ones pass on so that it can continue? Life is so weak. It is indifferent, and lawless. The good must die also, so the wicked can be born. There is no law. Not a good person for a bad one; that would be law. Good or bad, good and bad – these distinctions are our own! There are no laws in the universe. Chance reigns there still, even with the birth of man and free will. You make every effort to be good, but nature gains nothing from your effort. But mankind does, perhaps: yes, mankind! And, gentlemen, after you're gone? After your great wisdom? The new universe will be better because of what Dante has written? Michelangelo's Prisoners bear eternal night on their shoulders to keep it from smashing into the earth, which turns around the sun, the sun that turns around Hercules, Hercules that turns around – turns around what? – But you, a man, one who lives and obeys your conscience, knowing you improve nothing, you are a hero. You are totality, standing in the face of nothingness. You are God.

God? – But isn't it also true that you're living only because you're in the habit, and it bothers you to face the unknown? No, let's not get all grandiose; let's simply look at the way things really are. After all, life is very comfortable for those who don't know how to venture into the wider world. If you leave home, you could get lost, right? And along comes someone plenty proud of his brains and broad chest. Someone who lives on ambition; but if he were humble, he would die. In his pride, this person dreams he has a mission, and a path; but how much do you really matter? Without faith, without work, without love: just a heap of flesh! Your spirit is subject to chance. One person dies; and you no longer believe. You're just another form in the universe, one that can only prove itself superior in this way: by overcoming your proud habit, and dying. You can convince yourself of the mystery. You can give it all up. You can be humble and serene.

The abyss is not terrifying. One can slide right down. You just need to throw yourself outwards a little, so you don't carry stones rumbling down with you. Go down quietly. Don't disturb the silent chill of the universe. Be like water into water.

But, oh! – it could also be that you don't know how to bear grief, my friend. It could be, it's not absolutely clear, my dear. It could also be that it's only for fear of death that I'm speaking to you now. But what if it were true that you want to die because you can't bear grief – because you don't know how? Now comes the anguish. Do you feel it? The air trembles beneath its great hands. Clouds draw over the moon. Blood, dark. Silence. – God!

God still and silent on his throne.

I won't do it! It's cowardly to die without certainty. No one should; as for me, for me, I am not yet ready to die. Honestly no, or, honestly, yes: because this moment must be expressed. Expressed fully. All of life is expression. And so observe your death with the necessary calm, and get yourself into the right frame of mind. But why? I'll go on. I am a poet. Yes, I'll go on, without a doubt. The sea is in flames. The sky is vast. Night, gentle sister, and a little breeze comes and goes. How peaceful it would be to sleep.

Night! Mamma, I need you! Keep the light away, I don't want day to come.

I picked all the peonies of Lipizza, filled my cloak, and scattered them on her tomb.[16] "Mamma, tell them not to make any noise, I'm going to sleep. Goodbye, Mamma, farewell." All the donkeys carrying milk were coming

16 [Lipizza, Lipica in Slovenian, is a small village a few miles east of Trieste, in the Karst.]

down the road. Move, move! I almost climbed up on one, because I was tired. How does it feel to return from up there, and then on the stairwell – it reeks of burnt oil, or some other smell. But who's living in this huge apartment building? No, no, thanks, I'm not hungry. See you later.

Now the rain has won. A hot breath of wind rustles the pages spread on the desk, a breath that's sickly and damp.

From weary clouds, rain seeps down through the air. Everything is turning grey, in a disquieting languor, and people walk without purpose along long, silent streets.

We'll return to life like this, quiet and resigned, because maybe it's better this way, and both sorrow and joy are vain.

Once my studies are finished, I'll return to Trieste and become a teacher. I don't have a lot of needs, I live on very little, most of what I earn will go to my sisters. On Sundays I'll visit friends and we'll pass some time together, sitting close together and chatting affectionately.

This sweet girl is so happy that – after such a long time! – I've come to visit her. She takes my hands, gazing at me with such affection; and she asks me nothing, and does not pry. Maybe she knows, but she lets me enjoy the warmth of the heated room and the tranquility of her home in peace.[17]

"Let's have a cup of tea, would you like one? Wait: I'll have them tell visitors I'm not at home, I'm so happy!" No, why? Actually, I'd like to see a few people and have some conversation. I've been far away for some days. I've suffered a little; but now I've almost completely recovered. Let's drink this good tea; wait, this biscuit is even better.

And so, while we're talking like close friends, another girl comes in, the subject changes, and we talk for a while, and even argue a little. Then I say an affectionate farewell to them and return home, and smile at my family, and joke around with them. They are so happy.

Little by little, wondering at it together, they begin to speak again in their natural tone, without glancing at me or bending their heads at the table, embarrassed and not knowing what to say. Now little by little our life will resume its usual tone, you'll see, Mamma; and I'll work. I'm a little changed, it's true, but hope will also return, just wait a bit.

---

17 [The young woman is Maria Spigolotto, another friend of Slataper's. She should not be confused with the young woman of the same name with whom he was briefly engaged; see note 48. Spigolotto and Slataper exchanged letters until his marriage with Gigetta Carnel in 1913. See Slataper, *Le Lettere a Maria,* edited by Cesare Pagnini, G. Volpe, 1981.]

But my blessed soul still has enough strength to sternly refuse: no, no! Not like this. Keep away from people, until you can love them. Away! Have some respect for your own sorrow, at least.

Better endure this driving rain on my head, and go back up there, perhaps forever.

The dogs at night! I climb, away from the city, in my exhaustion forgetting to put one foot ahead of the other, and I don't hear the trees rustling along my ascent, I don't see the little solitary houses, locked up and shuttered as though a night-time murderer were always at the ready. I walk. The trail is muddy. I know nothing of the city that sleeps or glows or runs riot behind my back. I know nothing of the sky. I walk in faithful darkness, turning when the track turns – and I keep thinking it's about to end, leaving me trapped with no way forward. I walk on. The anxiety of uncertainty, the tension in my muscles have swallowed the sorrow. I only think of placing my feet with care so I don't slip. Ah, the oblivion of this breathless motion, with my chest thrust ahead to propel my whole weary body forward! The blood pounds in my temples. Faster! And suddenly in my ear, from right overhead, the cowardly howl of a dog.

A raucous howl, furious, almost desperate. A howl of revenge for the wasted nights of keeping watch. My soul starts up and trembles. What am I doing here at this hour? Another dog responds to the howl, one nearby that hadn't heard my quiet footsteps, and then another from somewhere opposite, this one higher up, young, joyous. The alarm has been given. And immediately the entire amphitheater of the hills is awake, and the night howls and barks against my poor footsteps, that were avoiding the dry brush so as not to awaken anything, just to pass through, alone and unnoticed. A window opens cautiously, and I rush away in fear, as though caught in the act.

It all comes back again. The sorrow and the anguish return. I'm afraid. There are too many unknown things, fraught with darkness, all around me. Am I really in the woods? I've never been here before. Nothing here is friendly. I touch damp, gummy tree trunks – surely this is an ash, its bark smooth as skin. Don't you feel it? Little white corollas, like tiny pearls, shower down. Everything is at rest. Don't move. Stay still.

Yet something is awake. It creaks and rustles softly. What is it, that even at night doesn't sleep? There's no breeze; the heavy air impedes movement. I stand still and listen, not breathing.

Who is hiding in the woods? But I have my knife on me. "Who's there?"

No response. And I tremble in my nocturnal wandering, in deserted places where only a fugitive would make his bed! As though I were plotting something against man. – No, no! There, I see the glow of a cigarette, a man is coming down the trail. He passes by me cautiously, glancing at me furtively. Why is he afraid? I'm not going to do anything to him! I listen to his steps grow distant and fade away … now he's already in his house, and he lights the lamp and watches his children sleeping.

And I? She could not sleep either. She too was lonely and sad. I watch over her night. I tread through the woods and underbrush like a night watchman hunting a murderer. I won't tolerate the night hiding any wrongdoer in its dark shadows. I search from dusk to dawn, and in the morning I throw myself down under a tree and wait for dark again. Some time or other I'll find him. Until then I have no right to sleep at night. She too could not sleep.

At night she would jump out of bed and throw the window open wide, seeking solitude with the wind in her anguish. She would watch the dark mass of the Karst spread out before her – but those who would pass by on the road below her house, and stop there on those nights, are all walking down in the streets, gossiping and pausing to discuss politics and business.

– This one lies down next to his plump wife. – Dreams that twenty of the most elegant young men are gathering around her, admiring her new hat. – Broods because he was unable to sell those boxes of citrus fruit. – Thinks now that university vacation is finally over, it's time to go back to Vienna. – Who knows why his sister stared at that man so intently? – You really must be more polite to him.

This is the life that made her smile. And she was meant to be happy. She had everything. There was even someone who studied the pencil marks in the books she read, and knew every street she took each day. She had everything. And she killed herself.

Ah! – Nature, my knife is bright! It reflects your eyes like the face of a brother. Its blade is unstained, like the point of a pickaxe. Solingen steel, horn handle, the sturdiest spring. Faithful and alert companion of my nights, stuck straight into the earth beside my right hand. Silent and steady. I asked a girlfriend for a pocket knife; she brought me these fifteen centimetres of steel. It has sharpened itself silently on branches and tree trunks. Now it laughs from cold and suffering. Silent one, want to warm up? Your ice-cold blade burns my lips.

Remember that night? It was hot, wasn't it, inside that marten fur? We'd pinned her down well! She leaped and twisted like a snake, and tried to wrench you off the ground. But with a good-natured laugh, I spat right between her bloody teeth and helped you plunge your fist down like a good brother, so your handle dug deeper into her broken back and her belly grew flat against the earth, as her screams grew more and more bitter, like a string being tightly strung. Saints alive! Have you forgotten? Her handsome rat's whiskers? Lying around has made you all stiff! Come on! Here's where you carve your neat triangle in the ash tree, so it seeps with whitish sap, like rotten blood. What's that? Oh-ho! You're thirsty for something stronger, Silent one? Vengeance dries you up. Come here: give me a kiss! How you laugh! Dear one. Quiet! The town clock is striking the hour. Good: now is the time. The filthy city lies below, lost in smoke and lights. Let's go, Silent one.

Nature, I thank you. You've made me free, and I thank you. I was full of rules and duties. I knew what was good and what was evil. But you create villains, then send others to wreak vengeance upon them. With one little act, you wrench men from their worldly preoccupations and make them all your own, for the sake of vengeance. You make the good die for your own just purpose. You torment us with anguish for your own just purpose. You create us and destroy us for your own just purpose. Nature, from the beginning of time you have been just, and I thank you for delivering me to birth. I obey you, O divine and good nature.

What do you want of this healthy child, whom you are raising to love you? Let's wait for him to grow, what do you say? Let's wait for him to grow, and work, and love. He's resting now. Let him rest, Nature. You're lovely as a bride in his eyes, and he speaks reverently of you. That little child believes, I assure you. He believes and kisses the flowers he comes across in the fields, and greets every person, marvelling at their beauty. He watches how the blacksmith works and how they lay paving stones in the roads. He wants to sit alongside the sturdy porters on the carts rushing by, and help that woman prop a washtub on her head. He wants to help everyone. Let's let him grow. I have time, lots of time, so let's wait. He was born here, right here in this big green house. You don't believe it? Why are you looking into my eyes like that? Is it dawn already? Soon it will turn a rosy red down below. We need to hurry. But don't look at me that way, don't be afraid! I'm a child who is waiting, who has time, lots of time, and expects to grow, and to love. Feel how cold my hands are already, I'm frozen through. I'm really cold. Give me a little fire and a little water, I beg you. Can't you feel how I'm suffering, my brothers? Let me sleep a few hours on your bed, I am so very tired.

Sitting beside the pond where the herd comes to drink, I stretch my hand out, take a rock, and throw it into the water. The rock makes a muffled plunk and disappears.

I walk with my head down, finding little shards of glass, stray blades of straw, clumps of hair mixed with gravel.

I snap a match in two, take my jackknife and cut the pieces lengthwise, then cut the new pieces; then I throw the whole lot away.

I wish I had some new beads to thread with string.

You will not rest. I can promise you that. You'll weep from disgust as you work, but you'll work.

You're tired and may no longer be able to do anything. Your hands are no longer strong enough to hold a hammer; your brain is foggy. You're a mortally wounded animal searching for a hiding place to die in. That's all right. But you'll work.

You don't know a thing. One small incomprehensible action has scattered the feeble truths you scraped together, your back bent. You're naked and alone. You stand motionless. You're confronted by a mystery that you will never be able to penetrate. That's all right. I know. But you'll work.

You don't know why grass grows or the world exists. You don't know whether the world really does exist. You don't know what you are. It could be that the universe was born from a curse. Perhaps your punishing work will be forever in vain. But you'll work, as though you were the last one remaining.

And afterwards – I don't know whether you'll rest there. But I promise you'll have no rest here. Here you'll work. That's certain.

I want to make myself tough and strong. The air of the Karst has already cleared the closeted colour from my face. My lungs draw deeper breaths. My back rests easily upon the stone. I like a robust body, able to suffer, resist, and work. Weak people disgust me, they're like creatures dependent on rain and sun. Health is a requirement of freedom. Let illness attack those who are used to staying in bed – my uncle always said – and keep them well away from me!

I like that I can snap a hazel branch across my knee, and heave twenty paces a stone I can barely lift to my shoulder. I like remembering that once there were men who pulled oaks right out of the earth to use as walking sticks.

It's a good thing to be able to defend your own life with your own fists. I don't like revolvers; it's possible I wouldn't be able to shoot a man. To defend myself with a knife, yes.

I could live up here on the Karst, alone.

Maybe I would find my real Vila, Carsina.[18] – She should not have died. She believed I was all strength and goodness. I'm not strong. I have need of love, like all men. I want life full and whole, with all its mud and

18 ["Carsina" was the title of a short story that Slataper sketched but never completed (Giani Stuparich, *Scipio Slataper*, Mondadori, 1950, 99).]

flowers. I'm not in thrall to death. I love a healthy body, suffused with blood and prosperity. I love my own body.

Carsina will be lively and have slightly resinous hair like tufts of spring juniper. Teeth white and sharp, for biting. A nimble waist, to collapse in rosy laughter with her head back in my embrace. It will be wonderful to wake up at first light, to see every stem of every leaf and the white sky between.

And to kiss each other in the dew. Carsina, as long as you're young, I'll live up here alone with you.

I should have watched over her sleep the way a dog watches over his master's bedroom to make sure no one enters. I should have held all of her in my arms, and planted her in the earth. When I kissed her, I couldn't imagine the thought of death might be in her heart. I didn't understand her. This is not grief, but punishment. I accept it, and I don't complain. I don't suffer.

The pain flares up from time to time even when I'm asleep, or idle, or physically exhausted. I believe it will be there even after my death. There's a clot of blood in my brain that keeps me from thinking clearly.

My love, I bless the day you were born and the day you chose to die. I don't question, and I don't cry out. I know you died confident and resolved.

Meagre words cannot explain your death. But every good act of ours comes from you, and you live on in the labour of loving. We will strive to be worthy of you. All our work is yours, and if we can be happy in our endeavour, your smile brings us peace and joy. Sister, we thank you, and we love your death just as we loved your life.

You are unaware of the mystery, but the sorrow that shut your eyes upon the void is also part of it; and if you express that sincerely, part of the mystery is unveiled. Because you can know the roots from the flowers, but you can't know the plant from the roots.

If your sorrow won't speak, then what good is your sorrow? Then it's all in vain, and so are you, your life, and the world. Just as in your sacred human form you must seek out the mystery, so sorrow and joy are the formless void from which you must conjure a new world. If you succeed, your sorrow will have given mankind a more intense eternity.

Because you don't know what the good is, but you sense clearly what is better. Suffering is good, if it demands a more profound duty from you.

Thus you immerse yourself in the mystery, and nourish yourself on it, so that its shadows become the sun for your soul.

For this reason, because you have to better yourself, you are a man among men. Now you can love them, because you have suffered and despaired. Bless your sorrow and descend, serene and severe, among them.

I'm lying flat on the grass. The sun fans my eyes with the diffuse flickering of the olive trees. The Adriatic mistral, full of health and joy, blows and blows. The green sea of Grignano shimmers and flares with countless flames and golden sparks, and its cool peacefulness penetrates me, loosening me like March soil.[19] To my lips comes an innocent, broken song.

How eagerly the body stretches out upon the earth! My arms open wide upon it, and my breath mingles like a prayer with the endless, playful breeze.

Mother, mother! If I curse you, your embrace is even more loving and serene. Your young trees surround me in whispering chorus, and the grain rustles and bends towards the red tasselled rushes, while in their dark foliage apples grow plump and dip down in the current of wasps and midges that freckle and dart across the blue deep. And with a sudden leap and trill, the wagtail bursts out over the sea.

It's lovely to rest like this, gently admiring the tall grass and trembling, forgetting myself as I gaze into the sky. I am a gentle prey that longs to be swallowed up in nature.

19 [Grignano is a small inlet located north of Trieste. On the tip of its promontory is the Miramare Castle, built in the nineteenth century as the residence of Archduke Ferdinand Maximilian of Habsburg and his wife Charlotte of Belgium.]

Karst, you are benevolent and strong! You know no rest, and lie naked to the ice and August sun, my Karst, broken and breathless towards a line of mountains as though rushing somewhere; but the mountains shatter, the valley closes in, and the stream vanishes into the ground.

All water plunges into your fissures; dry lichen turns grey on white rock, the eyes blur in the inferno of August. There is no respite.

My Karst is benevolent and strong. Each blade of grass has split rock to sprout, and each flower has sipped dry heat to open. This is why its milk is healthy, and its honey fragrant.

It has no flesh. But each autumn another brown leaf decomposes in its cavities, and its sparse reddish dirt still smells of iron and stone. It is new and eternal. And every once in a while a quiet sinkhole opens in it, and it lingers like a child among red peach trees and waving cornstalks.

Lying down flat on your lap, I hear the water drawn from your every crevice rushing away into the depths, one single, cool stream that brings your young health to the sea and the city.

I love the wholesome water of your caverns that tunnels through straight channels. I love these Karst women who come down to the city in groups, gripping their scarf knot in their teeth against the bora, with great nickel pots of warm milk on their heads. And the white stripe of dawn, and the mournful burn of sunrise through the smog of the city.

Here all is order and labour. In the Free Port at six in the morning, the pilot on duty, chilled to the bone and eyes glazed from standing watch, greets the gatekeeper on his way to open the storehouse. The massive brown-and-black oxen pull the empty carts slowly alongside steamships that arrived last night; and when the carts are in place, at six ten, the porters disperse themselves among the warehouses. In their pockets, all have their pipe and a piece of bread. The head of a work gang climbs onto a loading platform, and more than two hundred men gather around him with their workbooks held aloft, shouting out to be hired. The foreman, deciding quickly, grabs as many workbooks as he needs, and heads off followed by his new hires. The others remain silent and disperse. A few minutes before six thirty, the mechanic in dark-blue coveralls clambers up the ladder of the crane and releases the water lock; and finally, last of all, the wagons arrive, their flatbeds wobbling and crashing. The sun spills orange over the long grey line of warehouses. The sun is bright over sea and city. On the seafront Trieste awakens full of movement and colour.

Our big steamers weigh anchor for Salonika and Bombay. And tomorrow locomotives will thunder across the iron bridge over the Vltava, then rush alongside the Elbe into Germany.

And we too will follow our own law. We will travel, uncertain and nostalgic, compelled by hopeful memories that we won't recognize anywhere as our own. Where did we come from? Our country is far away, the nest undone. But moved by love, we will return to our country, Trieste, and from here we will begin.

We love Trieste for the tormented soul that she has given us. She tears us from our little griefs, and makes us hers, and makes us brothers of all countries riven with strife. She has raised us to struggle and fulfil our duty. And if from these plants of Africa and Asia that trade has sown among the warehouses, if from her stock exchange where telegrams from Turkey or Puerto Rico calmly lay the new foundations for prosperity, if from her life force, from her vexed and fractured soul a new will asserts itself in the world, then Trieste is blessed for having made us live with neither peace nor glory. We love you and bless you, because we are content that we may die in your fire.

We will go into the world suffering with you. Because we love the new life that is waiting for us. It is full of strength and sorrow. We must endure and stay silent. We must live in solitude in a strange city, envying the carriage driver cursing in the language everyone around him understands; and as we mingle in the evening, dejected, among unfamiliar faces that don't even dream of our existence, our gaze lifts beyond the impenetrable houses, trembling with grief and pride. We must suffer within our meagre human limits, unable to quiet the sobs of a sister, or to help a friend who's lost his way, and wonders *Why?*

Ah my brothers, how good it would be to feel confident and proud, enjoying our intelligence, plundering the vast lush fields with our young strength, to know, command, and possess! But tense with pride, hearts burning with shame, we reach our hands out to you, and beg you to be fair with us, as we strive to be fair with you. Because we love you, my brothers, and hope you will love us. We yearn to love and work.

PART TWO

From *Political Writings: Letters on Trieste*

Trieste Has No Cultural Traditions

Do you know Herzeleide?[1] She dressed her son Parsifal in fool's clothes and deliberately gave him poor advice so that he wouldn't be able to leave her in search of adventure and glory. And when he left – for good – his mother's heart was broken.

There is very nearly the same relationship between Parsifal and Herzeleide as there is between culture and Trieste.

Trieste, in the last few decades, has considered herself an important city. She woke up one day between a box of citrus fruit and a sack of coffee, thinking that she should – for the sake of her health – accord her life to another rhythm, beyond the blows of a steam engine, and delight herself with something more than the melody of silver coins jangling inside the pockets of her bulging vest. City of commerce, true: but so is Venice, and Genoa. And, for heaven's sake, even Florence at the time of Dante and Poliziano. More prominently in Trieste, more so than in Venice, Genoa, and Florence, the struggle for her own national identity – this Trieste realized in her awakening – could also give rise to her culture. And this was fortunate, because intellectual resistance is virtually the only force capable of withstanding the great incisive, dynamic virtue of the Slavs. Thus, Trieste noticed with joy that something haphazard, vague, at times feverish, was moving in her: a something that did not know its way. And her motherly soul grieved for not having known in time to guide her. This is Herzeleide: if her heart does not break it is because the young Triestine Parsifal does

1 [Reference to Wagner's opera *Parsifal* (1882). Herzeleide is Parsifal's mother. After Parsifal's father died, his mother raised him isolated in a forest, in the hope of keeping him safe. Wagner's operas were regularly performed in Trieste's Opera House Giuseppe Verdi. See Karyl Charna Lynn, *Italian Opera Houses and Festivals*, Scarecrow Press, 2005, 86–7.]

not yet have the strength to leave, in addition to not knowing the way. Trieste created him with too frail a soul.

He wanders in the forest, banging his nose against tree trunks; he sets out, but by now so many roads lead to the court of King Arthur! Whereas once upon a time ... Anyway, what was there then, once upon a time, we'll soon see.

A Celtic village belonging to the Carnia region, a small settlement stifled by the more dynamic Aquileia under the Roman Empire: in the Middle Ages, as soon as it was emancipated from servitude to the bishopric, it had to pay tribute to Venice; it did not develop into a true city until later, when Emperor Charles VI chose it as the Austrian commercial hub in the Adriatic, proclaiming it a free port. [2] And even more so under Maria Theresa, who extended the customs' exemption to the whole city, so that wares would not just pass through in transit. Some numbers: in 1717 (proclamation of the free port), 5,600 inhabitants; in 1808, 33,020; a collapse of almost 13,000 people during the French occupation, reaching 39,510 in 1818. In 1844 (the Lloyd had been established eight years earlier), 57,000; in 1857 (Trieste was connected by railway to the North Sea twenty years earlier), 123,108 inhabitants; in 1908, it had 220,000 people. Thus, an increase of 187,000 in a century; one can say that the complete development of the city took two centuries. This can be explained only through immigration.

But – it should be noted – because of its geographic, ethnic, and commercial position, its population of Italian compatriots did not increase, as happened in many cities of the peninsula; instead it assimilated people from all over the world, seduced by the ease of profits and by all kinds of enticing privileges and guarantees that Charles VI – clever beguiler – had issued.

And because the city, in all possible ways, enthusiastically embraced its hybrid development, it had no scruples – just as Maria Theresa wished – in accepting new citizens: so much so that it became a true asylum for crooks. I understand that Rome was its example! It is amusing to see how in some applications for citizenship (brought to light by Giuseppe Caprin) it was considered reference enough to have had a foreign police record. It's easy to see why Corfu does not have an intellectual tradition.[3]

2 [Carnia is the name of the alpine area in the north-eastern region of Friuli-Venezia Giulia.]

3 [Giuseppe Caprin (1843–1904), journalist, writer, and historian, author of many books on the history of Trieste. The comment on Corfu might be a reference to Tommaseo's *Il supplizio d'un italiano in Corfù: Esposizione e discussione di Niccolò Tommaseo* (Florence, Barbéra, Bianchi e Comp. tipografi-editori, 1855). In this text Tommaseo describes the tensions arising in Corfu between the Greek indigenous population and the Italian refugees who escaped there after the failure of the 1848 revolutionary uprisings in Italy. Tommaseo became for the Triestines of Slataper's generation the emblem of Italian patriotism and of that "cultural irredentism" that Slataper embraced.]

But even setting aside this fact of little importance, the many tens of thousands of foreign and business immigrants were certainly not a cultural asset for the city: more so considering that the bill of Charles VI relieved them completely of the honours and obligations of civic life. Obligations? Oh, then the original settlers were able to obtain from the goddess Maria Theresa equality in rights and duties: and so the Borgo Teresiano, a true German city surrounding the Italian city, was incorporated into Trieste, which had (and still has, luckily for her) the virtue of being capable of assimilating so indigestible a morsel. But how can we think about the development of the city's culture when a great number of families are neither Triestine nor Italian? And our surnames (like mine! pure Slavic) are evidence of this fact.

Assimilation, yes, but obviously in due time. In the meanwhile, every singular nationality lived its own separate life; each had its own cafes, and social clubs, and its own environment.

These are the conditions of our lives. But they would not count for much and would be greatly ignored if it weren't for the essential mercantile character of Trieste, which encompasses all, looming over everything like a leaden weight on our history. Mercury,[4] as in the nineteenth-century statuettes adorning our palaces and our wall niches (it was even discussed whether he should have a place in the new theatre!), always reigned supreme over us.

The importance of Trieste is due to its commercial victories. She takes life from the ashes of Aquileia, and the sunset of Venice is the light of dawn for her. She knows how to be a good advocate for her own interests, how to gain new railroad lines and exemptions at customs. She fights – sometimes bravely – when her wealth is threatened; but she is unable to protect her beautiful Ladin dialect,[5] her traditions, or her distinctive festivals. For Trieste, for a while, possessed – and might have had many reasons to express – her own unique character, different in particular aspects from that of other Italian cities. And even lacking an independent impulse or equal merit, it is certain that Trieste would have been able to compete somehow with Italy's magnificent literary production. But her soul, drained by its financial preoccupations, was too simple to discern greater aspirations, and she was too obtuse to see that at a certain point material development could not progress any further without the help of intellectual strength. For this reason, the story of Trieste is frozen: without an outlet for its aspirations, without need of art, without

---

4 [Mercury was a major Roman god, patron, among other things, of commerce and financial gain.]

5 [Ladin is a Rhaeto-Romance dialect spoken in north and north-eastern Italy.]

care of its soul. Slave to her compulsive thirst for profit, she could never look ahead boldly and imaginatively, not even to open new routes for her commerce; she never had even a minor version of Christopher Columbus or Marco Polo. The city does not possess a painting by an old master (my mistake: she owns one *attributed* to Giottino!), or a decent art museum: not only was she incapable of producing them, she would not even buy them – yet she could have afforded to, if she only had the desire.[6]

Istria was much more advanced: therefore, it was greatly damaged by the assimilating power of the city of Trieste as an administrative centre, capital of the Littoral, or of the province of Istria, depending on who was in charge: Maria Theresa, Napoleon, or Francis I. It was like an older sister, which is what Istria – and I don't quite understand why – calls us today. Istria, on the other hand, has a tradition of heroic deeds from pre-Roman times, and of Venetian art; we have nothing. The Genoese were right to steal our Lion of Saint Mark: for Triestines, it had no meaning.[7]

It is sad to trace the life of Trieste. She feels the need for independence, for emancipation from the bishop's rule, and more than once buys her freedom. In 1369 Venice lays siege to her, brutally, for six months; to surrender means to lose her trading identity, so instead she sells herself to everyone: to Leopold III, to the patriarchs of Aquileia, to the Carrara in Padua, to the Visconti, to Louis of Hungary, to Charles IV. All in vain: they wink at her and then they're gone. She calls out again to Leopold III, who finally arrives, but without result. Do you know the *Saica*, the *Beautiful Carinthian*?[8] It was a ship made of softwood, invented in Trieste, which would sell herself with all her wares, so that she would not have to make the return trip empty of merchandise. Trieste is a *Saica* throughout the centuries; but I would never imply that Trieste is the *Beautiful Carinthian*.

Instead she is a clever cosmopolitan: she understands that Venice accepted her independence in the treaty of Turin (1381) only because Venice was somewhat weak; and Trieste believes that she is ready for what's to come. Does she take up arms? No. Nor does she submit to the patriarchs of Aquileia who were her natural defenders, because they

---

6 [Giottino was the pseudonym of the Florentine painter Tommaso di Stefano (1324–57).]

7 [Reference to a statue of the Lion of St. Mark that belonged to Trieste. In 1380, when Trieste was under the control of the Venetians, the statue was taken by the Genovese troops during their occupation of the city. The Triestine historian Giuseppe Caprin, in his book *Il Trecento a Trieste* (F.H. Schimpff, 1897), revealed the unknown history of this statue, which became a symbol of the city's Italian identity.]

8 [Slataper's information about this strange ship designed to be sold with its cargo on its port of arrival comes from Giuseppe Caprin, *I nostri nonni*, G. Caprin, 1888, 23.]

were exhausted by squabbles, skirmishes, and debts. Instead she remembers the duke Leopold III; and her second submission to the House of Austria is a masterpiece of cleverness. Experience taught her that it was insufficient to accept the political authority of Austria to receive Austrian protection. It was necessary to submit to its dominion: Trieste would become Austrian; Trieste's interests would become its interests. Material assistance, soldiers, and weapons would follow; also, an increase in trade. For only the house of Austria could force the inhabitants of the interior to funnel all their wares through Trieste. Yet her autonomy and municipal government were firmly and undeniably respected. However, even at the truly glorious moment (perhaps the only one) when Trieste defended with her own blood the traditions of her municipality, not all her citizens were with her. Many, even then, remained shopkeepers, shopkeepers, shopkeepers.

A few decades ago, a Triestine remembering Dall'Ongaro stated, "Here, if a flower is born, it's turned into a business." Unfortunately, this is really true.[9] Some examples: at the beginning of the twentieth century there were three printing presses in Trieste. Internally, they were used to printing trade gazettes and notices; externally, to earn money, they printed the invectives of political refugees, without taking any interest in them. Also, in 1810, the Minerva Society emerges, thanks to the endeavour of Domenico Rossetti, a foreigner: Minerva the healer, vaccinator of children, goddess of botany, learning, and literature. In any case: Minerva. After a few years the conferences, art exhibits, and competitions promoted by the society are transformed into contests for writing business letters. Thus, all that noble activity of half the last century, represented by the *Favilla*, is the work of single individuals: Madonizza, Orlandini, Dall'Ongaro, Gazzoletti, and a few others.[10] And to entice

---

9 [Francesco Dall'Ongaro (1808–73) poet, intellectual and Italian patriot, was for a time the director of the Triestine literary and cultural journal *La Favilla*. He believed that culture could help foster a sense of Italian national identity within the multiethnic city of Trieste.]

10 [*La Favilla* was the first literary journal published in Trieste. Founded in 1836 by Antonio Madonizza (1806–80), it was financially backed by the Austrian Lloyd. The journal aimed at providing cultural and intellectual stimulation to the city's wealthy bourgeoisie. It also reported on the industrial and commercial growth of the multiethnic city. The title of the journal (The spark) was inspired by Dante's verse "Great fire may follow a small spark" in *The Divine Comedy, Paradiso* I, 34. Allen Mandelbaum and Barry Moser, *The Divine Comedy of Dante Alighieri,* U of California P, 1980. Giovanni Orlandini (1804–77) worked for a short time as the director of *La Favilla*. He was a romantic nationalist inspired by Mazzini and led the short-lived 1848 anti-Austrian revolt in Trieste. Antonio Gazzoletti (1813–66), a lawyer and collaborator of *La Favilla*, participated in that revolt.]

their followers to read the most serious articles, even they must pacify their subscribers with mundane gossip about fashion and business.

"Great fire may follow a small spark" was the journal's motto. Where is the great fire? If two or three personalities are still remembered, it is because of their activities in Italy; the others, who remained in Trieste, are unknown or forgotten. And this was the second time that everything seemed to point towards a life of scientific and intellectual achievement.

Nothing came of it, ever. For this reason, the (terribly damaging!) exodus of our best minds is understandable; and it is still going on, indeed it is encouraged – as Dall'Ongaro demonstrates – for political reasons.

We will soon analyse in other articles what it means to be a city fraught with such a historical burden, built of dry figs and carob pods, her legs ensnared in politics, with a soul so heterogeneous that leading figures take flight, rather than lose their bearings. These articles will state simple facts, as this one has: familiar to any Triestine who has read the three or four important books of local history, and especially familiar if they have looked around and within themselves with serious, honest attention. Simple facts, said without fear – not even the fear of addressing others, including fellow countrymen in Italy, who may already know these issues in great depth.

The Life of the Spirit

Finally! To delve deeply into this matter is like falling into a briar patch: it will scratch you. But it was my moral duty to be clear, against the usual myopic rhetoric: so as not to start down the path of a foolish idea, and then grope around for some stable ground, only to stumble and fall. Even so, after having filled my eyes with facts so as not to get lost under such a vast sky, I still can't find my way in the spiritual life of Trieste. Can you imagine a restless child, let loose in a dimly lit room, littered with obstacles?

Usually, to understand the culture of a city, you need to climb a bit above it, to the hill of abstraction; here, with the omnipotence of thought, you stop the continuous movement of events, separating two or three causes from the wagons of effect; you put on thesis-tinted glasses and go overboard.

In Trieste, I'm not able to do this. I would admit my ignorance and be silent if someone else could do it. But I am only acquainted with studies that reflect on the manifestation of the spirit from a literary point of view, which is the most obvious, and the easiest to address. Nothing, however, that deals with the entirety of the issue. Should I try? No, I'll just provide my notes. Whoever is more capable than I am can synthesize them in their argument.

So, we already understand each other: an all-encompassing inner life, not just a scientific or literary life. Whoever clings to the skirt of literature is unable to see or praise any other lady. And because in Italy we all cling to her a bit, even if the history of our communes or of the Hanseatic cities convinces us of the importance of economic culture, we ignore it because we are unable to acknowledge its role in the history of every city. Or we express it badly, just as I am doing now while writing about Trieste, because I cannot pretend it does not exist.

Trieste has a true commercial tradition that by now should have blossomed into a commercial culture. We struggled against much adversity for centuries: let's look there to discern our intellectual development. We see a pragmatic attitude everywhere. To satisfy a given need, a keen inventive genius creates the necessary means; a strong nose is shoved into the most tangled mess, capable of distinguishing what is profitable from what is not; capable, also, of choosing even the most tenuous-looking snare, if suited to attain the desired outcome; capable of offsetting an unforeseen disaster, with much anticipated profit; and not prone to losing heart, when clashing against an obstacle, but capable of turning back to look for a new, unobstructed path, willing it to be better than the first. As everyone can see, I am expressing virtues that run in the blood of every true businessman, and therefore, also in the blood of Trieste. Well, if such sharp intellectual skills could be applied to different fields, then sound artistic or scientific expressions have the potential to emerge. Our practical energy will not exhaust itself in business-like concerns: how wonderful is the sudden bloom of virginal spirituality in a fertile field, under a benevolent sun! I'm dreaming, looking to the future. I should focus on the present, which is unable to create an economic culture from its business in trade. Because the kind of heavy trading volume that compels the mind to more conceptual thoughts and wider ideas is still very young in Trieste. Furthermore – and this may be an additional cause – Trieste is poor in that conceptual *quid* that synthesizes intellectually what the senses are able to perceive.

Only in exceptional cases does an individual seek out in books a broad understanding of commerce as a human activity. Usually, an individual is unable to conceptualize general laws; his experience comes directly from the senses. He constructs his edifice: but he rarely adds a superfluous adornment to make it aesthetically pleasing. There are no tall chimneys reaching above, towards the heights, towards the eternal: what you see is smog! And, down below, no drizzle falls between the well-connected rooftops. Therefore when it comes to job qualifications, a person who spent his youth studying at the commercial institute is worth less than a person with a practical apprenticeship; master bricklayers are plentiful and supremely busy, while architects are few, and underemployed; and attendance is low at the Commercial Institute.[1]

1 [The Scuola Superiore di Commercio was created in 1877 by Baron Pasquale Revoltella (1795–1869) in order to meet the growing professional and practical needs of the Triestine business class. The institute focused on all business- and trading-related disciplines.]

Now, it is true, there is growth. And we even have a museum of commerce now. The yearning for a university like Bocconi or the German ones insinuates itself among the youth who would like to devote themselves to commerce. Because of these changes, an old classmate of mine, who is obsessed with trade, now feels very hopeful. I do as well, but I am not actually competent to evaluate these changes.

Moreover, even if to a lesser degree, Trieste lacks the disposition to forge an industrial culture. On these two solid foundations we will build our culture – which, for now, is not much, and is still uncertain. It is true that since I became more acquainted with the culture of the Kingdom of Italy, ours has not seemed so insignificant; for almost the same reason, I do not inveigh as much against the Austrian police, since I learned more about the Italian version. But it is always like a cutting planted in the wrong soil: the leaf hints at blooming, but without true vigour. In its veins runs the awful tension of opposing forces: the spirit that with the faith of a neophyte becomes restless and longs for power, versus the weight of the past that oppresses and stifles it. On top of this, Austria is crushing our bones. We awakened: from the open window a breath of air purer than the one wafting from ship holds and warehouses has flooded our soul. We gazed around us, at the strange, lively commotion, deprived of any apparent aim, all of it glowing with an enthusiasm that seemed beautiful, even to us. Could it be that this mental effort, which created a need in our souls, and a belief in realizing its potential through action, was the necessary training for an emancipated life? Then we realized that it would have been naive folly to trust lazily in the omnipotence of commercial prosperity alone, when our souls most needed respect from others, and self-awareness, which could only be achieved through spiritual activity aimed at a greater purpose. Domenico Rossetti (it bothers me to mention him constantly, but he is our greatest citizen), the members of the Minerva Society, which he founded, the writers of *Favilla*, and also – why not! – the German Count Stadion, governor of Trieste from 1841 to 1847, were the first to be convinced of this idea.[2] Then, as time went by, this idea gained the approval of the younger generation. This is true of Trieste: each generation is greater than the last. The son, in national and cultural endeavour alike, surpasses the father. The dawn of the new generation burns brighter than the sunset. We are rising.

---

2 [Domenico Rossetti: see *My Karst*, p. 39, note 19. Franz Seraph Count of Stadion (1806–53) was an Austrian politician. From 1841 to 1847 he was the governor of the Austrian littoral provinces (Gorizia, Gradisca, and Trieste). Here he demonstrated his talent and enlightened attitudes by adopting more liberal policies in matters of police control and censorship.]

But we want to achieve too much too soon. Without proper training at a lower altitude, we look for the highest handhold. We want to jump because others can do it. A young girl who wears mama's large hat and high-heeled boots to be as tall as her mother, that's Trieste. She found the latest trends of Italy's centuries-long cultural activity, in ready-made form; she added some scraps of cloth, and she dressed up. But it was *her* science, *her* literature that should have validated her Italian sentiments. Separated from Italy? But books have no borders. And she kept climbing upwards, also thanks to conferences that disseminated culture, the only thing that can nourish us. I already noted the work of the socialists in this regard; it is the best proof that our taste conforms to Italy, even if certain Graz beer drinkers would state the opposite. However, conferences, which are certainly a unifying bond, do not allow us to participate fully in the spiritual life of Italy. Even if they are frequent and important, they are just moments; they teach us, but their teachings don't become energy for thought or discussion. Sometimes, it seems to me – it might be a dream – that the conferences that come to us from Venice by train or steamer bring us boxes filled with butterflies: ideas that the lepidopterist caught on pretty Italian meadows. Shut in their boxes, they grow feeble and weak. But then, set free in Trieste, they become "So beautiful! So beautiful!"

And this affectionate curiosity that we show towards what is almost new, we also display towards books coming from Italy, even if they have nothing new to teach us. Trieste does not trust herself: Triestine publications are considered provincial and worthless; even if the local newspapers and their readers – sometimes joined in one limited conceptual sphere – let the bells ring out in self-celebration. A book published in Trieste is assumed to have been rejected by an Italian publisher. But this isn't the case: our editions of the Italian Classics (printed by typographers at Lloyd) are better than those from the other side of the Judrio.[3] A dozen Triestine books, published in Trieste, are worth much more than the many Triestine books published in Italy. But the prejudice against them is a foregone conclusion. Trieste does not have a cultured environment capable of giving confidence to booklovers. We don't have the brains to create it. The political parties hang on, even to someone who will shuffle them randomly without a clear vision. Felice Venezian, who, in spite of some mistakes, was a great thinker, was mourned by members of the Liberal Party as though they were mourning their own death.[4] The socialist

---

3 [See *My Karst*, p. 19, note 26.]

4 [Felice Venezian: see *My Karst*, p. 35, note 8.]

party has no intellectual tendency: very well! But aside from economic issues, they grope in the dark. Our political culture is still immature.

There is, of course, the school system. But we lack a university that could expand our culture and bring it to full life.[5] Our teachers either suffocate you under the weight of science, or ruin you with stale literary sentimentality; and they leave you so absolutely empty that, no matter who you are, you must recognize this once you're done with school. What about our gratitude? Keep calm. I for one can state that I only had teachers of the other type, those who are still men, even after earning a university degree. And luckily, there are some of these even here in Trieste; and happily, I had more than one of them, but the excellence of the few betrays my frustration with the many. But it is no matter. In this, I am in the company of all my fellow citizens.

That's right: when a group of young teachers boldly tried to publish *Il Palvese*, attempting to revitalize our culture by reconnecting it to the many failed attempts initiated by *La Favilla*, my fellow citizens were bored.[6] This proved that these teachers were not effective enough to support a truly innovative *Palvese*; it also proved that in the long run their *Palvese* was tiresome. Could it have improved with time? Well, Trieste, like almost all other financial centres, expects an immediate correlation between aspiration and action. What about education? "Listen, my child: you must have a career, a brilliant career!" For this reason, the theatre has always thrived and continues to thrive: it's entertainment, without any effort. However, our concert hall, for a nobler reason, is one of the finest in Italy: our citizens, for the large part, have a refined predisposition towards music. It suffices to say that it is taught in three conservatories and that the musical soirees at the People's University[7] are a delight for Trieste.

But I was talking about us, our tendency towards procrastination. Our cafes, as in all great capitals, offer hundreds of magazines and periodicals:

---

5 [See Introduction, note 26.]

6 [The *Palvese* was a literary magazine published in 1907 by Maylander (1877–1943), a Triestine intellectual originally from Croatia. Its aim was to give voice to the artistic and intellectual endeavours of the Italians who were living under Austrian rule. Both the poet Umberto Saba and Scipio Slataper published their first articles in this venue. The short-lived journal celebrated Italian literary figures such as D'annunzio and Carducci, but it also introduced its readership to the works of Scandinavian and other European authors.]

7 [The Università Popolari, or People's Universities, are institutions that became popular throughout Europe at the turn of the twentieth century. Their aim was to educate the masses by offering courses and conferences open to all. Trieste opened its People's University in 1900.]

truly ephemeral collections, as every collection of periodicals that wants to reflect the transitory nature of its holdings should be. When we were stimulated by intellectual desire, Italy quickly came to our aid, just like a mother runs to her daughter with coffee and buttered toast as soon as she, just awakening, rings a little bell. Getting out of bed, starting the fire, and making her own coffee? Are you kidding! So, we lack the spiritual perseverance that would strengthen our actions and allow us to achieve our desires. We are lazy: not because we are not doing anything, but because our particular situation requires much more. Aware of our Italian identity, we withdraw into the Italian way of thinking. We do not complement it with what would be our essence, if we were to express our painful existence with some force. At least we would gain a bit of respite for our little interior life! Instead, we are cowards. We are afraid of what surrounds us: if our spirit were to dwell on it, it would be shattered. There is a terrible anxiety in our affairs, but we keep it hidden, we do not probe it with any analysis. The complex reality remains concealed: today we see a part of it, and maybe we examine and understand it, and tomorrow we examine another part, and if need be, we remedy it: a small change to preserve our daily tranquility. But to look at all these parts in a comprehensive manner, within their context – no, that we won't do!

And yet, this is what we need to do! We must discover the cause of our restlessness, and fight it, without respite. Because Trieste cannot know a moment of truce; pretending might be necessary due to our fatigue, but it is incredibly damaging. Maybe we should shake the apathetic and lazy ones awake, grabbing them by the hair. Everyone who doesn't want to acknowledge the circumstances, and would rather endure them passively, is apathetic. We are in direct contact with other civilizations; however, the indolent ones, unable to confront and resolve the conflict between politics and reason until they can see that this conflict is only superficial, are unwilling to try to transform the damage produced by this direct contact into an advantage. Like all developing spirits we search for ourselves while becoming slaves to others. We speak German: we could command all Nordic literature; instead, we are indolent, and let ourselves become overwhelmed by it. Or, stupidly, we look down on it. We must defend ourselves from the Slovenes; but what if we let the Slavic genius and enthusiasm strengthen us? Our soul would expand if we could accept them as a new strength; they would replenish our energy, the same way our numbers were replenished by the assimilation of Germans and Slavs.

We must fight our own revulsion, and accept that Trieste is Italian in a different way from other Italian cities. This is more useful than fighting to convince some of the most reluctant in Italy that Trieste, even if in a different way, is indeed Italian. Then we need to express this difference.

Trieste does not know herself yet. She knows her history only in bits and pieces, but she throws herself headlong, with youthful enthusiasm, into big issues and ideas. Her natural beauty is still untouched by the human gaze or given artistic expression, because it is rarely discussed by guidebooks and almost never by poets. Instead, Triestines travel in search of places accessible to everyone for years now, thanks to Baedeker. Trieste ... but where else is existence such a dreadful torment of contrasting forces, overwhelming longing, cruel struggle and desperation?

Trieste feels Italy's heart pulsating in the coming and going of Adriatic waves: like a daughter clinging to her mother's breast. And the strong arms of the Alps hold her as to a mother's breast. Alas! The crumbling away of the pebbles in the Judrio's riverbed resounds with a wicked and ironic crackling. She is all alone. But she is inflamed with courage: she is *not* alone! Trentino, Friuli, Istria, and Dalmatia are with her. All close, a small family of brothers ... the mother is gone. She has her own affairs to attend to. A sob of agony? Down there is Dalmatia ... Well, let's defend what is still alive! Italian Trieste feels more and more, around her, inside her, the chill of death emanating from Istria, from Gorizia: like the gathering of the waves swelling against the cliffs.

But all this does not change anything: she is Italian. And she is also the end market for German interests. She must demand one, two railway lines that connect her to Germany. She must rejoice in the wares nourishing her commerce, and in the mixed race that brings her trade.

This is the torment of her two natures that incessantly try to annihilate each other: one business, the other Italian. And Trieste cannot do without either: it is her double soul, it would kill her. Everything necessary for her business is a violation to her Italian identity; whatever increases one undermines the other.

She recognizes the importance of the German but must fight it. She is afraid of the Slavic banks, but becomes their client. A relentless conflict: thus, the compromises, hopeless and sad, to lay it to rest.

Trieste is Italian: but she must find higher learning in Graz or Vienna. She quietly let the great events of Italian redemption pass her by, filling in the breaks with shouting and sighs: unredeemed! And irredentist consciousness rises once Italy is unified; it appears only when, in Italy, it is a memory of the past.

Unredeemed and Italian: she has four internationalist deputies and a Slavic one. She longs for Rome, but she must turn to Vienna. From Vienna she does not obtain anything, and she must struggle to survive on her own. In Trieste, like foreign currencies long ago, the languages, ideas, and customs of half the world can circulate freely.

This is Trieste. Composed of tragedy. In sacrificing the possibility of a straightforward existence, Trieste gains her own anxious originality. We must sacrifice our peace in order to give it expression. But express it we must. The first babbles in this idiom can be found at the time of the *Favilla.* Even if this is no longer the case, our dialect differed from Italian dialects. Let's not forget that it was once Ladin. Our soul is different, even today: it cannot contain all its contradictions within a single frame of thought, deriving from simpler circumstances. Trieste has a Triestine type. It must strive for a Triestine art capable of reproducing, through joyful clear expression, our fragmented and difficult existence.

When I think of her, I feel the pointlessness of these cold reports of mine. And I would gladly throw away my pen. But no: for the nightingale to sing, we must first quiet the squawking crows.

PART THREE

From *Literary and Critical Writings*

To Young Italian Intellectuals

And so we young people, showing disdain or outright hostility to critical work, turn to publishing the customary first volume of poems or short stories, a play or a novel: that is, given that our benevolent relative lends us two hundred lire, and our distinguished colleague or noble friend is already drunk on the vapours of our work, and ready to predict refulgent glory, we flash one glimmer of intelligence in an infinite fog of stupidity, and here we are, in the thick of life. Around this entanglement, sometimes, but often not, flitter about – like flies around something that stinks – some trivial little things: studies, and material labour.

We say: "We're young and want to express what we feel and what we think, not to rehash what so many distinguished authors worthy of oblivion have already expressed" – Good! But then, dear contemporaries, this clever premise leads to the following: If our lover scorns us, we respond with verses; if Italy needs ships, verses; and verses again, if our sister is about to die; verses for all our troubles! This belief, that poetry or that spur-of-the-moment literary work is to young people as babble is to a baby,[1] is a false truth owing to the exalted self-interest of both young and old: we are concerned with indulging the author-to-be, they with the already established author. Because it is not at all true that the fresh effusions of youth equal art. There might be some art there, if it could be expressed exactly as it is. But when we take up our accursed pen, few droplets of this fresh impetus trickle down: and how many of us have the courage to believe this is really the best that our personality can give at that given moment? How many are honest, how many are truly sincere, among us young people? So we yield up waves of reminiscences, like petit-bourgeois borrowing to look like big shots. Or we warp things,

1 [In the original, "*il pappo e 'l dindi,*" phrase used in Dante, *Purgatorio* XI, 105.]

trying to manufacture originality with mechanical processes and bizarre fakeries, disfiguring that new vision of things that is in fact common to all youth and that can be seen readily in certain naive activities, among friends, when we know no one who sees things another way and might mock us or condemn us is watching us.

Thus, we live in the company of ourselves and our friends. And if something stronger than fashion compels us, let's write for ourselves and our friends. But let's not publish. Fix this in your mind: the time of precocious, spontaneous bardic pronouncements is over, if it ever existed; modern poets are like Leopardi and Carducci: those who labour to eliminate all concerns and tricks that rot the artistic conception. It is no wonder criticism has infiltrated our blood. To pretend not to feel it is for cowardly fools. Or the very rare exception. And you, for example, you are certain of being the next D'Annunzio. And the success of "Vere novo" would be enough for you: one year of immortality.[2] If that is the case, you can stop reading me.

Yet I know that every young person worthy of life believes that life waits for him like a messiah. The admiration of a narrow circle of friends is not enough. He thinks of those who are far away; those who are far away matter more; and he cries out, because he wants to hear the collective soul resonate with his own.

I love this young man as I love myself. And to him I say: forgive me if this seems cruel, but the poetry of the twenty-year-old doesn't resonate with anyone. Old people are critical, and young people know how to be so with the works of others. Often the poetry you wrote and published doesn't move you any longer. When we do not yet have hands capable of crushing our passions, crushing them to squeeze out their juice to feed people, we must live them and suffer them ourselves, in the secret of our soul; not turn them into enemies and allow the sneering pity of others to spoil them and rough hands to molest our still inexperienced, delicate soul. Eagles or hawks are needed to soar among men: don't trust their obliging praise, because it's false. Sincere approval is a cry of commitment; and men fight more than ever today before they surrender, my friend.

So then what should we do? We write: but to clarify for ourselves who we are. And since to publish and become known is more essential than bread for us young people, on the side of this intimate art of ours, that

---

2 ["Vere novo" is the title of a poem included in D'Annunzio's first collection of poetry, entitled *Primo vere* (In early spring), published in 1879, when the poet was only sixteen years old.]

we alone know and imbibe as stimulus for our improvement, let's do some practical work.

No sooner have I pronounced the word "practical" than I already feel a collective churning of the stomach: is it you young unknowns, or close friends, or even this unknown and dear friend, myself? It's a little of all of them. How strange: it would seem that young Italians are a generation of cloud merchants and packagers of the void! And I haven't suggested at all that we become farmers or stevedores or bricklayers or pork merchants; and not even – but this would be so good! – talented engineers and courageous industrialists and traders. No: that would be too sudden a revolution. Instead, here and ready, there is a small, basic program that doesn't completely upturn our status as literary dilettantes, that is, as people living in a special world of ideas, which – it must be said – has begun to reek. It's not rotting yet, but it would be a good idea to throw open the windows and even the door, to draw in (from the *countryside*, Papini!) a good mountain breeze, even to give those weak in the chest a good sneeze. Let's edge into life, which whirls like an enormous spirit; the problems of the spirit are not worked through between a feeble chest and a dirty inkwell. There are so many acres of doubt and misery in Italy now, just waiting for someone to set a spade into the earth. Take heart! Do we really have to be so weak?

Listen: in all of us lives, more or less, a practical man we try to stifle in favour of a man of ideas. And by pushing far enough, many of us end up stifling him for good, and we end up staring at our belly button and believing it, round as it is with its edge squashed, to be a microcosm that reflects the macrocosm, and other similar idiocies. But we are artists, and this idea that art hides itself under action is a silly masquerade – We're all artists? By the nine Muses! all young people, you mean to say. And for my part, I prefer the mask to excessive makeup to appear beautiful. And what a mask! What is this piecemeal reduction of the spirit, which is one single formidable whole, complete in itself?

But you fear that it might crash down onto you; so give me the little tin sabre, good mother, and the cardboard hammer, and I'll shatter the block! And this poet, or whatever he is, who has no tolerance for the multifarious life of his time, and curls up like a snail in the damp cave of his own thought, perhaps sticking out his antennae to feel which way the wind is blowing? Or that other one, who withdraws into the country because he doesn't have the energy to consider the human problems that the city – monstrous dynamo of life – continually creates, smooths, roughens, and dissolves; he lies down among the trees because it annoys him to be dragged along by a wave of strikers, and he walks in the meadow because the city pavement is too hot? Yes to the countryside and to self-concentration; but only as preparation, as immersion. As soon as we come into contact with anything primal, we go back to our wild nature, we housecats and idlers. So that we can truly experience life today with a sense of wonder, of anger, reverence, and *love*.

To be moderns! To embody in ourselves the vital forms proper to our era: that is – don't twist your little mouths, dear contemporaries – asexual women turned off by the contact of man; workmen who extract from intense misery a ferocious new myth, a violent idealism; priests who have been defeated by life, wrapped in vestments embroidered in gold, gnawed by past centuries; one nation after another, rising with the sun; two populations glistening with heartache and yearning, each wielding rebar and heaps of coal to throw each other off their earthly throne, while one race favoured by the future looks on without sneering, and sees a civilization's coats of arms crumble – but does not gloat, and proceeds onward smiling, the cataphract of a new history; a reshuffling of the stagnant morality, because muck is necessary to fertilize new growth; a terrible seriousness that arrests us and entraps us in cheerful trivialities, so that we are horrified at the sight of this organism, made of humanity in pain and the ravishing agony of rebirth; flashes of childish innocence that burn or illumine us, frozen tremors, shouts, cries of anguish and joy; and yes, we too are returned to the pure absolute, to the brutality of the farmland, to escape this tragedy of houses each preventing the sun from shining on the other, to wait for the sun among the oaks, so that our spirit shines like that glinting plough ready to attack the grain.

This is the reality of today. And to probe into it, a knife takes the place of facts and figures. Alright then: we young people pour into our study the healthy qualities of our blood. And what about our poetry? If only humanity were so merciful! We would see things as deeply as Mazzini and Victor Hugo did. Not likely? Will we realize instead that we can only be submissive in life? If only Poetry were so merciful! Think of all the bad poems we would be spared!

To continually push forward and clarify this reality is our true culture. And you see right away that we have a responsibility to free others from false culture. To act: practical action, then. The latest clichés, like prostitutes, fools wearing teachers' wigs, empty Cupids publishing imitation Petrarch because their mother doesn't censor the press, professors who with every extra lira stoop over a little more … a whole world that has to be thrown onto the rubbish heap.

And then, yes, god what a bore! That art couldn't care less about all moral sermons of fat priests is something we know far better than anyone. And that Pindar only composed his odes on demand, just as, these days, that guy over there composes his slipshod comedies.[3] Only this is crucial: whether we're to be poets, or cobblers. These truths are no less true, no matter how old they become. But art has a morality of its own as well, a particular one, over and above human morality, because it outlives and precedes it: sincerity, freedom of the spirit from all moral judgments of the time, expansion of the unconscious like superheated steam, against the obstructive restriction of material needs, judgmental censorship, and the individual thirst for great celebrations resplendent with incense and gold. And when art is in the pulsing inner workings of a soul, and that person sees that by common consent art has become a business exchange between agents and bankers, he must feel his hands tighten and his fingers tremble with the need to grip these frauds by the neck. And yes: to strangle them.

Oh, you're an artist? This is our Rhodes, today. So jump to it.[4] Otherwise, there's a whip for you as well, my dear contemporaries: and we'll make you dance.

3 [Pindar (c. 552–443 BCE) was an ancient Greek lyric poet. "Slipshod comedies" is a reference to the dramas of Sem Benelli, whom Giovanni Papini compared to "nothing more than a used slipper of D'Annunzio, newly embroidered with some ugly Florentine lace." *Stroncature*, Valecchi Editore, 1920, 126.]

4 [Reference to Aesop's fable "The Boastful Athlete," where a man, after having spent much time abroad, boasted that while in Rhodes "he had jumped such a long jump that no man alive could equal it. A bystander, tired of his brag remarked, 'here is your Rhodes: go on and jump!'" *Aesop's Fables*, translated with introduction and notes by Laura Gibbs, Oxford UP, 2002.]

Futurism

I hope that sooner or later someone will take a closer look at the various poets who publish their verses in "futurist editions."[1] Their personalities are extremely diverse; so much so that if they were honest, the artistic vision of one of them would arouse in him an almost physical hatred for the others. Perhaps their alliance is merely calculated, in order to publicize their personalities, strengthening them here and there with bits that they have agreed to call "futurist faith." In reality, only their shared volume jacket can hold together a spiritually weak and consumptive writer, like Palazzeschi, for instance, with Buzzi, a young man with such strong lungs that he strives, no matter what, to ruin them by drawing breaths larger than his chest.[2] The jacket only holds them together; and also the obligatory homage to the leader Marinetti:

> So beautiful ... so Holy!
> Holy! Holy!
> Holy when you think of burning,

---

1 [Filippo Tommaso Marinetti (1876–1944), the spiritual leader of the avant-garde futurist movement in Italy, founded in 1910 the Edizioni Futuriste di Poesia (The futurist editions of poetry), a publishing house that supported the publication of futurist works.]

2 [Aldo Palazzeschi (1885–1974) was a poet and novelist who in his early work embraced the aesthetics of the crepuscular poets and also experimented with futurism. From 1909 to 1914 Palazzeschi and Marinetti were close collaborators. In 1911 the Edizioni Futuriste published Palazzeschi's *Codice di Perelà*, and Marinetti lauded the novel as a perfect example of futurist aesthetics. Their collaboration ended on the eve of the Great War. While Marinetti and the futurists embraced the interventionist position against Germany, Palazzeschi advocated a neutralist stance. Paolo Buzzi (1874–1956) was an Italian writer and poet who joined the futurist movement from its start in 1909.]

Holy when you catch fire,
Holy when you observe
your holy flames![3]

This reader comments: holy, according to futurist creed, is the one who pays. The reader is not trying to be witty nor does he want to speak ill of them. So-called futurism is just one attempt among many to create a spiritual movement whatsoever, only because you can afford it *commercially*. It arose from the vulgar misunderstanding that having the financial means to launch an idea is enough to bring it to fruition. It is the luxury of intellectuals who, having their veins filled with modern Milanese financial power, believed that they could assert their idea also in the highly aloof world of art. The futurists happily bare their teeth at D'Annunzio: however, they do not realize that D'Annunzio's desire to reform our drama by creating a Bayreuthian theatre, without Wagner,[4] matches their desire to renew Italian poetry by force of manifestos and clownish theatre stunts.

Because the futurist movement – let's call it that – lacks any true spiritual content. The very forms and practices of antagonism with which it tries to arouse awareness – the constant stream of manifestos, accompanied by the note that if someone will publish them, *Poesia*[5] will send as a gift this or that volume of their choice, etc., etc. – already reveal the lack of spiritual backbone in the movement they represent. And, if you look carefully, you will notice right away that this spirit – aesthetically – is an empty pretense of revolt, which plays with a very common critical truth, a truth that is transformed and then completely dissipated in these very commercial practices.

Their furor is not at all justified by a deep vision. After all, their historical world is an aestheticism puffed up into a boil injected with incongruous, repeated French expressions, which in France are the articulation of theoretical constructions that have been in place for a very long time. If their art was reduced to its core authentic expression, it would be imbued with a nostalgic feeling for faraway lands, where

---

3 [Aldo Palazzeschi, "L'incendiario," Edizioni Futuriste di Poesia, Milan, 1910. The poem was dedicated to Marinetti. English translation by Nicholas Benson, from Aldo Palazzeschi, *The Arsonist*, Otis Books/Seismicity Editions, 2013, 23–5.]

4 [Reference to the opera house that Richard Wagner built in the German city of Bayreuth in 1876.]

5 [*Poesia* was a journal published by Marinetti from 1905 to 1909. It hosted an eclectic array of poets from Italy and abroad. In 1909 the journal reprinted Marinetti's "The Founding Manifesto of Futurism," a manifesto that was originally published on 20 February 1909 in the French newspaper *Le Figaro*.]

adventures on land and sea are still possible: a decadent romanticism.[6] Their proclaimed love for modernity is nothing but an attempt to stifle this romantic content that they feel is dated, by overwhelming it with cars, airplanes, and torpedoes. They speak of freeing the spirit from the poetic myths of the past, but they are absolutely incapable of forging new myths from the new reality. Their artistic conception is filled with a materiality they are *unable to see*, or that they see as a wealthy bourgeois would: afraid of being struck by the newest car, he also buys one and, standing on his feet next to the driver, like a ruler, tall and portly, he spits on his equals who, frightened, pass by holding their noses. He spits on the frightened horror, in order not to get himself frightened and horrified by the speed.

They are very distant from the present reality. They don't think deeply at all because they are disturbed by a desire to act that is frustrated by their underdeveloped muscles. They attempt to believe, without conviction, that the meaning of our epoch, the one that could give a new Form to the eternal, constant, deepest insight, lies in its exterior appearance: the haste, the quick consumption of energy, Americanism, etc.[7]

This aesthetic pretence is based on a critical premise that, as I said earlier, is already a cliché. We all agree that academicism is an almost existential premise to the Italian spirit. Overall, our art and literature are deficient in works that do not express, in themselves, an absolute aesthetic value, but they do have an immense historical one: the liberating works of art, the ones that open up our crusted and decrepit soul.

The futurists want to free themselves from this state of mind. They put theory before practice; they immerse themselves in critical assertions; and they delude themselves or give the impression that they are inspired by a new god. Very true: we all want to identify ourselves not with Helios who drives his steeds across the sky, but with the labourer, who, sitting on a threshold, steadies his lunchbox between his tired legs, and gets his moustache dirty with *pasta e fagioli*. In this sense, we are all a bit futurist. We fight against ourselves and dig deep. On the contrary, Marinetti's futurists are completely unaware of their interior drama; rather, in order not to feel it, they shout. In order not to let it throw them into disarray,

---

6 [Here Slataper might have had in mind the young adult publication *Giornale illustrato dei viaggi e delle avventure di terra e di mare* (Illustrated journal of travels and adventures by land and sea), published from 1878 to 1931.]

7 ["Americanism" refers to superficial and often exaggerated admiration for anything American, at the expense of European cultural traditions. For Slataper's critique of Americanism, see Introduction, note 40.]

they make constant public statements that keep doubt at bay. To nourish themselves, they achieve an exterior certainty that is not there inside.

Because of this thoughtlessness, their books are read without any liberating joy. I do not believe at all that Marinetti's movement has any purpose, not even a historical one. Marinetti is the patron of the frenzied literary homunculus that lives in him as well as in all of his associates.

If the poet is really there, and what his value might be, that's another matter.

Crepuscular Confusion[1]

(On Guido Gozzano)

Corazzini, Gozzano, Saba, Moretti, Palazzeschi, F.M. Martini.[2] Let's join together these six little brothers belonging to the small Italian family of contemporary poetry; otherwise, one by one, they will get lost. Let's join them together, even if it is likely that one of the little brothers will raise his bald little head and, staring at me with terrified, big fearful eyes, will ask me in a high-pitched voice: Saba and Gozzano? Palazzeschi and Corazzini? How could they ever get along?

Because it's well known that the six little brothers look so much alike that family friends mistake them for one another, while they, the six brothers, counting each hair and the length of their noses, demonstrate their absolutely unique individuality.

Their personalities! Negative, passive, dull. Their ancestors had the loins of a buck and the stomach of a shark: as a result, their descendants are sickly, consumptive, scrawny, anxious, timid, diffident; at least, that's what they say. But we must understand: there is a moral law in man, and in all humankind, so that even poetry, the individual expression of human essence, has its history. You can't study a poet, not

---

1 [The term "crepuscular" was coined in 1910 by the writer and critic Giuseppe Antonio Borgese (1882–1952) to identify a new trend of poetry that privileged humble quotidian experiences, melancholic atmospheres, and a prosaic, understated tone. The poets identified as *crepuscolari* questioned the established trends of Italian poetry as represented by poets laureate such as Giosuè Carducci (1835–1907), Giovanni Pascoli (1855–1912), and Gabriele D'Annunzio (1863–1938). Crepuscular poetry emphasized the poets' vulnerability and inability to construct a totalizing coherent sense of the world they inhabited.]

2 [Sergio Corazzini (1886–1907); Guido Gozzano (1883–1916); Umberto Saba (1883–1957); Marino Moretti (1885–1979); Aldo Palazzeschi (1885–1974); Fausto Maria Martini (1886–1931).]

even from a formal perspective, if you don't know the historical trajectory of his spiritual demeanor. (This is why I believe that De Sanctis's work is great: precisely because he traces the singular poetic personalities, and their style, from the development of the Italian spirit.) But as with general history, so even with the history of poetry, it is impossible to simply apply the same law that works for the children of great men, or for American billionaires: after the greatest comes the least significant. In reality, even the least significant is, so to speak, a correction: it has a new, honest attitude that, returning to nature (i.e., resuming contact with life), opposes what is artificial in previous literary works. The incompetents, imitators who pass what is old and rotten for real blood, feed on this falsity; but the poets react with more or less violence and overblown criticism.

Let's admit it: our six child-like poets (I keep saying six, although the classical number should be seven; but not even for this reason can we include Guelfo Civinini) are indeed poets. At their core lies a shy human response, a sweet, feminine human response to the false, ostentatious magniloquence of Carducci and D'Annunzio.

From Carducci derives the annoying type the *prophet of the nation*, who clearly demonstrates that he does not believe in his homeland at the very moment he emphatically sings the nation's Roman origins, instead of just affirming plainly its modern greatness. Empty rhetoric, I believe, comes from this lack of active consciousness, this absence of passion, compensated for with clichés born out of habit; and it is immoral because it encourages weakness, while giving the impression of having instilled a moral value.

From Pascoli's bad seeds emerges the chalice of the humanitarian poet, who does not believe in humankind and acts out his afflictions badly, as if they were a small charity for the poor. From D'Annunzio we received as a gift the sylvan hero. Next to his imitators, animals with papier mâché horns, you can see Corazzini's heartfelt desperation. He is certain that "to be called a poet" it is necessary to live as they have sung. His naivety precludes him from seeing the emptiness of their poems! He believes them to be sincere – and because he is unable to live the way they do, he grieves sincerely that he is an inept at life. He gives up: "I am not a poet, then"; "All that I know, my God, is how to die."[3] Also, note,

3 [Sergio Corazzini, "Desolation of the Poor Sentimental Poet," first published in *Piccolo libro inutile* (Little useless book), Tipografia Operaia Romana, 1906; reprinted in Corazzini, *Sunday Evening: Selected Poems of Sergio Corazzini*, edited and translated by Michael Palma, Gradiva, 1997, 30–5.]

against his lamentations that disturb and dishearten us, Gozzano's own resignation and greater pride:

> Humanity? God? Country? Rhetoricians
> have mouthed the words so much they've made them nauseous!
> ...
> You seek an answer from the sorceress –
> the only truth worth knowing,
> Nature! – to have the power to catch in verse
> the mysteries she unveils to those who press.[4]

Here there is already hope for deliverance. And between these two extremes, generated by the same feelings – *I don't have faith: let's die! – No, let's start living again!* – with some rare attempts at well-being, unfolds the whole small and crepuscular activity of our "perplexed poets."

Uncertainty defines our existence. A word that belongs to the democratic era, that has rebelled against tradition and order, and cannot be reborn in an undivided faith capable of revealing the means and the aim of personal sacrifice. But these men are confused without noteworthy cause, like a man who, after a night spent drinking and womanizing, does not know if he should sneak off to the right or to the left in order to get home. Already in D'Annunzio we witnessed exhaustion after an orgy; but that was the exhaustion of a strong body, that had loved of its own accord; an exhaustion legitimized by the passion that produced it; here instead we witness the confusion of people who have watched others love and tire themselves out, and as they find themselves in the same exhausted condition but without having loved, they laugh a little, involuntarily, without noticing it, while longing for a true, grand passion. Even Corazzini – the most "heroic," i.e., the least ironic among them, because of his humility that allows him to recognize weakness as such, as something good, dear, and beloved – as soon as he finds himself in the presence of a woman, who is full of practical sense and flighty incomprehension, becomes a bit arrogant and teases her vaguely; but then, immediately, he becomes aware of his ridiculousness, of being a lover who arranges rendezvous "in the cardboard forest,"[5] and his small, tired heart does not reprove him, and instead sadly accepts the strange human fate that envelops everything. Of the six poets, he is the only one

4 [Guido Gozzano, "August Rain," in *The Man I Pretend to Be: The Colloquies and Selected Poems of Guido Gozzano*, translated by Michael Palma, Princeton UP, 1981, 161–3. Translation modified.]

5 [Sergio Corazzini, "Dialogue of Marionettes," in *Sunday Evening*, 49.]

in whom one perceives a glimpse of what we might call metaphysical meaning.

True, Saba also has the same religious humility that makes him open his eyes wide and gaze ecstatically. However, it is an ecstasy that can very easily appear – as it did to me some time ago – like the timidity of an insect that has fallen from a mulberry tree into a busy street.[6] His gaze still sees little.

Saba's poetic disposition is maturing with great difficulty. His small book of poetry ends with that litany that celebrates his wife as possessing all the virtues of wholesome domestic animals, and that he certainly believes is his best work, because he thinks that in it he expressed the beginning of his redemption. A modern return to St. Francis of Assisi. But without a doubt, his salvation is still all latent hope and will, and that poem, no matter how humbly I approach it, seems comical to me. As for Moretti, Palazzeschi, and F.M. Martini, they have been enclosed in their own limbo for the entirety of their short lifespan. They are little beings who either laugh, satisfied with their own nothingness, or have ossified in their initial pose. "The Sick Fountain,"[7] for instance, might well be rotten thoroughly enough to blossom into a flower: the flower, however, if Apollo is willing, will have a different name. Guido Gozzano? Perhaps …

Perhaps: that's his word, just like the past conditional is his tense. A circumstance that can no longer exist, that might have, perhaps, made him happy: to me this seems to be the height of his ultimate useless, implausible desire. The ambiguity of his similarly disposed fellows has found its form. There is a restlessness in them, an exhaustion, a tossing and turning of someone whose body is too delicate for a rough chair; and every one of them is looking for a way to rest. They do not know how to love; rather, they play with love. They can't stand the clamour of wagons, and therefore "they take shelter."[8] Moretti sits by the hearth, below the blue and white tiles, and begs his mother to stay a good housewife always, busy with humble tasks, so that he will not have to run away from that city of God where he can, for his peace of mind, transform every great thing into a little plaything. Then he picks up and goes to Flanders. Over there

6 [On Slataper and Saba, see also Introduction, 20.]

7 ["The Sick Fountain," published in 1909, is a poem by Palazzeschi in which the poet created a playful parody of one of D'Annunzio most sensual and musical poems, "Rain in the Pine Forest." Aldo Palazzeschi, "La fontana malata," in *Opere giovanili*, Mondadori, 1958, 35.]

8 [This is a reference to Gozzano's collection of poems *La via del rifugio* (The road to shelter), published in 1907.]

is peace, there is a canal with a sailboat and geese and a woman with an ample bosom and bright white bonnet. Ah, those strong, peaceful homemakers! (Signorina Felicita also has "a kind of Flemish loveliness." And ... "I do not want to be me anymore!")[9] The other one, Martini, runs away, holding the hand of a not overly sensual woman, among alabaster apples and postcards of a country inn. Umberto Saba in a summer twilight goes back to graze camels with his father Abraham, while Gozzano tries to travel back to 1850, which – he dreams – might have been his proper era.

Because, obviously, Gozzano's much-discussed romanticism is nothing more than a flight to shelter; his irony, a flight that never forgets that it is just a dream, "so to speak." Gozzano is always aware of the literariness of his longings. He is exhausted by present-day life – more eventful because it is the only one we do not read in books, but experience firsthand – by its human clashes, by the thousand doubts of a man whose emotional aridity won't let him become overwhelmed or enraptured by passion. His heart is without sorrow and therefore without joy ("The Two Roads").[10] He does not suffer; he presses his cheek to the banister, and observes the flowers in the garden:

> And now I'm not sad. Yet I feel
> so astonished to sit here and stare ...
> so astonished: I never did feel
> so much like a child before ...[11]

He is weak and apathetic: and so, long live the youthful maids! He looks for passion – and for quiet: opposing elements that come together only in his desire, and only appear to come true in his deluded dream. Look: books and romantic lore give him a woman filled with lively emotions, a chameleon, airy, free of fragile materiality; but what fiery little bites are contained in that hysterical mouth![12] On the other hand, at that time, especially in Turin, quiet inert objects still exist – dusty, fragile things that you only touch with your fingertips: "the collection of boxes without any candy, / the clusters of marble fruit standing under the bell jars'

9 [Guido Gozzano, "Signorina Felicita," in *The Man I Pretend to Be*, 89. Translation modified.]

10 [Guido Gozzano's "The Two Roads" is a poem included in *The Man I Pretend to Be*.]

11 [Guido Gozzano, "Absence," in *The Man I Pretend to Be*, 35.]

12 [Reference to Gozzano's poem "Una risorta," "A Woman Resurrected." In Michael Palma's translation: "the expert lips, and then / the little teeth that bit." Gozzano, *The Man I Pretend to Be*, 139.]

protection"[13] ... Let's throw ourselves on the bed and dream: a bit of pink, a pink crinoline skirt, hair parted in the middle, eyes lifted skywards: Carlotta! We live again.

But the poet is looking at a photo album. Beautiful, sweet, this youthful friend of Speranza; but Speranza is the grandmother ("My *grandmother*'s seventeen now"). The sweet romantic moon! But: "haven't you risen from the pages of *Novelliere illustrato*?"[14] The poet never forgets, indeed he takes pleasure in pointing out, by way of points of contrast that are always a bit corny, that his is a world made of paper.

With the exact same irony, he takes pleasure in lovingly poking fun at Miss Felicita's heart, because to him, being bourgeois and being romantic are the same thing. This longer poem disappoints, because it was already contained, with more finesse, within *Grandmother Speranza's Friend.*

Is all of Gozzano here? They've said so, and because his is a world of lemon candies, palates were soon irritated – and they thought that Gozzano had already had his heyday. But in my opinion, his romanticism is only a moment of stagnation and his poetry will continue to flow along what will likely prove to be his path. If you remember, his first volume, *La via del rifugio* (The road to shelter), opened with a beautiful lyric in which the poet, enthralled by his nieces' lullaby, tried to forget himself in dreams, and as the lullaby stopped and life resumed its course, he fell back, crushed, into the mysterious reality of the world – until finally, sadly, he gave up knowing and desiring. Now, it seems to me that this poem was his most significant. You can see how that man lying on the grass is revitalized by the lively grace of his little nieces. There is a youthful soul in him that bangs at the doors and would like to live! But there is also a soul, as there is always, in everyone, old, hopeless, and wise; the soul of a Brahmin from Pattar,[15] of Bevilacqua.[16]

Is this a drama? No. Rather, a sad, affectionate "colloquy" between an experienced older brother and a younger sibling. He briefly caresses Graziella with his eyes, before continuing on his path with his lady

---

13 [From the poem "L'amica di nonna Speranza," "Grandmother Speranza's Friend," in Gozzano, *The Man I Pretend to Be*, 99.]

14 [Gozzano, *The Man I Pretend to Be*, 109. Translation modified. The *Novelliere illustrato* (Tales illustrated) was a weekly popular magazine that printed short stories and romantic or adventure novels in installments.]

15 [Reference to Gozzano's poem "The Road to Shelter" that opens the collection of the same name.]

16 [Probably a reference to Pignatelli, an Italian peasant nicknamed Bevilacqua who modelled for Rodin for more than twenty years. When Pignatelli was old and worn out he posed for Matisse's statue *The Serf* (1900–04). See Hilary Spurling, *The Unknown Matisse: A Life of Henri Matisse, 1869–1908*, U of California P, 1998.]

friend.[17] This youth that smiles and surrenders right away, which is the theme of all Gozzano's best lyrics, has created a little masterpiece: *On the Threshold.* Listen to the ongoing counterpoint:

> My heart, such a merry young child who laughs as his own teardrops fall
> My heart, still a boy after all, so happy to be in the world,
> My heart, I might doubt perhaps, but it's only for you I'm concerned,
> that the Lady that humans have learned to call Death will quite shortly appear.[18]

Youth gives out a cry of joy, but immediately (what a difference between the two first "my heart" and the third one!) his voice lowers full of doubt, and he speaks with that sugary childish voice of an adult addressing a child. Then, take for instance "Totò Merúmeni," where youth has disappeared completely; all that is left is a desolate solitude. Here the poet studies the cocoons of butterflies and the life of crystals. He promises a new poem of Nature's small secrets, and as proof he offers a wonderful verse:

> To extend a blade of grass to the terrified // overturned beetles clawing at the air ... [19]

Is this his liberation? Maybe ... It is not that, by changing the object, the subject is able to rejuvenate itself; it is not that this is his belief; but it could very well be that Gozzano's youth begins with what he calls old age. What I mean to say is this: I have some hope. To surrender at the age of twenty-five, unless you have tuberculosis, is probably only an affectation.

Crepuscular confusion can occur not only before eight in the evening, but also before sunrise.

---

17 [Reference to Gozzano's poem "The Two Roads."]

18 [Guido Gozzano, "On the Threshold," in *The Man I Pretend to Be*, 45–7. However, Slataper here misquotes Gozzano's poem: in the original Gozzano wrote "mio cuore dubito forte ..." "my heart, I have the strong feeling that ..." while Slataper replaced *forte* with *forse* (maybe), adding to the poem, maybe involuntarily, another layer of existential uncertainty.]

19 [Guido Gozzano, "The Colloquies," in *The Man I Pretend to Be*, 167.]

PART FOUR

From *Ibsen*

Ultimately, what is Ibsen's "realism" or "prosaic" style, that critics always refer to?

Literary verisimilitude, when it is true art, is nothing more than the precision with which a poet stays true to his own way of seeing things.[1] As Ibsen states brilliantly: "Style must follow the same degree of idealism that is found in the representation." It follows therefore, that verismo, for instance, is not at all an art form capable of representing reality photographically – or of representing it at all.[2] It is not "truer" than other art forms – unless we compare it to idealism, which has by now become completely false and empty, and which verismo is a reaction against. As such, every reaction is "truer" than the previous, distorted action: everyone who is fed up returns to nature: the recognition of a falsehood leads to a more comprehensive truth. However, notwithstanding its historical meaning, realism is a new moral conviction, "a degree of idealism" that perceives the world differently. Every realist phrase or word is based on the premise that there is no hierarchy of human values: all things are equally true, good, and beautiful, or ugly, false, and bad, vis-à-vis an impassioned human solidarity, faith in God, or its absolute negation; or

1 Therefore the poet is always right – though blindly – when he states that only his art is "true"; and the critics are almost always wrong when they say that this or that work is "far-fetched," that is, it does not appear to be "true" to them, because their particular sensibility, taste, or experience goes against it. And I say almost always, because at other times "the shortcomings of verisimilitude" is nothing more than an imprecise expression for a criticism that is otherwise correct: the public cannot let go of its own particular concerns because the work, in itself, is contradictory, that is, not faithful to reality, it is far-fetched.

2 [Italian literary movement that corresponds to French naturalism. Italian verism drew its inspiration and subject matter from unique regional experiences. Its most important exponents were Luigi Capuana (1839–1915) and Giovanni Verga (1840–1922).]

vis-à-vis the pseudo-moral aesthetics whereby no value or reality exists aside from the purifying play of art for art's sake. These conflicting views yield the opposing lyrical realisms of Zola, Verga, Tolstoy, and others.

And so, Ibsen is also a realist. But closer – although at a lower level – to the Christian God who will judge our naked souls on Judgment Day. Thus, Ibsen is a realist in the same spirit as Dante, but without his prophetic violence. Indeed, those commonplace, humble words with which he repressed all his moral and poetic Catilinarian eloquence grow to an austere song when the intimate personality of his characters and of the whole drama is revealed in the final act of judgment. The act itself always begins with an almost hieratic solemnity, which corresponds to the solemnity of the circumstance. Every time Ibsen's characters must relate the backstory, or a hidden truth – that is, whenever they have to express a judgment on their own or on someone else's life – they sit beside each other and reveal their predicament, as we have already seen. It is right here, in this "sit here, next to me" (which the actors may express casually or emotionally), that the reader feels a shiver in his soul; here is the core of Ibsen's drama and of his characters.

This is Ibsen's greatness, where his prose becomes poetry, and his utter verisimilitude becomes an irrefutable truth. He is able to give to his earthly world the quiver of the divine. His judgment is so harsh and merciless that it becomes a song, as if the very core of a human being could transcend itself. It is like witnessing a miracle, like witnessing the birth of life under the yoke of the law. It is Kant in poetry. – Yet, at the same time, it is here, in this incredible effort, that the shortcomings of his art and personality also arise. That the highest provokes the lowest, that the most zealous purity goes hand in hand with the worst sin, is our bitter human fate. Brand *must* come to Gerd.[3] He never weeps, woe betide him if he does, but he should have wept. Brand must judge, it is the decisive force of his judgment that saves him from evil – but he should have loved. It is through goodness, through the love of God, that he is saved.

Ibsen does not cry, does not lose self-control, does not love. He would like to embrace life, he yearns for it, and calls out to it with the endless

3 [*Brand*, published in 1866, is a drama by Ibsen. Written in verse, it would, if performed in its entirety, have lasted more than six hours. The play is named after the protagonist, a pastor who sacrificed everything he had in order to follow his austere and uncompromising ethical vision. Written for a Norwegian audience while Ibsen lived near Rome, the poem expressed the love and frustration that he felt for his homeland. Gerd is the Gypsy girl who showed him a church "of ice and snow," erected on the mountain top. Her role in the play is to incite him to pursue his uncompromised and fanatical views. She caused the avalanche that killed Brand at the end of the drama.]

cry of all his sacrificed young creatures who long for the sun, the wide world, the sea, and for freedom. But he cannot love life, he cannot let himself become immersed in it. His artistic creatures are born not in his heart but in his unwavering convictions. All he knows is one core idea, a fundamental conflict between truth and lie, courage and cowardice, individual and society, joy and narrow-minded duty, and this shapes his whole world. This vision does not allow any interference from an abundant reality that would imbue it with experience, to the point, maybe, of becoming disorientated or lost, if it were to be revealed inadequate and insufficient; or, if it should prove itself well defined and coherent, it could conquer and hold all reality in its hand, and Goethe-like, force it to become clear and eternal.

But instead, it remains steep and intractable, wary of being caught off guard and dismantled. Look at Brand, look at Ibsen: this man who goes through life closed within himself, with his hands behind his back and a sneer on his lips, a vigilant terror in his eyes. His life has no life; and his art is just as poor.

When his characters are shaped by a theoretical assertion or doubt, and they are confronted with reality, Ibsen does not allow them to live, but diminishes them, according to the drama, stripping them to the bone, ossifying them, to the point that only their white skeleton remains, petrified by sorrow. His dramas are certainly neat and compact, but there is not a syllable or a movement that does not serve to fulfil one, two, or three functions. All is connected, developed from scene to scene, from drama to drama, all is justified, perfectly constructed; but it reeks of death. If we pay close attention to his characters' first words, we can certainly predict the tone with which they will utter their last. If we scrutinize a character in depth, we realize immediately which other characters he will have to interact with. One mathematically influences the other. They have their plot. After all, there are no more than a dozen of them. And the new clusters, that is the new dramas, the new dramatic qualities of his characters, correspond to each new phase in Ibsen's core belief.

In sum, this is an impoverished world. A world deduced and not induced. Lutheran aridity and not Catholic compassion. Reading, rereading Ibsen over and over again, you are suddenly seized by an indescribable restlessness: give me some air! some blood! Go back to Shakespeare. Look at this joyful poet, who lets all his characters roam around the world, without a worry, without fear of losing control! The good shepherd does not keep his sheep locked next to the arid rock where he is sitting, but lets them graze free on the mountains, each searching out the grass it likes best. Live as masters of your own lives, my brothers! Attend to your business, your loves and your sorrows – cocky and strong, beaten and hesitant, ridiculous, bestial, or delicate – but always filled with your rich and full potential. Get lost, as you please, in the world. The poet loves you just as you are. He has only love for you. He gives himself wholly to you. We cannot find Shakespeare, the poet, in you, because he disappeared in you, and has identified himself with our life. He had so much faith in himself that his genius, with his cheerful voice, could instantly summon all his creatures back to him. Wherever they are on earth, from the densest thicket, from the most remote oblivion, he can revive you and show you that you have always been in the right place, within the living organism of his kind laws. From a tavern to the court, from marital bed to battlefield, for him it's just the calm blink of an eye. What do theatrical unities matter when there's unity of love? Every moment and every perspective contains in itself the totality of time and space, and his repertoire "is full of songs." How catholic is this love of his, how warm with grace! This little-known man has the arms of a god. His kingdom is wide, and every vice and virtue has free access there, because vice and virtue are connected within this certain, internal, essential faith. Life, all of it, is truly holy.

Ibsen aspires to this holy life, but he is unable to enjoy it: he needs to judge it.

Well, it's true: there is only one law and there is no escaping it. Judgment is necessary. Men exist, hell exists. Even Brunetto, Francesca, and Ugolino must be condemned to hell.[4] Compassion is dead; one does not

4 [Brunetto, Francesca, and Ugolino are three historical figures that Dante encounters in his journey through hell in the *Divine Comedy*. Brunetto Latini (c. 1220–94) was a Florentine scholar and important political figure active in the Guelph party that dominated Florentine politics during the Middle Ages. He was Dante's teacher, and as such he appears in Canto 15 of Dante's *Inferno*, where he is condemned among the sodomites. Although Dante condemned Latini to Hell, the poet chose to emphasize the respect and love that teacher and pupil had for each other. Francesca is Francesca da Polenta, the daughter of the lord of Ravenna. Not much is known about the real Francesca, except that she was married to Giovanni Malatesta in order to strengthen the alliance between the two families. Francesca fell in love with Paolo Malatesta, her brother-in-law. The lovers were both killed by Giovanni. Dante puts the two lovers in Canto 5 of the *Inferno*, where they are punished with the carnal sinners. Here too, instead of focusing on their sin, Dante allows Francesca to tell the tragic story of their romantic ill-fated love. Ugolino della Gherardesca, count of Donoratico (c. 1220–89), was an important political figure in Pisa and Tuscany during the second half of the thirteenth century. His political scheming and betrayals to maintain power in Pisa came to an end when Archbishop Ruggieri, a former ally of the count, turned against him and accused him of treason. Imprisoned with two of his sons and two grandchildren, they were left to starve to death. Dante includes the episode of Ugolino in Cantos 32–3 of the *Inferno*, where he is punished together with Ruggieri among the traitors. The poet allows Ugolino, who is gnawing at the head of Ruggieri, to recount the anguishing experience of being a helpless witness to his children's death.]

cry in hell, there is no compassion for evil. But notice how Dante has his assassins confess! How his humanity makes him tremble in front of the creatures he must judge, and how he suffers in them, feeling their terrible punishments in himself. Even if he is misguided, his human compassion redeems him; if he is proudly cruel against himself, his holy beatific love leads him to the stars. Because he loves, he has the right to redeem Francesca and Ugolino from their inevitable and necessary damnation: this is why Farinata rises up straight, above the inferno, and you can see him whole, not just as the heretic destroyer of Florence, but also as the outspoken defender of his homeland.[5] This is not to say that the *poet* rises next to the Catholic; rather, it is the man in his totality, alive, who must judge and love. Not even in hell is the poet's love extinguished: and therefore, goodness is not extinguished either. For this reason, because he has judged but loved, because he has judged but suffered in doing so, he rises to heaven, where love and judgment are one. Dante too is the poet of judgment day, but as a minister of God on earth.

Ibsen judges, but does not forgive. When vivid, dreamy creatures enter and crowd his solitary study in the evening, asking to be taken and sent fraternally into the world to lighten and to comfort man of his manly sorrow – the poet seems almost ready to smile, surrender, and join them lovingly. But it is only for an instant: the mirror shatters, broken; "and therein [reflected in the mirror,] stood a stodgy guest / with blue-grey eyes, with a buttoned-up waist coat, / and with felt shoes."[6] And this brotherly world disappears, next to this unsmiling and pitiless man: "Only buildings. Nothing green."[7]

5 [Farinata degli Uberti (early thirteenth century–1264) belonged to a powerful ancient Florentine family that supported the Ghibelline party, and played a pivotal role in the political life of his city. Dante belonged to the opposing political party, the Guelphs. Canto 10 of Dante's *Inferno* re-enacts the political tensions that plagued Florence during Farinata's and Dante's times. Farinata is being punished as a heretic follower of Epicurus, the Greek philosopher who rejected the immortality of the soul. Although in the canto Farinata expresses his antagonism towards Dante and the Guelphs, he also reveals his passionate and uncompromising love for Florence, a sentiment that still consumes him in the afterlife. He reminds Dante that he alone defended Florence openly when other Ghibellines proposed to destroy the city. When the Guelphs regained power, Farinata was exiled for the rest of his life.]

6 [Ibsen, "Fra Mit Husliv" (From my home life). I thank John Sundquist for his help with the translation from the original. Slataper used the German version of Ibsen's poem, "Aus meinem häuslichen Leben," in *Henrik Ibsens Sämtliche Werke in Deutscher Sprache*, vol. 1, bd. 1, edited by Georg Brandes, Julius Elias, and Paul Schlenther, S. Fischer, 1903, 85.]

7 [This quote comes from Ibsen's fragmentary autobiography "Childhood Memories" [*Barndomsminner*] in *Henrik Ibsens Skrifter*, vol. 16, edited by Vigidis Ystad and Narve Fulsas, H. Aschehoug & Company, 2010, 496.]

This comes from the reading of a poem ("From My Home Life") whose painful meaning has so far escaped everybody. He would like to love, he feels the desire to love, but can't. The person in the mirror will not allow him. Ibsen is aware of his destiny but is too proud to succumb to it. One must endure to the very end, all or nothing. You must will your destiny, no matter what it is. It is this heroic fortitude that saves him, alone within his decadent and love-deprived spirit.

He is the man who cannot pray without condemning. His doubting soul (although only love leads to faith) must be constantly on guard. Deep down, despair, scepticism, and distrust brood, and the smallest admission, the tiniest surrender to other human beings, to the world, or to life, would destroy his edifice. His faith is that of Luther or Calvin, of all the great desperate upholders of faith. In their souls there is no joy, no breath, no humility. All their lives they must fight against Satan, against the evil powers of the mind and the flesh. As inquisitors of themselves, they are intolerant and without forgiveness. The whole world needs to believe, at any cost, because one single unbeliever would undermine their faith. There is no communion with other people, whatever is born jointly has no value, and eternal law or traditions don't help: the individual is alone in his terrible struggle, all in vain. In their arid, agonizing, preaching hearts, Satan is still present; the evil little I is still there; you don't reach God through deeds. The deed is not truth, it is inadequate, no matter how much you torment it with the most complex scruples or impose on it the strictest ideals. This is the Protestant rhetoric of ideals people always talk about. However, the deed is holy for the Catholic: the deed is God incarnate, which in turn allows us to ascend to God. This results in love of action, the sensuality of the act, the beautiful bounty of art, and the richness of language. Two churches, Catholic and Protestant. Redemption, quiet joy, happiness through toil, freedom from Jehovah's damnation; toil without reward, without respite, American toil, technical, soulless, German, European.

Because of this inability to love, and because of the inadequacy of mankind, Protestantism, which freed the individual – as we've been told – had to manipulate him in the most brutal manner, so that he would not lose himself in desperate anarchism. Behind the vaunted German order lies the despair of all strong individuals who, by themselves, are deemed worthless. The state has had to bind itself into a thousand associations, leagues, and regulations. The German policeman represents fear of anarchy; the barbarity against the Poles and Danes and the unique character of German anti-Semitism are triggered by fear of extinction, of disintegration. The same doctrine that proclaimed the value of the individual also negated him.

And because of the inadequacy of man, the anguished plea to God becomes necessary. Absolute grace, without which nothing can be accomplished, always finds its reason to be in the lovelessness of moral intolerance. If this were not the case, it would be impossible to explain how a spirit who has given everything to God, who has deprived humanity of every authentic possibility, could then be so intolerant towards it. The Protestant should love truly, and in every place. But Christ has returned as a Jewish prophet in the texts of Protestantism.

All is God, and man, ill treated, is powerless. This is not religion. There is no authentic communion with God, because every instant of life is outside of it, and only when you pray are you with Him. Fichte demonstrates this: the Protestant priest cannot absolve you. Dante can, but not Ibsen. And when this God falls, when we do not believe in Him anymore, He who was everything, only aridity and the taste of ashes remain: an indifferent despair that preaches and judges. An intolerant severity rules, strict as in the Foreign Legion. But this is not a true judgment, because there is no love for the judged; because the one who is judged, once redeemed, is not truly embraced by our faith; he is excluded, and distanced, and each of us withdraws into ourselves. Because there is no love, no belief or joy. This is the desperate, technological civilization of positivism that judges all.

Man has no value in himself; he is shaped by everything except himself. He is what he was seven thousand years ago, he is only what someone else remembers of him, moulded by both a causal and arbitrary conjunction of things. And which he must, because of a fleeting chance, eternally remain. How can one build a morality, a culture, a society on these premises? A mother will forbid her child to climb a tree because he could fall. Education will be reduced to this: impeding at all costs the possibility of sinning. We will write the Baedeker of life; the rules, but not the Book.[8] Society will become an always more perfected corpus of prohibitions. Everything will be explained; life will have no mystery, due to the hubris of the new society of the blind: precision and passivity will be the rule. Morality will be reduced to hygiene and charity. Kant turned into Haeckel.[9]

8 [The Baedeker is a series of popular guidebooks published by the Baedeker publishing house starting in the 1830s.]

9 [Immanuel Kant (1724–1804) was an influential German philosopher whose work revolutionized Western thought. Ernst Haeckel (1834–1919) was a German biologist. His works were widely distributed (they were also translated into Italian) and contributed to extending and vulgarizing the concept of evolution in Germany and in Italy. He used Darwinism to promote scientific racism, noting that "the Caucasian man" was the highest ranked in terms of development and achievements.]

Clearly in Ibsen, a sound moral conscience, a consistent strength persists: there is, without a doubt, a tragedy in *Ghosts* (Helene), and there is a collective human fault; there is a heroism that will not yield and die stifled; a reality, maybe religious, sombre as the metaphysical beliefs in Hedda Gabler, unbearable as the Christian original sin. Yet this new Oedipus Rex does not lead to Oedipus at Colonus.[10] Jesus has no place in this world, nor does Siegfried.[11] There is no point in Ibsen's asserting that he never depicted the theory of heredity, but only portrayed its consequences: isn't the dreadfully strict responsibility of man reduced here to nothing more than the edict: be careful that you don't catch syphilis? And yes, there is a catharsis: it's this, which the audience ponders on its way home from the theatre: let's fight alcoholism and prostitution; follow the order of the day regarding the question of gender and sexuality; and think of Herlich-Hata![12] It's pointless: this is a mechanical vision of our fate.

Positivism represents a weariness, a moral laxity, a jarring halt in the endeavours of humankind. Positivism, always latent in Ibsen's dramas, although almost always defeated, is undoubtedly Ibsen's weak element. Even Helene, who epitomizes the drama, must die the same day Oswald can be cured. Here one can see how Ibsen was influenced by his times with all its "isms." Here the poetry of his prose turns into the common speech of the day, where the dry, flawless rationalism of all his motivation comes from (of course he is always frustrated because it is impossible to empty the sea with a little pail); and also where his realistic scenarios originate, which is why the colour of the carpet is so important for the qualities of the characters, just as are the given time of day and the weather (these are Ibsen's words). In conclusion, it's here that his reason becomes stifling mathematics, and the individual comes undone. It is here that Brand dies.

---

10 [*Oedipus Rex* and *Oedipus at Colonus* are two tragedies by Sophocles. In *Oedipus Rex,* Oedipus, king of Thebes, gouges out his own eyes after realizing that he is, although unwittingly, responsible for sleeping with his own mother, Jocasta, and for the consequent plague that is ravaging his city. In *Oedipus at Colonus* the exiled and blind king accepts his fate and is able to experience a peaceful death and forgiveness: he is escorted to the underworld by divine intervention.]

11 [Siegfried is the fearless hero of the medieval German epic poem *Nibelungenlied.* He is also the subject of Richard Wagner's opera *Siegfried,* which constitutes the third drama of his *Nibelungen* cycle. It premiered in Bayreuth in 1876. Many of Wagner's operas, including the *Nibelungen* cycle, were performed at the Teatro Lirico Giuseppe Verdi in Trieste in the late nineteenth century and early twentieth century and, together with Verdi's operas, became the "pillars of the operatic seasons." Karyl Charna Lynn, *Italian Opera Houses and Festivals,* Scarecrow Press, 2005, 87.]

12 [Paul Herlich (1854–1915) was a German physician and scientist. In 1909, together with Dr. Sahachiro Hata (1873–1938) he discovered and synthesized arsphenamine, a drug that could effectively attack the bacterium that caused syphilis.]

PART FIVE

From *Political Writings*

Irredentism Today

Anti-Austrian Sentiment

Anti-Austrian sentiment is definitely present in Italy today. It has not been extinguished by diplomatic obligations, nor by the humble declarations of the Italian government, nor by the fraternal and cosmopolitan affection that characterizes the spirit of our century. Austria is the clerical, papist state, par excellence, incapable of any artistic expression. It is logical that almost thirty years of political alliance has not produced any sort of emotional bond.[1] Italian political circles did not even attempt to consolidate the Triple Alliance with pro-Austria propaganda, as had been done for Germany (taking advantage of the intellectual appetite for everything Teutonic), and as is usually done, successfully, with unpopular alliances. It is true that there were, and there are still, two philo-Austrian currents: first, the pacifist one of the *Vita internazionale* (T. Moneta), which attempted to create friendly understanding by bringing together a group of intellectuals and politicians (the Austro-Italian committee is under the direction of Bertha von Suttner).[2] Their premise was to maintain peace at every cost, but even the smallest reality check undermined their best intentions. I think that the committee still exists, but in name only. The second philo-Austrian current is the moral

1 [Reference to the Triple Alliance. See Introduction, note 19.]

2 [Ernesto Teodoro Moneta (1833–1918), chief editor of the newspaper *Il Secolo* and founder of the Società internazionale per la pace (International Society for Peace). In 1890, he founded the review *Vita internazionale* (International life), which focused on European political and national issues. He was awarded the Nobel Peace Prize in 1907. Bertha von Suttner was an activist, a journalist, and novelist from Prague. Her 1889 novel *Die Waffen nieder!* (Lay down your arms!) launched her as a leading figure in the pacifist movement in the Austro-Hungarian Empire. She was awarded the Nobel Peace Prize in 1905.]

struggle for the spiritual education of all Italians, which is the more implicit than explicit agenda of *La Voce*. Even if Austria at its most fierce extreme does not appeal to our intelligence and more liberal upbringing, the Cavour-like spirit (as opposed to the spirit of Garibaldi) sees in Austria a perfect example of anti-rhetorical determination and political effectiveness.[3] This is an example that should be appreciated and studied in anarchic Italy, where a punch thrown at a demonstrator by a policeman can threaten to bring down the government. Perhaps this is the only sentiment that might have some value; but only if Italians learn from it. For now, even those politicians who know how to delve profitably into the current political reality, no matter what their experience has been, cannot feel sympathy towards Austria. It has always been said as simply as this: there is no other way.

The Triple Alliance was and still is a harsh necessity, which seized our nation the moment she started meddling in European affairs. It is a prison and a cage; a type of external bondage in exchange for domestic freedom. The alliance allowed Italy to recover financially, but it deprived her of her prospects. Italy feels that she is not yet free. Freedom is the ability to communicate with others independently, according to one's own convictions. It is harmony between domestic and international life. Instead, Italy's existence is determined directly and harshly by the will of other nations. Her foreign policy cannot develop along a clear path that might allow her the peace of mind necessary to make all kinds of decisions, because she must change her position as others change theirs. Every honest manifestation of her soul goes against her own interest. She must impose upon herself a false persona and kiss the hand of those who force it upon her; she must roll with the punches and, her cheek bruised, negotiate the terms of her European existence.

The violent duress that keeps Italy inside the Triple Alliance exacerbates her natural anti-Austrian sentiment. In Italian memory and imagination Austria is still loathsome. All the hateful details and phrases from 1848 and 1866 are still vivid: the lacquered moustache of the Germans,

---

3 [Camillo Benso, count of Cavour (1810–61), was an Italian diplomat who served as the first prime minister of the unified Italy. Together with Giuseppe Mazzini and Giuseppe Garibaldi, he was among the most important leaders of the Italian Risorgimento. As a diplomat for the Kingdom of Sardinia and Savoy, he worked to free northern Italy from the yoke of Austria and was able to secure the support of France in the struggle for the unification of Italy. In 1860 Cavour supported Garibaldi's expedition to southern Italy to liberate the Kingdom of the Two Sicilies, which was still under the control of the Spanish House of Bourbon. However, Cavour did not want Garibaldi's success in the south to hinder his vision of a unified kingdom of Italy under the rule of the House of Savoy.]

"with the heads of the Germans, we will make bocce balls …"[4] Radetzky is still alive and well.[5] So is fondness for the nations we hoped would help us during our Risorgimento: the brave Hungarians, the hapless Polish homeland. We continue to have contradictory feelings towards our Slovenian brothers, who are incited against us by their oppressor, or towards the damned Croatians, who, wherever they go, bring lice and bedbugs. Those "who were there," who fought in the wars, have not yet all passed away; and Austria does not allow the younger generation to forget. Austria does not respect us: first of all, because of our never-ending unpreparedness, upon which, like a rhetorical weathercock, our constant yapping about preparedness founders, when in fact the opposite is true. Secondly, because of our diplomatic naivety, which is anti-Machiavellian and underlines our weakness, but without the courage to take advantage of the political opportunities that our weakness makes possible. Moreover, Austria adheres to a traditional perspective that is becoming delusional and that will probably end up leading it astray. Austria is only able to understand and grasp the reality of the day; but she laughed at the state of mind necessary for the rise of a leader like Cavour. For all these reasons, German Austria (that which rules today) is afraid only of Germany, of its domestic Slav population, and of Russia; but of us – Mother Rome, forgive me! – she doesn't give a hoot. The slightest hint of respect would have created an Italian university in Trieste or would have conceded autonomy to the people of Trento. Or at least it would have made the Austrian police stop putting together unbelievable trials, breaking up cultural societies, and prohibiting excursions. Austria does not lessen its inflexibility except during the weeks preceding a new commercial treaty or a diplomatic conference, and this is done for appearance's sake only, to convince us to accept implausible deals.

As a result, the Italian people, especially in the Romagna region and perhaps also in southern Italy, are always alert. They do a lot of yelling. But that's all. Anti-Austrian sentiment is only a feeling, not an awareness building towards war: thus, no irredentism, but the constant possibility of irredentism. In truth, they do not care much about Trento and

4 [The years 1848 and 1866 are important dates in the Italian Risorgimento: 1848 marks the beginning of the Italian uprisings against the Austrian Empire, and 1866 is the year of the Third War of Independence fought by the recently formed Italian kingdom against Austria.]

5 [Johann Joseph, Graf Radetzky (1766–1858) was the Austrian general in charge of the Italian campaigns during the Italian wars of independence. He defeated Italy in the battle of Custoza in 1848 and in the battle of Novara in 1849. He served as governor of the Austrian occupied Lombardo-Venetian kingdom from 1850 to 1857.]

Trieste, and they never thought to willingly arm themselves to go to their defence. Their own freedom is too recent, and their sense of national identity is too strong for the irredentist struggle not to have a painful resonance for them. But – what about Malta? Or Tunis? and many of their immigrants?[6] The "Austrian" factor is essential to the Italian irredentist attitude. Moreover, Austria is the master of Italy's borders, and Italians well understand, certainly due to the expense of reinforcing the border, the fragility and uncertainty of their survival.

We should also not forget that we are troubled by a great moral malaise, one that seeks its resolution through a violent shock that would bring forth a new, clear, and precise moral value. Revolutions or wars are what deliver spiritual shocks to a whole population.

A revolution with Paolo Orano at the head of an inexistent syndicalist movement seems impossible even to those who wish for it.[7] War against Austria – thus far we don't see any other probability, or possibility; or desire, or fear.

In conclusion, all these issues create very favourable conditions for an irredentist party that clearly knows what it wants, whatever that might be.

Contemporary Irredentist Movements

However, as I look for this clear will among the various affirmations of irredentism, I find only haphazard, contradictory declarations, caught between reality and aspirations that do not take reality into account; finally, I see truncated declarations or intentions that, in making beautiful statements, neglect to illustrate the moral premises, or the conditions necessary for their fruition, or the potential consequences, or all three factors together.

Republican Irredentism: this, in its most sincere part, is the closest to the popular anti-Austrian sentiment. It continues the Garibaldine democratic tradition. It does not prepare for war, but dreams of it in the future.

---

6 [Italians had been present in Tunisia since the early Renaissance. In the late nineteenth and early twentieth centuries the Italian Tunisian community grew to more than one hundred thousand people. Although in smaller number, many Italians, mostly from Sicily, created a flourishing Italian colony on the island of Malta. Both groups maintained strong patriotic ties with Italy. See Robert Franz Foerster, *The Italian Emigration of Our Times*, Harvard UP, 1919, 206 and 214–16.]

7 [Paolo Orano (1875–1945) was an Italian sociologist, journalist, and writer who was, for a short period, a militant in the Italian Socialist Party. He soon became a strong supporter of fascism and its anti-Semitic doctrine. In 1937 he published *The Jews of Italy,* which Italian fascists used to legitimize their anti-Semitic politics.]

It believes in the Nazione armata,[8] even if it sees that the nation is not arming itself. Overall, it ignores the existence of Slavic populations in the Adriatic provinces. It tries to keep the memory of Oberdank alive.[9] It believes that the Italian monarchy is still anti-irredentist, and that if we want to free the unredeemed regions, we will have the Savoy army against us: this is what it believes, or pretends to believe, because it does not want to see the contradiction between republican and irredentist ideals. It views as a political sell-out any "unnatural" diplomatic effort: that is, anything that does not favour the French republic. It would like to see an alliance of all Latin lands, and it believes this will happen when Italy and Spain become republics. For the most fervent believers, irredentism is a pedagogical tool useful for the patriotic education of their children.

When it is not politically naive, republican irredentism reflects the ongoing frustration with Italy's unification under the monarchy. It does not have a will of its own; it only reacts to the attitudes of the House of Savoy.

[...]

Masonic Irredentism: Prezzolini already wrote about this in his article "Austria or France" (*La Voce*, 15 December 1910). I will add a few facts. Its close association with monarchic irredentism is absolutely clear, as can be seen, for instance, in the essential relationship between Trieste and Freemasonry.[10]

The liberal-national party of Trieste is monarchic. It states so every day. What upsets local republicans the most (so much so that a few years ago they even felt an affinity with the Triestine socialists) is the fact that the liberals took part in all the mourning and all the celebratory events of the Savoy monarchy. As an excuse, the most forward-thinking liberals use the fact that, right now, the House of Savoy represents Italy; and they're right. Many members of the liberal party, especially the leaders, are Freemasons. Felice Venezian himself was most likely a Freemason. Whoever seeks a position controlled by the liberals must first ask the Masons. They are the founders of the Triestine chapter of the association Libero Pensiero.[11]

---

8 [The Nazione armata (Armed nation) was a revolutionary society founded by Garibaldi in 1859 to counteract the Società nazionale (The national society), which was ideologically closer to Cavour's ideals.]

9 [See Introduction, note 81.]

10 [The Freemasons played a pivotal role in the unification of Italy.]

11 ["The National Association of Free Thought" was an Italian association that came together for the first time in 1869 in Naples to protest the First Vatican Council. At that point Rome was still an independent state and the pope refused to recognize the legitimacy of the Italian state. In 1903 it became an official organization, and it added to its title the name of Giordano Bruno. It brought together many anti-clerical and liberal intellectuals. The members of the association had close links with Freemasonry.]

The connection between the Triestine Masonry and the Roman Masonic lodge is the so-called Triestine Club in Rome, which is led by Mayer (who is the owner of the *Piccolò* and of Stefani, is a friend of Nathan and Rava, and has been received more than once by the king) and by Barzilai (previously a man of letters and critic on the staff of the *Tribune*, suddenly elected Triestine deputy in order to fight against the dissolution of the Pro Patria association).[12] Mostly because of them, Italian Freemasonry contributes to the electoral campaign of the Liberal Party. Barzilai (so they say) is republican; 33 per cent of Masonry (so they say) is republican; Trieste has a true Republican Party. And yet, *against it*, Italian Masonry finances the liberal *monarchic* party. The Triestine republicans (who are incredibly naive) send their articles and letters to the *Ragione*, and they appear there, edited with a liberal spin. It should be noted that Masonry has an important role in the ways the Italian newspapers publish news about us.[13] As a result, the Italian public is almost always informed with a liberal bias (and this holds true also for the many socialist newspapers).

It is obvious that Masonic irredentism is like Masonic anti-clericalism: it is the corrupted extension of its founding principles, now utilized to hide intrigues and favouritism, and to seduce the gullible.

The Savoy dynasty, with its changing domestic and foreign politics, and no longer fearing the Republican Party, has understood that it can take advantage of both the obstructive and the Francophile strategies of Masonry. We must admit that the House of Savoy understands one thing: it recognizes the predominant mood of the country, and, in order to maintain its control over it, adapts its politics accordingly, even if they go against traditional sentiments and desires. Aside from Umberto (and the German Margherita), who might have had the will, no positive or negative

---

12 [Teodoro Mayer (1860–1942) was a Triestine journalist and politician. He founded the newspaper *Il Piccolo*, the most widely read paper in Trieste. He was a member of the Liberal National Party and from 1906 until the beginning of World War I he was a city councilman. He owned half the stock of the Italian news agency Stefani. Ernesto Nathan (1845–1922) was an Anglo-Italian Jew who became an Italian politician and a strong supporter of the irredentist cause. He was a Freemason and held the post of Grand Master of the Masonic Grand Lodge Grande Oriente d'Italia. From 1907 until 1913 he was the mayor of Rome. Luigi Rava (1860–1938) was an Italian politician and Freemason. Salvatore Barzilai (1860–1939) was a Triestine politician and intellectual. He was one of the founding members of the Italian Republican Party (1897). The Pro Patria association was an irredentist association active in Trieste from 1885 to 1890, when it was dissolved by imperial decree.]

13 [*La Ragione: Giornale di politica e di cultura* (Reason: A journal of politics and culture), founded in Rome in 1907, was the official newspaper of the Republican Party.]

initiative ever comes from the House of Savoy. It is the most inert monarchic dynasty, and for this reason it may turn out to be the longest lasting.

When the House of Savoy is represented by Carlo Alberto, who is strictly bound to anti-liberal and Austrian traditions in a time of strong liberalism and Italianism, we witness a great crisis.[14] When it is represented by Vittorio Emanuele III,[15] we witness the slightly uneasy idyll of divine grace merging with the democratic, bourgeois, nationalist will of the nation. In other words, useless medical assistance in Calabria, rather than the necessary, decisive political leadership in Rome.[16]

Ferrari and Labriola[17] have clearly pointed out that the history of the House of Savoy is defined by a constant shifting from France to Austria and back again. Even here it has taken on the traits that are typical of Italian history. Now, with its failures in Africa, the Mediterranean Sea, and Austria, the House of Savoy has turned its focus to the Balkan region, the Adriatic, and France. But it is obvious that the Italian people would not support a war of national oppression, nor would they vote for its financing. Thus, the House of Savoy is simply using Trento and Trieste as a lure. I doubt that Vittorio Emanuele III is truly irredentist. But his government excites irredentism. The association Trento-Trieste is obviously monarchic.[18] The hot-headed Venetian irredentists (such as Foscari) are also monarchists, because for (right) now an anti-Austrian irredentism can do nothing effective other than favour Italian over Austrian shipping

14 [Carlo Alberto of Savoy (1798–1849) was the king of Piedmont-Sardinia. Politically conservative, in 1831 for fear of republican revolts he signed a treaty with Austria stating that, in case of war, Austria would defend his kingdom. In 1848, he supported the first war of independence against Austria.]

15 [Vittorio Emanuele III (1869–1947) was king of Italy from 1900 to 1946.]

16 [In December 1908 a strong earthquake devastated the cities of Reggio Calabria, Messina, and other coastal southern Italian towns. The king and his wife reached the area and offered their support to the many victims. Slataper himself, together with other university students from Florence, went to Calabria to help the wounded and the homeless victims of the earthquake. He described the devastation of the region in his article "Una notte all'ospedale di Napoli" (One night in Naples's hospital), published in the Florentine newspaper *Nuovo Giornale* on 5 January 1909. Reprinted in Alessio Quercioli, "Scipio Slataper e il terremoto di Messina," *Belfagor*, vol. 65, no. 2, 2010, 205–12.]

17 Ettore Ferrari (1845–1929) was a mason and an Italian politician. Arturo Labriola (1873-1959) was a socialist and an Italian politician. He founded the weekly magazine *Avanguardia Socialista.*

18 [The Associazione nazionale Trento e Trieste was active in Italy since 1903. Its aim was to disseminate the irredentist cause within Italy. On the eve of World War I, it played an important role in promoting Italy's intervention against Austria.]

routes; which, in the future, would necessarily make Macedonia another port of resurgent Venice.

Under these circumstances, it is natural that the monarchic government, which wants to befriend the Slavic states, does not want to allocate finances for an Italian bank in Trieste, and does everything it can to hinder the movement of Italian capital in the unredeemed provinces. It is a natural consequence of our servile, exceedingly unwise current politics.

In reality, an effective way for the king to support the Italians living in the unredeemed regions would be to conduct politics astutely. Those who do not defend themselves cannot defend others.

Imperialist irredentism. As everyone knows, its scope is vast: the Adriatic and the Mediterranean seas, beyond the Alps, perhaps to the centre of Europe, all the way to where Italy can expand its borders and the imperialists can draw their breath: towards the infinite and the undefinable; the absolutely anti-Italian aping of pan-Germanism; an exaggerated monarchism; in sum, the automatic response to Italy's centripetal politics. Trieste and Trento are small, even negligible parts of the whole. Because when imperialist irredentism refuses to confront reality, it reduces itself to the trivial monarchic irredentism that I have been discussing.

Its newspaper was *Il Regno* [The kingdom], which some would have liked to call "L'impero" [The empire]. Then, thanks to Corradini and his followers, it was reborn in Turin as *Il Tricolore* [The tricolour], and it is becoming even more deflated. It is not necessary for me to remind you of Corradini's renunciation, confirmed in the interview published in the *Nuovo Giornale* [New newspaper] on 6 December 1910. (See also Viani's indignant response – poor chap! – on the pages of the *Tribuna* [Tribune] on 7 December 1910.)

Moral Irredentism. This is the irredentism of those more concerned with ethical issues than territorial conquests, and who believe that war is necessary to provide a nation with new ideals. This is the type of irredentism that Caroncini already articulated in *La Voce*: a practical offshoot of Corradini's nationalist-syndicalist vision; the other side of anti-war propaganda.[19]

---

19 [Alberto Caroncini (1883–1915) was an Italian journalist who collaborated with *La Voce* and the right-wing newspaper *Il Regno*. He was a member of the Nationalist Association and strongly supported the idea of going to war against Austria. See the article "Ancora del nazionalismo," *La Voce*, 21 July 1910. Enrico Corradini (1865–1931) was an Italian politician, novelist, and journalist. In 1903 he founded the newspaper *Il Regno* and was one of the founders of the Italian Nationalist Association. Influenced by the ideas of the French revolutionary intellectual Georges Sorel (1847–1922),

I am not discussing the moral value of war. I believe that if the war is sincere, even if it ends with a defeat, it can be good. In the same way an individual can be reborn with a new ethical vision after his "absolute negation," as long as this negation is not false, literary, or exaggerated, so can a whole nation after a catastrophic war, as long as it had clear historical premises and aims. We must remember Italy's understanding of its own national identity. It is the reason for its existence, it defines its role within Europe. Mazzini is Italian. We became a nation with the words of Vittorio Emanuele: "these broad principles of nationalism."[20] We hate Austria mostly because for us it embodies the government that suppresses national identities. We supported the Boers, and we may be with the Indians against the British. Nothing is farther from us than the Roman spirit; we even felt sympathy, against our own interests, for the Abyssinians. We are anti-imperialists. Is this just a detrimental sentimentality? I believe it shows our most profound respect for our own history. Against the Austrian campaign towards the east, we did not have, and will continue not to have, any other option but to defend the national freedom of the Balkan peoples. A war against another ethnic nationality, even if it is a victorious one, would be a war against ourselves: and proof of that would be our inability to govern the vanquished.

We should also not forget a point that may have become trite, but that unfortunately we must continue to repeat: that the heroism of "musket shots" is useless in modern warfare. Present-day war heroism is made of discipline and mathematical precision: qualities that are still lacking completely in Italians today. We are still saturated with Garibaldinism. Before we start a war, we must expend great effort to adapt our spirit to the new necessities of war. War may lead to defeat; we must at least be able to prevent the most tragic consequence of defeating ourselves first. This training is much more important than increasing our arsenal of weapons.

Cultural Irredentism. This is the Triestine form of irredentism, embraced for the first time by the socialists, who refuted the importance of political borders. It is also the irredentism *La Voce* supports.

Corradini tried to bring together syndicalism, socialism, and nationalism. In a conference held in Trieste at the Minerva Society in December 1909, entitled "Syndicalism, Nationalism, Imperialism," he emphasized how revolutionary syndicalism and class conflict could also energize a nationalist and imperialist effort. For Corradini the irredentist cause was a necessary step towards a wider imperialist agenda. See Corradini, *Discorsi politici 1902–1923*, Valecchi Editore, 1924, 51–69.]

20 [From the address of King Vittorio Emanuele II to the Congress on 10 January 1859. Vittorio Emanuele II (1820–78), the first king of Italy, reigned from the unification of Italy in 1861 to his death in 1878. He played a pivotal role in the unification of the country.]

We do not deny the importance of political borders; but we strongly feel that they do not contain the homeland. The love for one's homeland is the coming together of every individual activity in one single historical tradition in accordance with everyone's needs and desires. It takes that unique form through which our contemporary ideals can be realized in the future. This is what is important for humanity, and for the time to come; the rest is dictated by everyday, practical needs, which both nations and intellectuals recognize more and more as ephemeral. We live internationally, there is no sense in denying it; between a smart German and a stupid Italian, we prefer the German. So, in a certain sense, the confederation of nations has already been accomplished.

More to the point, this cultural irredentism, whose aim is to educate Italians to small sacrifices, is the most effective groundwork for any future events. If a hundred thousand Italians were to join the Lega Nazionale,[21] a war would be less fearsome. And so, our "idealistic notion," in truth, is the most pragmatic course of action. So much so that when nationalist irredentism manifests itself in some proposition, it is transformed into Sighele's cultural-pacifist discourse,[22] while the nationalist anti–Triple Alliance sentiment becomes the pro–Triple Alliance exposition of De Frenzi.[23] This is the vengeance of the real.

But we have integrity; that is, we are *sincere*.[24]

As far as the provinces of the Venezia Giulia[25] are concerned, the irredentists find themselves in an embarrassing predicament: on the one hand, they feel that the Italian people should believe that the whole of Istria, Friuli, and Trieste are Italian, and therefore they make the Slavs

---

21 [Founded by Carlo Seppenhofer in Trieste in 1891, the National League replaced the previous association, Pro Patria, disbanded by imperial edict in 1890. The league was active in the regions of Friuli, Trentino, the city of Trieste, and Istria. Its aim was to promote Italian culture and to organize Italian patriotic demonstrations in the areas that were still under the Austrian Empire.]

22 [Scipio Sighele (1868–1913) was a sociologist and criminologist. Slataper here refers to Sighele's paper "Irredentism and Nationalism" that was presented at the congress Il nazionalismo italiano, held in Florence 3–5 December 1910 and then published in *Il Nazionalismo italiano: Atti del congresso di Firenze*, A. Quattrini, 1911, 80–95.]

23 [Giulio De Frenzi (1878–1967) was a journalist and politician. Slataper here refers to the speech "The Politics of Alliances" that De Frenzi delivered at the congress Il nazionalismo italiano, in *Il Nazionalismo italiano*, 105–27.]

24 [Reference to Prezzolini's article "La nostra promessa." See Introduction, xxiii–xxiv.]

25 [The Venezia Giulia region comprised Trieste, Istria, parts of the Dalmatian Coast, and Gorizia. The term itself, coined by Graziadio Ascoli, a Gorizian glottologist, had strong nationalist implications: "Venezia" referred to the city of Venice, which controlled most of these areas in the Middle Ages, and "Giulia" denoted the ancient Roman settlements in the region.]

appear to be an invention and provocation of the Austrian government; on the other hand, because they want Italy to be involved, and to help their subjugated brothers, it is incumbent upon them to clearly describe the quality and the magnitude of the threat they live under. And so, they move ahead, only to hem and haw. And at the same time, they complain of the indifference and ignorance of the Italian people!

Italians must know the truth. First, because it is immoral to incite a nation with fictitious representations, and to provoke unforeseeable and unwanted consequences. Let them say what they will: but this is the reality, this is the crux of irredentism for Venezia Giulia. This irredentist conviction that cannot stand objections is too naive and insecure. "Truth cannot be avoided or upended: one must climb over it."

Preparation

First of all, the need to be prepared. We have already talked about moral preparedness; as for military preparedness, I recommend the brief volume *Nationalism and the Problem of the Italian Military*, by Fabio Ranzi. Carlo Placci, in his inquiry on the Italian-Austrian relationship, published in *Il Regno*, quoted the opinion of a high-ranking officer:

> It is madness to encourage and even tolerate this spreading animosity towards Austria, if we do not have the intention to back it with military intervention at a later date. Are we prepared to wage a victorious war? In all confidence, I will tell you that at the beginning of March 1904 (to say nothing about four years later!), when our political relations with Austria were especially tense, not to say alarming, I was very worried. Only we soldiers knew the exact state of affairs, the real state of the military and the navy. Today, after the public critiques by Ricotti, Candiani, Palumbo, Taverna, and others, not even a layman can have any illusions. We are not sufficiently ready!

Let's say that the condition of our military improves. But what irredentist propaganda can be considered *purposeful*? We all agree that real propaganda does not consist of simple demonstrations where, at worst, the protestors' bellies suffer no upset, and those arrested are let out the back door of the police station after having been brought in, in grand style, for some pressing diplomatic reason, through the front door. Why don't the irredentists take on the humble task of spreading their ideas among the people? Why doesn't a serious pamphlet of irredentist propaganda exist, to counter the many socialist pamphlets against "wasteful expense"? What are the members of the Trento-Trieste doing? I've leafed through all its sporadic output of pamphlets, and this is what I've seen: (1) a great display of duties and obligations; (2) huge ignorance regarding all irredentist issues; (3) donations to social funds at times of political strife; (4) the absolute incapacity to coordinate, in the moment, all the conflicting demonstrations (after the events in Vienna would it not have been logical for the Trento-Trieste to organize and coordinate all of these rallies?); (5) following Borelli's 1911 proposal, an exhortation to all Italians to send their business cards, stamped by the Lega Nazionale, to the mayor of Rome.[26]

They will respond that the most valuable work is also the most secret. That may be true; as long as the secret doesn't consist of giving Masonic support to the Liberal Party in Trieste, which is the anti-irredentist party par excellence!

Then there are the various kinds of "volunteer battalions." I do not doubt that some of these divisions might be dependable. But as soon as these battalions are utilized in any national interest, we witness the heroism of theatrics. Salvemini[27] has described them in the town of Molfetta; I remember how the university students in Florence treasured their bold rifles! But what about studying some border geography and tactics?

Should we mention target practice also? It has become the legal means of enlisting in the volunteer corps. Every year I see the invitation to join posted in the halls of the university; but I asked, and it turns out the results are dismal.

Let's suppose that all this training is going as well as everyone would like; let's see what the conditions for war would be.

Conditions for War

There are still those who hope for the destruction of Austria. They say it was that gossip, Emilio Castelar,[28] who was the first to assert this would happen with the death of Franz Joseph. Today the only ones who still believe that are the few latecomers who do not know, for instance, that

---

26 [Giovanni Borelli (1867–1932) was an Italian nationalist and monarchist who participated in the Nationalist Congress held in Florence in 1910. The mayor of Rome at the time was Ernesto Nathan (see note 12).]

27 [Gaetano Salvemini (1873–1957) was an Italian intellectual and politician. He believed in the socialist cause and fought against the miserable conditions of the peasants in southern Italy. During the fascist regime he lived in France, where he founded the anti-fascist newspaper *Non mollare* (Don't give up). He was born in the town of Molfetta in Puglia.]

28 [Emilio Castelar (1832–99) was a Spanish politician. He was president of the First Spanish Republic.]

Austria is governed by the hereditary archduke. But this idea was pretty much what the millennium was for Catholics; and Austria continues to live on, essentially unaltered, under different forms.

The truth is that the Latin populations, and especially the Italians, have created a mythical idea of Austria. Austria, from Mazzini onwards, has been perceived as a kind of opposite of our soul; the devil of our god. In 1848 we believed that all the non-German people of the Austrian Empire would have fought with us against it. Today we continue to take comfort in Hungary's outcries against the Austrian government, and in the notion of Austria as apathetic and obtuse. Now, all of this will be of great interest to historians of our ideals; but politically, this attitude is a mistake.

Some well-intentioned nationalist should engage in this very useful enterprise (as Papini has already suggested): to write a serious book about Austria. Austria has a wonderful tradition of government. It has absorbed all the teachings of Roman law and of Machiavelli, while we were just talking about Rome and Machiavelli. Internally, with universal suffrage and workers' protection laws, it absorbed the two opposite political movements of clericalism and socialism into state parties. Its most serious threat comes from its multi-ethnicity, of which it has made use for its own existence and purposes. The colonial policy of the Roman Empire was to unleash the various ethnicities against one another, and to dominate them. Like Rome, but less than Rome, Austria was not able to impose a common language; but it has been able to impose a state bond based on respect, fear, and veneration. With discipline, it has unified all its disparate parts: it has created a national army.

It is a state governed by a Germanic bureaucracy. But it is a nimble bureaucracy, that knows how to shrink itself and become a dictatorship when necessary. It's German, but it has incorporated into itself the most useful elements of its various nationalities: Istrian or Dalmatian admirals, police officers from Trento, Czech university professors. It has acknowledged and exploited the political value of its different ethnic groups. It is blindly devoted to its own country. It is much more honest than other bureaucratic states; faithful and united within itself, from the prime minister to the gendarme cast into the heart of Croatia. The Austrian government is one unified force. Swiftly, it builds sturdy roads and railways, combining commercial and military needs. It does not yield an inch to the Parliament's orders, if it considers them damaging in any way; if the deputies do not approve new funds for the fleet, Trieste's arsenal, *at its own risk*, continues to build new battleships.

It follows that its diplomacy is always confident. Its mandate has been straightforward for decades. Pushed towards the east, it has not made a hesitant step since 1870. Over the last thirty years, it prepared for an annexation everyone had already recognized as de facto since 1878.[29] Thus, it acquired Bosnia and Herzegovina without any internal protest: Bertolini notes that in Sarajevo the citizens glancing over the annexation proclamation were much more interested in tasting his "koňak."[30] These are the same lands for which Austria had to sacrifice thousands of soldiers in 1878.

So, no Austrian collapse. Instead, the possibility of war. And not an Austro-Italian war; a European war.

Austria and Germany are a coalition that has silenced all of Europe. It is the epicentre of European politics. Italy has not been able to take advantage of its position. Italy, renouncing its so-called compensations, and for the time being reneging on its objectives in the Balkans, could have been compensated for these losses in the Mediterranean. It did not know how to, or was not able to; recriminations are pointless now – or so it seems – and we should turn, resolutely, to other possibilities.

We have already recognized our dilemma: either Austria or France. This is an invitation to honesty. This is how we can move forward. *L'Italia all'Estero* was born with a clear philo-Slavic and philo-French agenda.[31] In its first issues the irredentists were represented by liberal Croatians. It knew what it wanted. But the irredentists complained, and as a result its agenda was muddled.

Now the same thing is happening again: we desire and proclaim war against Austria in every way, but we end up saying that France does not matter, that we cannot count on the Slavs, that war against Austria is pure madness, that we have to remain in the Triple Alliance *with dignity*. We want to fight against pan-Germanism, but we go after the Slavs: we incite irredentism, and we want to remain with Austria. In the same way, we advocate liberalism while opposing German capital imported into Italy.

The Nationalist Congress has voted against "sentimental alliances," and Corradini stated that he is particularly opposed to Francophile sentimentality. Very well, but what are we playing at? Unless we truly believe

---

29 [After the end of the Russo-Turkish war in 1878, the Austrian Empire engaged in a war to occupy Bosnia and Herzegovina, which were part of the Ottoman Empire. At the end of the war these provinces became de facto Austrian colonies. On 5 October 1908 they were annexed to the rest of the empire.]

30 [Reference to Gino Bertolini's travel book *Tra Mussulmani e Slavi in automobile attraverso Bosnia, Erzegovina, Dalmazia e Croazia*, Fratelli Treves, 1909. "Koňak" is the Czech word for cognac.]

31 [*L'Italia all'Estero* (Italy abroad) was a biweekly newspaper addressing foreign and colonial politics. It was established in 1907 to foster the nationalist and colonialist spirit of the Italian people. It closed in 1913.]

that Germany and Austria will give us Trentino and Istria on a platter. If we're not that naive, then the only solution is to be Slavophile – a position which I will summarize here, in a rough parenthesis.

Except for the Masons, we all agree that France is spent with comfort and misrule. England is a power that must be allied with a terrestrial army, but it would be able to serve its ally only secondarily, as a threat to fourth and fifth parties. Russia, having renounced the Far East with the Korean Treaty, is recovering slowly. Montenegro, Serbia, and Bulgaria are insubstantial. It is possible that with such an alliance, a well-prepared Italy could engage in a "victorious war." Moreover, a Czech and Croatian-Slovenian uprising is possible, but of an exclusively national character, more pro-autonomy than anti-Austrian.

Clearly, if Italy wants this alliance, it must call principally on the Slavs. De Frenzi rightly noted that the Slavs are not a nation, and that aside from some isolated and generous attempts, the majority of Slavs, because they abide by the church, are anti-Italian. In reality, a united Slavic nation would not be necessary for us; but a union of Russia, the Balkan states, and the Austrian Slavs would be useful: that is, a political, temporary union against the common enemy. Also, we must make distinctions: the Czechs, for example, are not clerical, and they have great sympathy for Italy. We must also remember that the Slavs love anticlerical France.

However, to achieve this alliance, Italy must absolutely renounce Trieste, Istria, and its aspirations in the Balkans. Its strength would come from stirring up and assisting Slavic identity. It would block Austria's eastbound advance with independent nation states. It could annex Trentino and Friuli up to the Isonzo. In this way, it would be possible to gain the support of that Slavic Austria that would very soon rule the empire.

This too is an anti-sentimental attitude that runs counter to the interests of the irredentists of the Adriatic coast, and maybe it shows sentimentality towards the Slavs, but it is logical and, I think, unequivocal.

There is one other serious objection, brought forth by Bertolini: what would the moral consequences be, for Italy, of forging a union with a passionate and feminine race like the Slavs? How could we control pan-Slavism, if Germany is weakened? Personally, I don't really believe in the moral effects of political alliances. It seems to me that the very fact that we are united with Austria is the psychological obstacle to strengthening ourselves with its virtues. And the cultural reality of pan-Slavism, whether imminent or already present, is a serious historical and geographical mistake, politically. Slavic freedom on the other side of the Adriatic may signify Italian security within the rest of Europe. But at this point, to be concerned with *race* presupposes events that are still well in the future.

The National and Political Future of Trieste

If one is concerned with the question of Trieste, one notes first of all that the conduct of Trieste, its routine, daily life, regulated by prevailing interests, contradicts how we Triestines here in Italy depict our situation. We like to emphasize our rebellious, enthusiastic spirit, forced to suppress its brotherly affection for Italy, yet poised to rise up heroically at the right moment. This contradiction between Scipio's helmet and Mercury is to an extent very natural, because the few, or the many, who work for a new historical settlement for sentimental or political reasons are so completely convinced of the validity of their own beliefs that they accept them blindly as the only possible option.[1] We must not forget that it is natural to want to embrace the most congenial and popular opinion, rather than giving ourselves the uncomfortable task of studying, and doing a little soul-searching, to accord our actions with how we would like to be, and bring our words in line with how we're sure we must act. This unconscious dissembling, however, and this natural tendency to comfort (habits rather than actions, too-quietist habits, facile, deluding, that end up producing too much that is negative) do not altogether explain this contradiction: and that is truly essential in the soul of Trieste today.

Trieste is a place of transition – geographical, historical, cultural, and commercial – that is, of struggle. Everything is dual or triple in Trieste, starting from the flora and ending with ethnicity. As long as Trieste has no consciousness of itself, as long as the Slavs speak Italian and its culture consists of and fulfils itself in business, in commercial interests, then life is fairly peaceful. As soon as the need arises for an independent, non-commercial culture, the frozen crust breaks and anxious debates erupt.

1 ["Scipio's helmet" is a reference to Mameli's "Canto degli Italiani" (The song of the Italians). See *My Karst*, p. 37, note 15.]

Obviously, at the beginning of its history, it was impossible for Trieste to know the full significance of its complexity. One could have certainly hoped to quiet those debates, not in the name of some religious or moral ideas that could bring them in line with loftier aspirations, but in the name of and with the allure of profit. Catholicism has always been remote, too remote for Trieste's atheistic indifference, just as the Austrian state, in its most advanced form, is not much more than a commercial contract between multiple ethnicities.[2]

The Austrian government, having failed in its most serious attempts, and unable to hope any longer in a broad Germanization of Trieste, had every interest in promoting an Italian identity that could break the unity of the southern Slavs along the coast, which would in turn allow Austria's trading routes in Central Europe to remain open. Although to us today this seems absurd, this is the reason why Governor Stadion was philo-Italian and why the whole government supported the Italians.[3] For their part, the Italians too had every reason to treat the Slavs as fellow citizens, in order to keep the enemy and trouble at bay: hence the sympathy and the philo-Slavic compassion that all the inhabitants of our provinces felt towards them once they started to feel Italian. But this was a very contradictory attitude because it combined the ideals of ethno-national equality proper to the revolutions of 1848 with the right to one's own country or political autonomy.

This conciliatory effort could not bear fruit. Thus, the Slavs, as soon as they learned to read and write, did not genuflect in front of ineffectual Italian sympathy, but became aware of their own rights and started to dream their own future. Consequently, the Austrian government, in its typical German manner, had to weigh the will of the Slavs against the size of the population, which, besides, was very faithful to the state. Thus, in order to save their own nation, also threatened, they sacrificed the Italians, who, meanwhile, had started to question the legitimacy of the Austrian state. Because in the meantime the Italians had followed their own path, and their cultural awareness made them realize that through Dante and Machiavelli one had necessarily to arrive at Mazzini, and that a national consciousness could not be constantly obstructed by a way of life not its own, forced to tiptoe so as not to disturb an archaic human balance, prevented from discussing things freely, from looking forward,

2 This holds true for Austria's most advanced elements: the rest sees in the Apostolic Emperor the embodiment of religion, homeland, interests, in such a way that we can talk about an "Austrian" sentiment.

3 [Baron Franz Stadion von Warthausen (1806–53) was governor of Trieste from 1841–47.]

existing, and acting openly, under the sun. Why did Austria, after having taken away our freedom, deny us our right to our own cultural education? Simply because we Italians were much more culturally advanced than the majority of all the other peoples of the Austrian Empire. We liberals had to carry on our shoulders a reactionary and clerical Austria. What was still necessary for many, was for us oppressive.[4]

The educated classes, as soon as they satisfied their basic material needs, became aware and conscious of their right to exist. Other concerns started to become more predominant. The idea of the nation started to develop not only as a right of peoples whose geography, history, and traditions are similar (a fatherland is precisely this interpenetration of geography and history), but also because it was the only way to satisfy all their various human necessities. It is true that the Triestine lawyer, in case of Italian annexation, would have to contend with competition from the many colleagues in the kingdom, and that the elementary and high school teacher would become a state employee with a salary lower than the present one. But in history, as soon as people have reached a state of material comfort appropriate to their social class, strictly financial factors do not count any longer. What counts instead are the passions (which can be influenced by ideas, not by hunger), the ambition – for instance to be able to expand one's influence to a broader group of compatriots – and the desire for wider renown, for more important social possibilities. For these reasons the majority of men of letters, journalists, teachers, lawyers, politicians, and all other so-called free professionals have been irredentist. It follows that all news reports were and still are exclusively irredentist.

But opposing this class there was all the rest of Trieste; there was the collective interest of Trieste. She did not even discuss, except in times of financial crises, what would happen to her without the connection with Austria, because such a change would have been a disruption and a disturbance to all aspects of her life. Commerce is linked to relationships with clienteles, and obviously, there is no other class, in its totality, that is more conservative than the business class, for whom a period of war devastation is enough to undermine its prosperity. Also, this class is

4 [The word "liberal" in this context carries a different meaning from the contemporary usage in the United States. Here it refers to the nineteenth-century secular political and economic ideology, which embraced "constitutional and parliamentary government, economic individualism and the distinction between religious and political authority." Andrew C. Gould, "Origins of Liberalism: Concepts and Explanations," *Origins of Liberal Dominance: State, Church, and Party in Nineteenth-Century Europe*, U of Michigan P, 1999, 3.]

completely shaped, in both its individuals and customs, by the present situation, so much so that the great Triestine commerce is for the most part in the hands of a mixture of Germans, Greeks, Hungarians (German, Greek, Hungarian Jews) and it is supported by Slavic and German capital. Therefore, the irredentist thesis is no less than the danger of an axe on its roots. Moreover, the mass of the people, almost completely lacking culture, follows the instinct of "who cares who's on the throne as long as the dog gets his bone," and the habit of its dynastic affection.

However, a few years ago the intellectual class was able to count on another factor, and a serious one: the Slavic population. Irredentism, confronted by the implacable resistance of the whole Triestine way of life, had almost completely fallen asleep, and now found new nourishment. A businessman can easily answer in this way a man of letters who shows him the need to unite with Italy because in Austria there is no freedom of speech: "these are concerns for jabberers, not for doers. Here, I can tend to my business very well." However, he will start to worry when his supremacy is wholly threatened and, in order to avoid the danger of one death, he accepts that within his home he must build another perhaps even more secure one. Four or five years ago, the old irredentism made use of the traditional 1860s double-edged sword of "the rights of all peoples to self-determination," and therefore had to ignore the Slavs in order not to compromise itself as logic would require. Now, the new irredentism, with the aid of imperialist principles, proclaims its national necessity, scorning any ideal of justice towards others that might weaken itself.

We have this dilemma: to choose between a national (and also financial) existence that the irredentist cause could most likely secure, and a financial existence (at least in part also national) that would most likely be destroyed by the national one. In front of this twofold historical demand, the majority of Triestines have chosen the most comfortable position: an equivocal one, living from day to day, acting in the interests of the nation as long as it does not conflict with their petty financial interests, and supporting financial initiatives as long as they at least appear to support national advocacy. Thus, the parents who send their children to German schools are chastised, while financial wealth, even if it is Austrian, in circulating should benefit the "National League," at least in small part.[5] The liberal-national party is the political product of this way of thinking. In it (notwithstanding some give and take, benefiting Italian identity or business needs, depending on the predominance of certain people or

5 [See p. 134, note 21.]

specific issues), the Triestine dilemma is alleviated, and the city is able to continue its daily life. Therefore no one with some common sense can despise the liberal party, which, gathering very different perspectives, raises the national identity of the city only very gradually. As a matter of fact, I am certain that any politician, no matter what his ideal view for Trieste, would join its ranks. At the same time nobody with some common sense can forget that in politics accepting things as they are is only a first step. The work of this politician would produce the same poor results that we are accustomed to seeing now, if he, like our contemporaries, did not understand where and how to lead the majority, and if he, permeated by legalese and cheerfully condescending complacencies, did not place himself squarely before the dilemma I am talking about.

Doing this, we notice at first only these two fundamental positions (because we cannot take into account fantasies of economic sacrifice or of national identity, as they belong to the neglected margin of comfortable individual dreams): irredentism, which must demonstrate that Trieste would not suffer too much financially once it is united to Italy, while from a nationalist perspective it would be saved; and the attitude known as socialism, which must demonstrate the damage that the city would suffer from joining Italy, and at the same time emphasize its ability to maintain its Italian identity under Austrian domination. Irredentism, by nature, is not restricted to a political party, but is very widespread, and only in the last few years and among a small minority is becoming a true political conviction. This other attitude, admittedly or not, is that of the socialist party and of some other groups and individuals who are philo-Austrian, or indifferent – or sincerely, critically, solitarily Italian: those whom their adversaries, simplifying complex doubts and discussions, inaccurately define as *Vociani*.

Obviously, we cannot expect the irredentists to provide much detail on their agenda. But we cannot just give them a pass when they accuse those who write against them of cowardice, espionage, and of being pro–Austrian authority.[6] First of all, it is not true that whoever wants a revolution must avoid all revolutionary means, because that would damage their cause. Similarly, it is not true that who goes against the public, popular opinion should be quiet every time his ideas could make him

6 I am referring here to R. [Ruggero Timeus], the author of a long article published in the *Idea Nazionale*, who uses this argument against Vivante without, however, ever citing his book. I have surmised and summarized the irredentist theses from that article, as well as from other articles, essays, and especially from constant debates with irredentists.

lose a job or limit his options. First, because no one can ask someone else to be a hero when he himself is not, we are all ready to recognize that the irredentist has the right not to sign his propaganda; but, at the same time, the irredentist does not have the right to accuse those who sign their own of cowardice. Second, a large number of Triestine irredentists who have "emigrated" to free themselves from Austrian clutches now live here in Italy. Why then is irredentist literature in such short supply? The truth is that in fact the majority of irredentists are not at all sure what they want; they are lazy, and they are selfish.[7]

On the other hand, Vivante has analysed the other perspective in a very important book.[8] His book, together with Benco's monograph on Trieste and Pasini's study on the Italian university in Trieste, allow all Italian citizens to get to know the city well.

Vivante, as he honestly declares in the preface of his book, is a socialist. An isolated socialist, in many ways "hateful to God and to His enemies."[9]

His experience comes from real political experiences: as an irredentist and political editor of *Il Piccolo*, and as a socialist and director of the *Lavoratore*. His book offers a wealth of psychological insights on this particular milieu. In order to complete it he worked for two or three years in the libraries of Venice and Trieste. Reading it, one feels the certainty of walking on solid ground. To the inherent merit of the book, we can add the fact that Vivante is not a man of letters. His position as maverick socialist strengthens the quality of his criticism. Because socialism, like any other new social movement, had to reassess reality all on its own and instil fresh energy into society. The false assumptions that informed this socialist approach are well known to everyone, and we will have occasion to point them out later.

So, the book has a documentary quality, and the archival research has been so precise and extensive that it is the first time that entire periods of our history (such as 1848) have been brought to light and men and ideas discovered. It is difficult to summarize in an article, especially for the readers of *La Voce* who already have read some excerpts, and have been informed, by me and others, of the issues concerning our region. Here is the gist of the book.

Irredentist propaganda revolves around two lies: one national and one financial. It is absolutely not true that the whole Julian region sees it as

7 Irredentist literature is more frequent in Trentino because over there the national question is much clearer, and the irredentist ideology can solve it easily.

8 Angelo Vivante, *Irredentismo Adriatico: Contributo alla discussione sui rapporti austro-italiani*, Florence: Libreria della Voce, 1912.

9 [Quote from Dante's *Inferno* III, 63.]

economically advantageous and desirable to be unified with Italy. Mixed together with the Italians, living next to them, are the Slovenians and Croats, who are the majority of the population, contrary to the statistical sleight of hand and the cultural injustice that the Italians perpetrate against them, which is obviously greater than anything they can perpetrate against the Italians.[10] These Slavic populations are not a government invention, nor did they arrive just yesterday: for the most part they have been here for eleven centuries. Abused by the Italians, it is not true that they are uncivilized; on the contrary, in some aspects they are more civilized than the Italians (for instance, in the district of Gradisca, which is almost completely Italian, 31.66 per cent of the population is illiterate, while in the Slavic district of Tolmino, it's 28.67 per cent); the banks in Carniola in 1888 had a market worth of 32,480 crowns, which in 1902 increased to 44 million!

As for the financial question, the whole history of Trieste and the scientific study of the current commercial situation demonstrate that the port's prosperity is not at all *natural*; it is instead a product of the state that Trieste joined, out of necessity, the same state that controls its hinterland.[11] Therefore, Trieste is inextricably tied to Austria, and even the Triestines who would like annexation by Italy must also want railways that will make it more Austrian. If in the near future Austria no longer sees the need to favour Trieste, because the port does not belong to her any longer, what today still appears as a remote danger (for instance the canals that could connect the northern German ports and the Black Sea with northern Austria) would become a reality. Moreover, Austria could develop any port on its coastline, unless Italy also saw fit to annex Fiume and Dalmatia; but even this would not be enough.

One cannot say that unification, under these conditions, would be to the great advantage of Trieste's Italian identity, because Trieste was able to assimilate the Slavs only because of its activity as a great commercial city. The next day we would again have a grey and stagnant city. Instead, right now, although the Italian population cannot any longer count on an en masse assimilation of the Slavic inhabitants, it can very easily coexist with

---

10 [Vivante and Slataper were well aware that the Austrian authority identified national identity through the use of the *Umgangssprache*, the language of everyday use, instead of the mother tongue of their subjects. Because in Trieste the Italian Triestine dialect was the lingua franca used in everyday exchanges, the official statistics always showed a disproportionate number of Italians, while the Slovenes were always counted as a small minority.]

11 Vivante's book is the first comprehensive study dealing with the economic life of Trieste. Besides the articles of early irredentists, this is, although imperfect, the first study in Italian on the Slovene question.

them as they fight for the most basic equal rights, not for dominance. We should not think that the Slavic population is growing; it is just becoming more visible. Moreover, with the industrialization of their original regions, Slavic immigration into the great urban centres is abating. We must then embrace the true national and political tradition of Trieste, which is, in the thought of Valussi and Tommaseo, to attain equality between the two peoples and to spread eastern culture (Slavic, Greek, Albanian) within western culture.[12]

Alongside these ideas there are those expressed by irredentism understood as the only effective defence of national identity. This kind of irredentism, which Vivante does not discuss sufficiently, is different, as we have seen, from the original irredentism, because the latter was born out of Christian principles influenced by the romantic movement and by the ideals of popular self-determination promoted by the French revolution. It is also different from the second irredentism, developed in the last two decades of the century, which, while still maintaining the same principles, acknowledged that their realization would obstruct the rights and the will of the Yugoslav population; it misrepresented the Slavic reality, reducing it to the ugly implementation of mass immigration and false Austrian statistics. The Austrian government – which in reality *helps* the Slavs in everything – was the lifeline of this propaganda. In fact, if the Slavs were there naturally, how could it be possible to speak of a genuine Italian spirit yearning to reunite with Italy? And if the Slavs were not there, for what purpose, against whom, could we pretend to need constant help from our Italian brothers? The Slavs were there, but only thanks to a government ploy. Without the government they would have not been dangerous; in fact, they would have disappeared, immediately absorbed or pushed back. The new irredentism has not completely abandoned this double position, and the old irredentism continues to set the general tone. The persistence of this contradiction shows, among other things, how the irredentists themselves feel that the Italian mood is little inclined towards imperialistic claims; but it must be noted that the

12 [Pacifico Valussi (1813–93) was a journalist and politicians from the Friuli region. In 1838 he became the editor of the *Osservatore Triestino*, the official newspaper of the government in Trieste. During his time in Trieste, he recognized the importance of Trieste as a unique borderland where various national identities and ideas could come into contact and circulate. He was a close friend of Niccolò Tommaseo and joined him in Venice in 1848. Tommaseo (1802–74), originally from Dalmatia, was an intellectual, politician, and writer. He participated in the 1848 revolution in Venice against Austria and published the most important dictionary of the Italian language of the nineteenth century. He was one of the first intellectuals to defend the independence of Dalmatia against Italy's nationalist vision.]

new irredentist propaganda, following its own logic, is openly imperialistic. The propaganda states: the Slavs are here, and they are dangerous. It's true, the government helps them quite a bit; this is to be expected: because the Slavs are naturally its supporters (this is because the government must do at least part of what the majority of its population wants). Alone, we cannot defend ourselves against some barbarians supported by a whole barbarian state apparatus. We must reunite with Italy, and not worry at all about the inevitable ruin of the Slavs who would be annexed along with us. Let there be no doubt: if the Italian state intervenes in our fight without any false scruples, in a few decades the Slavs who have immigrated recently will return to their country, and the others will assimilate. Moreover, this political change will not have any serious consequences for commerce. If Trieste goes to Italy, Austria will either break into many pieces, from which new nations will be born, or it will continue to exist, but in a different configuration. In either case, it is impossible to see why Austria, or the countries that are now under Austrian power, would engage in a trade war with Trieste, i.e., with Italy, as though defeated countries could continue to resent victorious nations for a prolonged period. But even if they wanted to hold onto their resentment they could not, because Trieste is *naturally* the best harbour in the Adriatic. This is because Fiume is without an effective railroad infrastructure on Hungarian soil, has cumbersome customs taxes, and is situated on the Kvarner Gulf, with very rough seas. Dalmatia should not even be considered, because it is too far away. Like Antwerp and Rotterdam competing with Hamburg for the same German market, Trieste would continue to have its commerce with the immediate hinterland (Yugoslav lands) and faraway lands (the alpine provinces, Moravia, and Bohemia). After all, it is a question of life and death. Because it is foolish to kid ourselves: the Slavs do not only demand that their rights be recognized, they want to throw us overboard. Today they are not that important, but given the inevitability of a Yugoslav state (which would include Trieste) in the near future, this new nation would be naturally imperialistic; that is, it would seek, with all its state power, to seize *its* port, and it would succeed in a relatively short time.

Now, I believe in good conscience that I have weighed these two positions for quite a while, with enough honesty and seriousness to be able to discuss them with some clarity. I'd like to point out right away that Vivante's economic reasons are too serious to be undermined by these statements from his opponents. They delude themselves that they are able to talk about very complex issues whose analysis should be based on very specific knowledge, in the same way they talk with regularity of diplomatic prospects at the cafe. For instance, the fact that Austria or

Yugoslavia could not make use of Fiume seems strange even to people who do not know much about the issue. Even admitting that Hungary could infiltrate into Yugoslavia all the way to the Adriatic, it would have no reason to obstruct the development of a port that belongs to it. As for railroads, apparently they are still being built, and the fact that the Kvarner Gulf is turbulent would only matter if coffee too could get seasick. But Fiume too enjoyed the same state protections as Trieste (for instance, the preferential customs duty on coffee),[13] so why doesn't it thrive like Trieste? Because Trieste is already there; it's a port with a stronger commercial tradition and clientele. Fiume *right now* has poor rail connections, while Trieste has good if not excellent ones; Trieste, *right now*, with equal state support, can take advantage of its better geographical position. What about tomorrow? Today Austria favours Trieste. But tomorrow, why couldn't the northern ports extend their commercial dominion to Moravia, Bohemia, and the alpine provinces? Not as an affront to Trieste, but as a more natural commercial relationship? The only serious objection could be Antwerp and Rotterdam;[14] but what's the use of casting around assertions without any evidence? What's the purpose? Why do it? Are those port cities truly in competition with Hamburg for the German hinterland? For what reasons? In conclusion, we must start to discuss Vivante's argument. Those in the know should speak.

I am not in the know, and I cannot commit myself to further studies that could distract us from what is of central importance to our case. Vivante himself admits in his preface that if his socialist ideal were realized, if there were a system of free trade, all of his reasons would become meaningless. It is true that this is a far-fetched possibility. There is one possibility, however, that *could be* much more realistic: that Austria advances to Thessaloniki. I am not saying that this will happen. I am stating that, in line with the traditional political agenda dating from 1870, Austria's internal turmoil and its fragile political equilibrium are not enough to keep it from adding new, restless elements, as long as Austria gains new and indispensable wealth. But what about the Balkans? Russia? England?

---

13 There is less duty paid on coffee imported into Trieste and Fiume than into other European ports. This is the most obvious example that Vivante cites in order to demonstrate how commercial trade depends more on the handling of taxes (and freight) than other particularities of geography and traditional functionality.

14 [Antwerp and Rotterdam are cities whose important ports continued to thrive in the nineteenth century thanks to their strong international commerce with Germany and other European countries. Slataper here notes that one could object that Trieste could become the Antwerp or Rotterdam of the Adriatic Sea.]

Italy? Let's not dwell on it: it is self-evident that it is a possibility.[15] What would happen to Trieste? Not just Trieste, but the whole Adriatic Sea would lose all its commercial importance. Let's concede that it might not lose it completely; in any case, Trieste could, without any loss, or even with some advantage, join Italy.

What I am saying is that it is very difficult to foretell the economic future of a city. The only certainty right now is that commerce in Trieste, as in all other ports of the world, is not an absolutely natural phenomenon. What we can predict today, accurately, based on actual data, supports Vivante more than his adversaries. It is unlikely that Trieste will become once again a fishing village, but having to endure the competition of the northern European ports and of a new Austrian port on the Adriatic, it would be less important than Fiume is today.

But we must take into account the national struggle. Here things get much more complicated. We are confronted with two different states of mind: the nationalist one, which sees in national strife nothing more than a power struggle, and believes that any kind of fairness towards one's rival will turn into an act of injustice against us; and the other state of mind, the truly socialist one, which cannot accept that others will have to endure what we would not ourselves, and sees in nationalist hatred only the contempt that city dwellers feel towards country peasants, and the effects of injustice perpetrated by masters against servants. Naturally, the socialist feels more sympathy for the aspirations of the latter, because they are oppressed; therefore, they tend to inflate their numbers and their righteousness, both as a reaction to the nationalist rhetoric that wants to deny their existence and because doing so tends to project their aspirations into the present. Thus, they err on the side of exaggeration for the same reason that the nationalists, for whom the past was more favourable, tend to err on the side of minimizing their numbers. The irredentist mindset is more acceptable as an ideology in Italy now that the events in Tripoli seem to support the right to oppress other nations (whereas it's nothing more than an instance of the constant war that European civilization, more resilient and industrious, has inevitably waged against less active civilizations). The socialist mindset, on the other hand, is far less acceptable because the norms of absolute justice have not yet regulated the actions of their internationalist agenda, not even

15 It would be useful for Austria to conquer only a strip of land from Sanjak of Novi Pazar to Thessaloniki. Albania would be free, within its geographical and, almost completely, its ethnic borders; Greece's eastern borders would be rectified; Bulgaria would take charge of the rest of Macedonia and also of the ports that have direct connections to Plovdiv and Sofia.

in the case of national strife. It suffices to remember that the Austrian-German socialists would like to treat their Czech comrades the same way the Austrian bourgeois treated their Czech enemies). To choose a clear position between these two mindsets would mean resolving the anxiety and uncertainty around ideas of nationality, country, moral and practical action, and much else besides all this.

[...]

We should not be afraid of our own civilization, which allows us to correct our failings, which are as strong as our virtues. The fact that socialism is strong among us should be a reason for joy, not condemnation. That there is more debate and critique means that our thinking is more engaged, and that we are more human.

Why then should we be afraid if the Slovenes become more human? You say: "it's a bad idea to arm them with their own culture" (but you give them access to Italian culture, you do all you can to give it to them, to educate them, and because of this cultural imposition they end up resenting you even more because you have taken away their identity). Do you really believe that their culture could become a strong weapon against you? And yet you also say that their strength lies in their blind solidarity. Following your logic, you destroy their individuality as much as possible. You encourage the tensions that already exist among them. According to you this will make them weaker. In reality, what you propose will make them much stronger, because their blind solidarity is a cause of weakness, as is the lack of individual identities that still keeps them from artistic and industrial endeavour. From a civil perspective, they will become much stronger, without a doubt. As a result, you should not worry; the current strife will lose its tone of intolerance and will become the struggle of two more advanced societies. The Slavs' current resentment is the result of the contempt and repression that they feel all around them, as they suffer from lack of agency, of continuity, and of the stability that only a national identity with its coherent laws can provide.

You are harsh towards them just as they are with you, and you fear their culture, because you lack your own national consciousness and feel incapable of sustaining this rational antagonism. Deep down, the reason for your dismay is that you doubt yourself and shroud yourselves in twenty centuries of civilization because your small and feeble spirit is afraid that you will not be able to survive another five years. You want to keep the Slavs uneducated just like the masters want to keep their servants castrated. You're like kings living in fear of their butlers.

Your civilization is growing very little, and you don't try to develop it seriously. You're always on the defensive. You focus completely on the national struggle, and you have put at its service everything that could be used to nourish your civilization: art, science, education, and character. For questions of national defence, you keep an Italian secondary school in Pisino, in such a condition and with such standards that it's a miracle if the students who graduate have the moral strength to save themselves. That's how you create the champions of the nation.

You do not try to improve yourselves and do not let serious criticism rise from the ill-natured gossip of the coffee house. You will accuse me again of being an enemy of the country, because woe betide our opponents if they catch wind of our pettiness. You think about little other than superficiality and display. Otherwise how could you explain your delusional perception of the Italian language, understood as something in itself, separate from real life? Your blind faith in the Lega Nazionale exempts you from thinking of all the other means, less obvious, but deeper, like the plough that doesn't glimmer while it's digging. On every national matchbox you can read Gioberti's phrase: "The death of language is the death of the nation."[16] But you have removed this phrase from its context, in the same way you have uprooted language from real life. You forget that for Gioberti the death of a language is the sign that a nation is dying as well. Thus, for the defence of your national identity, you've crowded into the trenches on the periphery and forgotten to cook rations in the centre; that is, to carry out the deeds that will ensure your life tomorrow. This is how you nationalists conduct yourselves. Luckily, even the German Triestine shopkeeper expanding his clientele, which is Italian, strengthens and enlivens the Italian identity of Trieste, and is a stronger nationalist than you are.

I am not saying that we should not think about defending ourselves. I am only saying that whoever thinks only about defence, does it badly. The best defence encompasses also the dedication to culture, to the best culture. Without this desire, our national struggle becomes a lavish form of charity: for the cause of our country, just as it's done for prostitution. We become like the lady speaking German to befriend the postal clerk mailing her letter, which, however, bears the stamp of the Lega Nazionale.

A newly born people must be by necessity completely armed and has no time to think about anything else. But they will have to pay for it at the time of victory, when they'll need to reinvent themselves *ab ovo*. Indeed,

16 [Vincenzo Gioberti (1801–52) was an Italian politician and philosopher. He was a strong supporter of the unification of Italy under the kings of Savoy. The quote comes from his volume *Del rinnovamento civile d'Italia*, Paris and Turin: Giuseppe Bocca, 1851, 359. Here he emphasized the importance of a national linguistic identity to create a unified Italy.]

they will have to accept the social norms that the defeated put in place before them, and only after centuries will they be able to achieve their ideal. But a people living already for centuries cannot wage wars in this way, unless they want their own destruction. They must strengthen themselves and support the cultural centres where their ideals can develop. We must go back to ourselves, and improve, and enrich ourselves, in order to maintain our power to do good in the world. What kind of civilization is this, that has a dingy room for a library? We must respect our own culture, if we want others to respect it. (Today, once again, from a more mature standpoint, I repeat this necessity more emphatically; and I still approve of and stand by the young man who, three years ago, scandalized you with his *Letters on Trieste*. But I can't defend his harshness and impulsivity.)

This is how we should view all our national issues, first of all the issue of assimilation.

It would be interesting from many points of view to discuss whether we can still assimilate the Slavs. I agree with Vivante who believes this is possible, but only in a scattered fashion and with a short-term effect. I also agree with Vivante's intuition that except for the first half of the nineteenth century, assimilation was much more superficial than we think. In any case, today a Slavic way of life exists, almost perfect in itself, with its own capital, workers, schools, banks, theatres, associations, shops, professionals, cafes, hotels, pubs, newspapers, writers, and politicians. Despite all this, the nationalist struggle is conditioned to believe in the possibility of assimilation.

And this is, in any case, a mistake. Whether or not it is possible, it would be good for some and sad for others; but it isn't something that we should spend time on. Even when a government with the necessary means wants to implement it, forced assimilation is not successful. In Germany and Russia, Poles are thriving; they are not just surviving. If we no longer want to concern ourselves with this option, which as we just pointed out is quite difficult to achieve, we will put the Slavs on the defensive, and only add insult to injury. We will fall back into the old patterns and beliefs. We will rely on the Lega, and if a Slav addresses us in Italian and wears a Dante pin[17] on his lapel – because in the Dante Alighieri Society there are beautiful girls and many dances – we will rejoice in our accomplishment. And we'll organize more and more dances, with beautiful girls, and we'll invite the Slavs and they will come, with Dante

17 [The Società Dante Alighieri was a cultural association whose aim was to propagate Italian culture and further the Italian identity of Trieste.]

pinned on. And the next day, it will take you by surprise that all the Slavs, even those who joined the Dante Society, voted for their own candidate.

We must stop with these clever stratagems. We should not be concerned only with our success, confusing its superficial rewards with what we can gain only by doing good.

But this is all just idle talk, boring, never-ending philosophical blabbering, while the political reality is that we are alone. A few thousand, separated from the rest of the nation, surrounded on all sides by Slavs. The reality is that in the near future these Slavs will be the third largest nation in Austria, and we will have to obey them as subjects, while they, as masters, will do with us as they please. Then, the intuitive truth, that two people cannot coexist in the same place, will have its proof, against our best arguments, to our disadvantage and ruin. Forget about justice and tolerance.

I do not think that two people can coexist when their level of culture is so different, as in our case now. But French people and Germans coexist in Switzerland, as French people and Flemings do in Belgium, although with some instances of struggle.[18] The national struggle is a struggle of civilizations that will diminish and settle down, once a certain equilibrium is reached. I'll never be like the socialists, I'll never waste a minute of my time preaching peace between Slavs and Italians: but I am certain that we can achieve peace, once war is taken more seriously.

---

18 Speaking of Belgium: Gino Luzzatto, in a long critical essay on Vivante's book, published in the *Unità*, although noting that the argument is "susceptible to doubts and further discussions," answers with the following quote to the nationalists' objection that Trieste could forge with Austria the same relationship that Antwerp, in Belgium, and Rotterdam, in Holland, have with Germany: "whoever thinks this, does not realize that Belgium and Holland are two countries essentially devoted to trade, and that they are interested in facilitating export trade in any possible way. They forget that Germany is a great industrial power and that although Hamburg is its greatest seaport on the North Sea and serves all continental Europe, its very small ports are not big enough to handle all the international traffic, and therefore it needs the great ports of Antwerp and Rotterdam. They do not take into account that the great river Rhine, which cuts across the most industrialized region of Germany, by necessity must depend on the great harbours in Belgium and Holland. None of these conditions would be present once Trieste becomes Italian; she would be surrounded by two highly protectionist states, while her natural hinterland would be all within a foreign land that, in order not to have to pay custom duties constantly, would have every interest in finding and developing with any possible means their own port, similar to the port of Trieste." [The book review by Luzzatto, "L'irredentismo adriatico," appeared in *L'Unità*, no. 25, 1 June 1912, 97–8, and is reprinted in A. Saitta, *Storia e miti del '900: Antologia di critica storica*, Editori Laterza, 1960, 66–73.]

Will the Italian people throw us overboard? Why would they! Aren't they behind us, aren't they with us morally, even if from a material standpoint they, a European nation, help us very little and cannot do much for us politically? How could Italy stand by as these outposts vanish, not due to natural causes like unproductivity, but because of a state's intervention? In Austria, Germans and Hungarians will continue to exist. As Vivante rightly notes, they would never allow their primary point of commerce to become Slavic.[19] Faced with the possibility of a new Austrian state, the Germans could easily grant some sort of autonomy to the north-eastern Adriatic coast, as Hungary did for Fiume. But there is no need for some poorly based prognosis, this is the historical truth: in Austria, neither the Germans nor the Slavs will have the upper hand, because Austria ensures a balance of power between Russia and Germany in terms of geography, ethnicity, and history. Our own position, like that of all other minorities, is ensured not by the sympathy that the Germans or the Slavs might feel for us, but by their ongoing conflict.

Italy: we always repeat her name and start and end all our thoughts with her, because before being Triestine, we are Italian, and we must be ready, if necessary, to renounce our own interests in favour of her political and national interests. Italy can and must help us for her own sake in every possible way. But today we cannot in all honestly see the possibility or benefits of a possible annexation. Italy must be certain of the autonomy of the north-eastern Adriatic, and be a close ally of Austria, today and for many years to come.

So, in the end, are you an irredentist or not? Are you a socialist? What *are* you, so help you God!

My dear friends, you who are irredentists, how do you behave? Are you throwing grenades? Are you risking your own lives? Are you risking your financial interests? Are you losing your jobs? In what ways are you spreading your heroic propaganda? True, once in a while, some of you act heroically, but you all agree that as things stand today this behaviour is naive and often useless. Nor do you deny the fact that to have the reputation of being an irredentist, sometimes it might be very useful to find a job.

So, what do you do? Acts of intolerance against the Slavs and protests against the government. That's all you do as irredentists. If you're serious, then you work hard, and you organize yourselves to live as much as

19 That is, Austria would have no interest in helping to dismantle the present state of affairs, which affords it an expansion of capital and influence, since that would have the effect of making a part of their empire so unified and autonomous that it could become an independent state tomorrow.

possible as Italian and free. If you're superficial, you spend your time playing billiards. This irredentism, which you believe is the general mood of Trieste, does not increase the heroic status of the city one bit. Triestines continue to listen to military bands performing in city squares, attend battleship launches, swear loyalty to the emperor, educate their children in pragmatic necessities and send them to German schools, and continue their daily lives – as the reader knows much better than I. For too many people this vaunted heroic feeling is such that it does not interfere with their day-to-day life as Austrian citizens focused on their own interests; as a result, both possibilities and both advantages remain open. Nourishing within oneself a heroic sentiment means anguish, distress, anxiety; and, except for some socialists, I have never found soul and body more perfectly equilibrated than among irredentists. They enjoy both the present reality and their vision of the future.

I am not saying that this is true for everybody. I myself am too hesitant not to give credit to those who have truly found the right path. What I am saying is that our existence is probably harder than others, and that we should not accept peace if this aspiration, in which we would find tranquility, remains only a good idea, nurtured by us, but with no viable future. If I recognize that I cannot act as an irredentist, because my actions *could not* achieve any success, not even if I sacrificed myself as a martyr, I know that I cannot act like the majority, and continue to profess myself an irredentist in Italy, or in Trieste, among a few trusted friends. Instead I must renounce my beautiful, false dream – and continue to work, tirelessly.

And so, I am not an irredentist. But if you are truly irredentists, you must want, together with me, a life that is more arduous, more heroic, and more impartial. You must want, with me, a new life: clerks who accept work in state-run firms, because a secluded existence is an easy and damaging egotism, but who will not flatter their superiors; people who refuse to speak German just to earn respect; young people who do not renounce their ideas in order to find a good job. Less servility even if it means some loss, more honesty, and more sincerity. Don't learn ethics, politics, or even etiquette from the Austrian government. Our life should be independent honourably, so that it might become independent legally. Our children should be brought up thinking of sacrifice, not about their personal profit.

If you are truly irredentists, you must be certain, with me, that this is the only possible way for you to act. I cannot foresee the future. I must admit that all my predictions and opinions might turn out to be wrong. Italy might free us one day, or the Slavs might destroy us. But I know, and

I am certain that no matter what our future will be, it will be better than today only if we prepare ourselves.

And just as I am not an irredentist, I am not a socialist, because now the socialists accept the status quo and no longer work to transform anything. They too have their secret internal compromises, their economic codes, and their national pacification, all of which greatly aid them in avoiding hostilities with the government that uses them. In Austria and in Italy, they're doing fine, and one can no longer hope their work will transform the state in any way. But I too can see clearly, along with Vivante, and even with Valussi and with Tommaseo, that the historical mission of Trieste is to serve as crucible and source of civilization – of three civilizations. It is marvellous, and almost dizzying, to think of how, in this little corner of Europe, the forces and problems that may be the most serious in the western world today are being struggled over: Germanism and Slavism, the Balkan problem, economic hegemonism, the future of Austria – and of Italian identity. The great, full, rich, restless Latin civilization, which must not die on the other side of the Adriatic either.

But if it is doomed to die, and we Latins of the Julian lands must vanish, then it must not die before having given as much as it can of what is good in it: if possible, some decades before vanishing, but certainly not after an ignominious, suffocating agony. Then we will be worthy of being remembered; and we will live on, in what the Slavs will have had to learn from us.

But even so, we must live in our own body.

National Rights Are Affirmed with War

So, the *Times*, the *Globe*, the *Nation*, the *Outlook*, the *Echo de Paris*, and some Russian newspapers continue to warn us that, because of our prolonged inaction, the number of Slavs on the Adriatic is increasing by the thousands every day. We Italians immediately hastened to show that the Italians instead are in the majority, that the culture is completely Italian, etc. If such amendments were of any use, then to the philo-Slavic article by Steed, director for foreign affairs at the *Times*, we could oppose this passage by the same author from his excellent book *The Habsburg Monarchy*:

> After the loss of Lombardy in 1859 and of Venetia in 1866, the demand for Italian officials decreased and with it the "usefulness" of the Italian element. The authorities discovered that the Italians in Dalmatia formed an insignificant proportion (little more than three per cent) of an overwhelmingly Slav population – a population then pitifully ignorant, uncultured and backward in every respect. It was therefore decided to let this population loose upon the highly civilized minority, and the bitter struggle between Slavs and Italians began, the government supporting and encouraging the Slavs and at the same time doing its utmost to foment discord between them and the Italians.[1]

However, this is not the time to indulge in these little satisfactions, nor to engage foreign newspapers about statistics or the history of Italian or Slavic predominance in the north-eastern Adriatic. The discussion must now have another basis: war.

---

1 [Henry Wickham Steed, *The Habsburg Monarchy*, 2nd ed., Constable and Co., 1914, 125–6.]

This is true not just because of the old saying that he who does not act may as well not exist, but for two specific reasons. The first is that nationality and the principle of national identity are real rights in themselves, but at the same time they are very broad concepts, vague and susceptible to many interpretations, contradictions, and limits. The second reason, which follows directly from the first, is that, based on the theoretical and emotional premise of nationality, various antithetical political solutions can coexist; of these, only the one that proves its strength with real force and effort is destined to win.

So, yesterday, in the name of nationality and with great fanfare, French, English, and Russian newspapers had us well established in the Adriatic region; today, in the name of nationality, they expel us or threaten to expel us. And we cry out: this is how they show their good faith! It was enough for the nightmare of a potential occupation of Paris by German troops to be averted, or for the Russians to enter Austrian territory, and their [French, English, and Russian] arrogance flared up again. This is a true statement and may serve as a cold shower for those who just hope passively that everything will work out well in the end. However, the contradictory stance of these newspapers should not be taken so literally as to lose its meaning. And the meaning is this: with you, we're willing to play the card of Italian identity in the Adriatic against Austria; without you, we're willing to play the Slav Adriatic against you. These words might appear contradictory, but their meaning is not, at least for those who understand that emotional reasons are only the pedestal and the facade of politics. Pedestal, because it is impossible to engage in a lasting politics unless it is consistent with the nation's centuries-old spirit, instincts, and needs. Facade, because in politics we always talk about public opinion, foreign and domestic, although actions are dictated by the will and intelligence of the few.

This is the sense in which our foreign friends talk to us about nationality. We must be realistic about what this means. We should not delude ourselves by affirming repeatedly that this war is simply a war of national identity against the principle of authority, and that therefore Trento and Trieste will be Italian no matter what. Without a doubt, the statement is true. Therefore, for Austria (and for Turkey, if it gets involved), this war is the spike that will loosen its grip; while for Serbia, and possibly for us too, it will mean national realization. But this will be true only for those who act to make it true; it will not be realized by those who are contented with its truth alone. Nationality in itself is far more of a duty than it is a right; it is a fixed force that wants to be put into action with a sacrificial effort. Our right to the Adriatic, even if the whole of the eastern Adriatic were Italian, would come to nothing if it weren't felt as a duty, serious and essential – a solemn duty, at a historical time such as this one. And if we can talk about it today as though it were our right, against which no one can make any valid claims, that is hardly due to our public irredentist demonstrations, at which we shouted out our right to Trento and Trieste; rather, it's because of actions taken by Rome and Venice, whose virtues we still enjoy, although we've done nothing to merit them. And actions by our irredentist brothers in unredeemed lands, who have felt the nation as a tremendous, anxious duty, every day, and every year. And have we really helped them, we who stand to benefit from the fruits of their labour?

For all these reasons, to discuss the right to nationhood at this moment is already a demonstration of weakness and laziness, if not an aggravating lack of seriousness. That English or Russian public sentiment should be more on the side of the Serbs than ours, or vice versa, can take up only some of our attention. Public opinion is a reflection of political utility and of how emotions run at the time. For every Serb who dies in battle, the English people are willing to accept a thousand more Serbs in Dalmatia. And with reason. And against that, no argument based on geography will be effective. We need to be proactive as well, and we need to reap the same benefits. We can have the discussion when the war is over, when we will put in the balance not only the weight of our numbers and our civilization, but also our sword of victory. In fact, in this war, which is said to be about nationality, who else but us is discussing nationality at this moment? Are the French perhaps preoccupied with demonstrating that all of Alsace-Lorraine is French? Is Russia debating whether there are many hundreds of thousands of Germans in Poland, Galicia, and Transylvania? Is Serbia recognizing that philo-Serb Croatians are a tiny minority, in comparison with the huge numbers of Croatians who do not want to hear talk of Serbia, in Croatia, Slavonia, and Dalmatia? So, let's not be the only ones doing this Mazzinian theorizing; let's behave like everyone else, like practical followers of Mazzini. Let's wage war.

By now one can say that there is no national territory in Europe (except perhaps certain parts of Poland, in the broadest sense) that has not been unified with its motherland. The great, classical nations have their borders, one way or the other. Now, if at all, what is discussed is the need to complete them, according to their natural borders (as for example with us, France, and Romania), or to allow them their natural, essential outlets that would ensure their true independence (as for Serbia). And although up to a certain point nationality is a secure enough marker of where the border should be – when war is strictly between nations – borders, ports, and national spheres of influence can never be pried apart in such precise and peaceful segments. We have seen it in the Balkan wars, which was indeed a war between nations, but also what we would call an imperialist war. We will see it even more clearly in the current war, in which it will not be those who have the greater claim, but those who have demonstrated greater power, who gain the larger share. And with complete, righteous, and holy justification: because what better argument could there be for one's right to grow, occupy new lands, take on new powers, and expand one's influence and responsibility, if not through victory in war, with the demonstration that we are worthy and capable?

These are the reasons that only someone who practises politics without understanding anything about it would call "immoral," smiling idiotically.

PART SIX

From *Letters to Three Women Friends*

To Elody

Florence, 6 June 1912

I'm studying. But your letters give me much pleasure. Whenever you express your anxiety, your style becomes more complete and mature. The love you have for *My Karst* (which has pleased quite a few, even those who are more severe, and by temperament further from its flights and outbursts of lyricism: Amendola, Papini even, Pasini, and others; though it seems Benco didn't like my fictional representation of the *Piccolo* – but enough about that!) increases my desire to write something more organic, more mature; something balancing joy and torment, like my life, burning in its impetuous and regular ways: a work that, more than artistic, is *moral*, the product of victory; not an outburst, but a restraint; not extension, but *intention*, fully tensed to spring out in a small cry only at its most extreme points; very much like the gentians of the Karst. But I don't know yet whether I'm talented enough to nurture and give strength to what's arid and dry; just as, many times, I'm unsure whether my passions are such that my moral behaviour could serve as an example for someone who is truly suffering. And this doubt saves me, often if not always, from moralistic narrow-mindedness, just as it saves me, I hope, from simplistic art forms that quickly turn into rhetoric: because the latter are nothing but a pedestrian imitation of the simplicity of the great poets, who were able to bring to life the whole world in a single verse – an imitation by hand of inadequate poets who are unable to capture anything in a word but what it ordinarily says. This is why *My Karst* is so sincere, and in its effusiveness there is far more modesty than there would be if the story were related in a quieter tone; and those sections that I tried to tell in another way I removed, convinced that they were dishonest. (An example: the scene with the woman, in which I wanted to convey the impartial, the epic, the dramatic, whereas in reality all I was happy about was that she loved me while I didn't love her, and so I should have written a rhapsody to my self-satisfaction instead.) *My Karst* is the work of my self-centred life as it was, and in part, still is; but its closing words must be prelude to a new work, just as from that moment, with that return, for me a new, more purposeful life began. Because after the death of Anna, I lived a period in which only the sense I had of myself, that I was capable of doing something beneficial for others, saved me. And perhaps you do not realize how much good it did me to be with you those afternoons in Grignano under the acacias, in our hidden place, the sea full of sunlight and you, restless but gentle creature, nearby. (Now that it's hot again, Grignano returns to mind.)

To Gigetta

Florence, 8 February 1912

Gigetta, why don't you write me? I'm eagerly awaiting a letter from you. In recent days I've sent you a letter after having a conversation with Amendola; a letter on the occasion of your party; and third, a postcard from Vallombrosa, and lots of notes. Did you receive everything? Maybe tomorrow I'll receive a letter from you. Sometimes in the evening, or after dinner on a Sunday when I don't know what to do with myself and a disheartening grey inertia seeps into me, I call out to you with little cries. Sometimes, I feel that I would be desperate without you. Made desperate by my poor intelligence, my terrible memory, my obtuse sensitivity, I pass entire days in which nothing stirs me from my insignificance. Made desperate by my many acts of cowardice, my pointless, continuous dreaming. I turn over in bed, my eyes staring off.

Anyway, I would not ask for sympathy from you. I ask nothing but to feel your warm presence in my room, to see your hand on the table, to follow your eyes. I would want you to remain quiet. Maybe I'd want to cry, that sorrow no one can name, that comes from human weakness, arrogance crushed, and fear, as when I read Dante, and feel myself small and helpless. It's not the beauty that frightens me, the way the mountains do: it's the greatness, the fullness so complete that it trembles. I don't love my humility, but I have to accept it, I have to feed it with my work that costs me some struggle, I have to celebrate it in myself because I'm honest, I'm serious, and I have to recognize that this is right; instead, my whole soul tends towards arrogance and pride. It wants certainty, it wants to be assured of my truth; it wants to be able to respond to anyone who opposes me in some way without sliding into a state of weak humility, without getting tugged into the adversary's flow of reasoning, but remaining firm and strong, like a catapult.

However, right away, I rise from these moments of hesitation and doubt, and I set to work. I'm a dreamer, it's true. But for me the dream represents the need to upset the whole of the upper atmosphere where my work has managed to create a little disruption. My dream is in part an abstract taking of possession, temporarily, of the piece of sky onto which the little field I know how to work is projected, so that it seems immense; in part, a segment of road that I then must actually travel, with my gaze straight ahead; and that act encompasses hundreds of miles, a prohibition against stopping, an impetus, recognition of the greatness I must aspire to; which, if I were forced to renounce, I would still always recognize as greatness. What I'm trying to say is that this dream gives me a sense of peace, but only briefly; and it doesn't let me sleep.

The other evening, I was telling Stuparich my ideas about communal endeavour in Trieste, and ... as happens every time I speak with someone younger than me, I saw the pleasure that my ardent ideas fired in him, all his hope and despair. You know my thinking well; you are already working alongside me. You I can tell about this thought, which I dream: it is to live, organically, all the complexity of human life (through its history and its people, through friends and through adversaries), such that I'll be able to express myself, and to work, for all. *To be a man.* Whatever else life gives me, I would not be completely content when my time comes, I would not have arrived, I would be lacking. Art would not be enough for me. Action would not be enough. Nor would knowledge. And not a formal plan; but the blood of the earth, harmonized in my veins. So that it would make no difference if I were writing, speaking, acting, thinking, wanting, desiring. To such an extent that, in essence, my life's legacy could be a history book my children could read, and my friends could comment on. When I think this grandiose and sorrowful thought of mine, it unfolds and humbles itself; it turns into the endeavour of ten friends each of whom knows a language outside common circulation, who can explain what's going on and has gone on in the world. And this in Trieste.

Trieste is my country. Every day I find more of Trieste in myself. Trieste, which is the obstacle to victory, and could be its symbol. In Trieste, everything is yet to be done: starting with action. It is a crossroads of civilizations: they should be studied live. Trieste needs teachers: and so let's teach. The city contains, restless, the elements that disturb us moderns: we must truly reconcile them. I can try to convince myself that I'm calm, while I write in Italian and read German books, and I contemplate our nation with a human conscience, but unless I am able to realize and spread this balance of mine, it does not really exist. Also, if I am not able to encompass all the complexity of human life, witnessing and participating in all its apparently contradictory forms, commerce and literature, salon and tenement, Karst and pavement, Slovene and Italian, I am not a *poet.*

All this has only to do with me. But I yearn with desire for others, for health, for beneficence, for love of my fellow man. And we have to begin with our own country, right from here, because if not, we're just pretending. We must be prophets in our own country.

Ah, Gigetta, Gigetta! It could be that all this is nothing but the preparation for a work of art, but how I would like to be one of those great men who can shake my poor humanity from the roots. Aeschylus, Dante, Goethe, and more: Christ. Christ and Goethe. Insane stuff, of a beast possessed by demons, by fallen angels; but the dream alone makes me tremble as though I were at the edge of the universe. Ah, my famished youth, if one could see you in your intimate hours, in your god-like suffering! But you know that it's necessary to stay humble, that it's necessary to study French verbs, that it's all necessary. But I'm not willing to give up. Sometimes I think: what kind of life of anxiety will I give Gigetta? Sometimes I think: what kind of life of tranquility will my family give me? Sometimes I think: whatever will become of me? I don't know, but it's better to die striving and failing, than to live as the bourgeois keeper of one's own soul. Better return to God's embrace, like an anguished child. I won't renounce the mystery, or my own humanity. This is a man: this being who combines tragic opposites and gives a cry of joy. *Homo sum.*

Goodnight, Gigetta. Do you love me very much? And so, every night, I open up myself to you, begging your eyes to look on me lovingly, to love me well. Goodbye, my pale, gentle little one.

To Gigetta

23 November 1915

I found a piece of paper with a bit of your writing on it: "comfort."

I want to write you a bit more today and to be with you, my dear little one.

In a soldier's uniform, unshaven, revolver on my hip, alpenstock in my hand (that I found, near the little Fort of Podgora,[1] the first terrible battlefield that I saw on the 5th, having just arrived, after the attack on the 3rd), I would look much thinner and more exhausted to you. This time I really felt the war more intensely. To return to war after being injured is truly a more difficult or at least more sombre affair. And we arrived already reeling from mud half a metre high, in a terrifying rain, without knowing where or how. The arrival in Ca' delle Valade near Brazzano was really heartbreaking, though the places I knew (the abbey of Rosazzo, the house of my aunt) comforted me a little. But above all, thoughts of you, of mother, and of the little one made me more thoughtful, that is, more of a man. The first years of youth might have ended with *My Karst*, my whole youth finished in the Modena hospital, and now I feel like a man.[2] I no longer have that twenty-year-old rash-and-ready imprudence. My courage is now more a matter of character and resolution than instinct.

Otherwise, now that the first days of dysentery and confusion have passed, I feel well. I am calm, as always, perhaps the fundamental trait of mine that never abandons me. Too calm, but also efficiently calm. I get

---

1 [Podgora was a hill on the Italian front. It is here that Slataper died, on 3 December 1915.]

2 [Slataper suffered an early injury while at the front, in June 1915. He was sent to the military hospital of Modena to convalesce. After recuperating, he returned to the front.]

along well with all the soldiers. Guido too comports himself well; though he may be a bit too giddy.

Of the war, as I've written to you a few times, I have more peripheral than direct impressions. A thousand little, important things come to mind, that I'm reluctant to write down because I'm in the midst of them. I don't really understand the ongoing debate about the war by those who are fighting in it. Maybe it's because even in war – though it seems impossible! – I'm quite lazy. But what's certain is that I see just about everything with my own eyes, and I don't impose on new experiences the old rhetoric of city life. If you pay good attention, you'll see that almost all the letters from soldiers are written not by those who are fighting, but by those who receive them. Almost everyone sees the things that they were prepared to see; but unlike many others, I have a totally different sense of the war than the one experienced every day, made up of little miseries and weaknesses that are also felt by those who then write those fervent letters. And these men consider those who believe in the words of glory and victory, which they may have once written themselves, to be greenhorns and fools. But I do not. I see that we are all men, that war demands more than human strength, that it has in it something higher and far more frightening than one single man can, by himself, offer or bear. But it is the community of men that succeeds, it is the collective effort of mutual help, of support, of cooperation that brings out our love for each other, and this is the real war. This is the purpose of military discipline, which is carried out like any other human undertaking, but under conditions that transcend the human. To excavate a tunnel requires cooperation and order, reinforced in taking shifts; but capturing a stronghold requires a desperate and sacred collaboration that seems to have the rhythm of an invocation, in which no one reasons any longer, but everyone acts together as though inspired by a sacred terror. You can feel that God is near the battlefield. And this is what I don't find in Tolstoy, who was too much of an impressionist to be religious.

Dear little one, now you know how I am thinking and feeling in these days of rest alongside the soldiers. And I feel a great sense of calm and faith, almost as though I had returned to your side, because I have never once felt the sense of my own death amidst so much dying. At the most, I could be wounded, but not more.

Dearest, call our son the name you wish; if it's a girl, Giovanna rather than Clementina. Tell me about yourself, even if there's nothing important, but write to me. By now I'm used to receiving a letter from you almost every day. Don't cry, my little one. Dr. Pestalozza's[3] medical certifi-

3 [Probably Dr. Ernesto Pestalozza, the obstetrician who was attending to Gigetta.]

cate won't mean anything unless we return to some Italian city and the furloughs begin. I hope and I think that we will have them soon. I'll have my monthly pay at the end of the month, and then I hope to be able to send you three hundred lire.

I kiss you with my whole heart and soul, my love. Be well, always. Goodbye.

Index

THE LORENZO DA PONTE ITALIAN LIBRARY

General Editors: Luigi Ballerini and Massimo Ciavolella

Pellegrino Artusi, *Science in the Kitchen and the Art of Eating Well* (2003). Translated by Murtha Baca and Stephen Sartarelli. Introduction by Luigi Ballerini. Foreword by Michele Scicolone.

Lauro Martines, *An Italian Renaissance Sextet: Six Tales in Historical Context* (2004). Translated by Murtha Baca.

Aretino's Dialogues (2005). Translated by Raymond Rosenthal. Introduction by Margaret Rosenthal.

Aldo Palazzeschi, *A Tournament of Misfits: Tall Tales and Short* (2005). Translated by Nicolas J. Perella.

Carlo Cattaneo, *Civilization and Democracy: The Salvemini Anthology of Cattaneo's Writings* (2006). Edited and introduced by Carlo G. Lacaita and Filippo Sabetti. Translated by David Gibbons.

Benedetto Croce, *Breviary of Aesthetics: Four Lectures* (2007). Translated by Hiroko Fudemoto. Introduction by Remo Bodei.

Antonio Pigafetta, *The First Voyage around the World (1519–1522): An Account of Magellan's Expedition* (2007). Edited and introduced by Theodore J. Cachey Jr.

Raffaello Borghini, *Il Riposo* (2008). Edited and translated by Lloyd H. Ellis Jr.

Paolo Mantegazza, *The Physiology of Love and Other Writings* (2008). Edited, with an introduction and notes, by Nicoletta Pireddu. Translated by David Jacobson.

Renaissance Comedy: The Italian Masters, Volume 1 (2008). Edited with an introduction by Donald Beecher.

Renaissance Comedy: The Italian Masters, Volume 2 (2008). Edited with an introduction by Donald Beecher.

Cesare Beccaria, *On Crimes and Punishments and Other Writings* (2008). Edited by Aaron Thomas. Translated by Aaron Thomas and Jeremy Parzen. Foreword by Bryan Stevenson. Introduction by Alberto Burgio.

Leone Ebreo, *Dialogues of Love* (2009). Edited by Rossella Pescatori. Translated by Cosmos Damian Bacich and Rossella Pescatori.

Boccaccio's Expositions on Dante's Comedy (2009). Translated by Michael Papio.

My Muse Will Have a Story to Paint: Selected Prose of Ludovico Ariosto (2010). Translated with an introduction by Dennis Looney.

The Opera of Bartolomeo Scappi (1570): L'arte et prudenza d'un maestro cuoco (The Art and Craft of a Master Cook) (2011). Translated with commentary by Terence Scully.

Pirandello's Theatre of Living Masks: New Translations of Six Major Plays (2011). Translated by Umberto Mariani and Alice Gladstone Mariani.

From Kant to Croce: Modern Philosophy in Italy, 1800–1950 (2012). Edited and translated with an introduction by Brian Copenhaver and Rebecca Copenhaver.

Giovan Francesco Straparola, *The Pleasant Nights,* Volume 2 (2012). Edited with an introduction by Donald Beecher.

Giovan Francesco Straparola, *The Pleasant Nights,* Volume 1 (2012). Edited with an introduction by Donald Beecher.

Giovanni Botero, *On the Causes of the Greatness and Magnificence of Cities* (2012). Translated with an introduction by Geoffrey Symcox.

John Florio, *A Worlde of Wordes* (2013). A critical edition with an introduction by Hermann W. Haller.

Giordano Bruno, *On the Heroic Frenzies* (2013). A translation of *De gli eroici furori* by Ingrid D. Rowland. Edited by Eugenio Canone.

Alvise Cornaro, *Writings on the Sober Life: The Art and Grace of Living Long* (2014). Translated by Hiroko Fudemoto. Introduction by Marisa Milani. Foreword by Greg Critser.

Dante Alighieri, *Dante's Lyric Poetry: Poems of Youth and of the* Vita Nuova *(1283–1292)* (2014). Edited, with a general introduction and introductory essays, by Teodolinda Barolini. With new verse translations by Richard Lansing. Commentary translated into English by Andrew Frisardi.

Vincenzo Cuoco, *Historical Essay on the Neapolitan Revolution of 1799* (2014). Edited and introduced by Bruce Haddock and Filippo Sabetti. Translated by David Gibbons.

Vittore Branca, *Merchant Writers: Florentine Memoirs from the Middle Ages and Renaissance* (2015). Translated by Murtha Baca.

Carlo Goldoni, *Five Comedies* (2016). Edited by Gianluca Rizzo and Michael Hackett, with Brittany Asaro. With an introduction by Michael Hackett and an essay by Cesare de Michelis.

Those Who from Afar Look like Flies: An Anthology of Italian Poetry from Pasolini to the Present (2016). Edited by Luigi Ballerini and Beppe Cavatorta. Foreword by Marjorie Perloff.

Guittone d'Arezzo, *Selected Poems and Prose* (2017). Selected and translated with an introduction by Antonello Borra.

Giordano Bruno, *The Ash Wednesday Supper* (2018). A new translation of *La cena de le ceneri* with the Italian text annotated and introduced by Hilary Gatti.

Giacomo da Lentini, *The Complete Poetry* (2018). Translated and annotated by Richard Lansing. Introduction by Akash Kumar.

Remo Bodei, *Geometry of the Passions: Fear, Hope, Happiness: Philosophy and Political Use* (2018). Translated by Gianpiero W. Doebler.

Scipio Sighele, *The Criminal Crowd and Other Writings on Mass Society* (2018). Edited, with an introduction and notes, by Nicoletta Pireddu. Translated by Nicoletta Pireddu and Andrew Robbins. With a foreword by Tom Huhn.

Gasparo Contarini, *The Republic of Venice: De magistratibus et republica Venetorum* (2020). Edited and introduced by Filippo Sabetti. Translated by Giuseppe Pezzini with Amanda Murphy.

Donatien Alphonse François, Marquis de Sade, *Journey to Italy* (2020). Translated, introduced, and annotated by James A. Steintrager.

Scipio Slataper, *My Karst and My City and Other Essays* (2020). Edited, with an introduction and notes, by Elena Coda. Translated by Nicholas Benson and Elena Coda.